TRANSFORMATION AND REACTION

TRANSFORMATION AND REACTION
America 1921–1945

GLEN JEANSONNE
University of Wisconsin—Milwaukee

HarperCollins*CollegePublishers*

To Hannah Pace Jeansonne, who matured, like America.

PHOTO CREDITS
Page 13, Culver Pictures; page 21, Ohio Historical Society; page 36, Brown Brothers; page 45, UPI/Bettmann; page 63, Courtesy of the Ford Archives, Henry Ford Museum, Dearborn, Michigan; page 71, Museum of Modern Art/Still Film Archive; page 75, Library of Congress; page 84, Beinecke Rare Book and Manuscript Library, Yale University; page 85, Aubrey Bodine; page 115, Acme/Bettmann; page 126, Franklin D. Roosevelt Library; page 145, Culver Pictures; page 146, Bettmann Archive; page 167, Library of Congress; page 177, UPI/Bettmann; page 194, Official U.S. Navy photo; page 203, National Archives; page 206, Wide World Photos; page 226, Official Coast Guard photo; page 230, Bernard Hoffman Life Magazine ©1945 Time Warner Inc.

Senior Editor: Bruce Borland
Project Editor: David Nickol
Design Supervisor: LaToya Wigfall/Heather A. Ziegler
Cover Design: LaToya Wigfall
Cover Illustration: Library of Congress
Photo Researcher: Michelle Ryan
Production Administrator/Assistant: Valerie Sawyer/Hilda Koparanian
Compositor: University Graphics, Inc.
Printer and Binder: R. R. Donnelley & Sons, Company
Cover Printer: Lehigh Press

Transformation and Reaction: America 1921–1945

Copyright © 1994 by HarperCollins College Publishers

Library of Congress Cataloging-in-Publication Data

Jeansonne, Glen, 1946-
    Transformation and reaction : America, 1921-1945 / Glen Jeansonne.
        p.   cm.
    Includes index.
    ISBN 0-06-500142-7
    1. United States—History—1919-1933.   2. United States—
    History—1933-1945.   I. Title.
E784.J43   1993
973.91—dc20   93-25508
                                                                            CIP

93 94 95 96 9 8 7 6 5 4 3 2 1

CONTENTS

PREFACE

✣ APPROACH

This book arose from my experience of nearly 20 years teaching American history covering the period 1921 to 1945, and from my desire to write a clear, comprehensive, succinct history with a strong theme characterizing that era. It is a distinctive era, a dizzying trip through prosperity, depression, reform, and war—a lifetime of peaks and valleys packed into twenty-four years. Rural America became an urban nation, tempered by moral rebellion, transformed by a collective approach to economic problems, and thrust upon the world stage as the foremost power.

What strikes me most about the period is its convulsive change balanced by resistance to that change. Other periods, such as the era since 1945, have experienced rapid changes, although by 1945 there was a precedent for accelerated innovations, and people expected them. Remarkable change occurred largely because of two world wars. As with any great changes, there were winners and losers—those who gained prestige and augmented their power, and those who lost both. Young people and women were in the vanguard of change and derived the most benefits from it. But those who opposed change—fundamentalists, Klansmen, fiscal conservatives, and isolationists— were not left out of the process; they often influenced the nature and pace of change.

There were physical, spiritual, emotional, intellectual, and personal changes, not all of them salutary. Technology changed most rapidly; religious and political institutions lagged. No change had so many ramifications as urbanization and the consequent shift in economic, political, and demographic influence from the town and country to major cities.

The fabric of society was torn by dissent, factions, and interest groups; the American system oscillated between change and inertia, between forces of progress and forces of order, and was tested by a dynamic tension between transformation and reaction. These conflicts existed within individuals such as Henry Ford, an industrial innovator and a social reactionary. Some mounted the ramparts as cultural revolutionaries while defending the barricades as political reactionaries. A nation that danced the Charleston and drank bootleg liquor voted for Harding, Coolidge, and Hoover.

World War I divided Americans in the postwar decade, yet the depression brought sacrifice and reform, preparing them for the challenge of another world war. World War II united them to a degree not matched before or since. It was the greatest collective experience of their lives and a force that shaped not only the country, but the world. It tested America's human and natural resources and the people—who learned more from their mistakes than from their successes—found inner resources they had doubted they possessed.

✧ FEATURES

I have tried to write a book that students will read for pleasure, not merely because it is assigned. Its themes are meant to provoke class discussion. I have attempted to advance my thesis without forcing events to fit within that thesis.

I have tried to make this era of colorful personalities come alive through biographical sketches of such memorable characters as Henry Ford, Clarence Darrow, Charles A. Lindbergh, Gertrude Stein, W. E. B. Du Bois, and Douglas MacArthur. Believing that many histories slight popular culture, I have attempted to describe what was important to people during their lifetimes as well as those things valued by posterity. Thus there are vignettes not only of such famous writers as Ernest Hemingway, F. Scott Fitzgerald, and Sinclair Lewis, but of those who dominated sales in their time, such as Zane Grey, Edgar Rice Burroughs, Geneva ("Gene") Stratton-Porter, and Harold Bell Wright. I have described popular black leaders such as Father Divine and Marcus Garvey as well as the more historically significant W. E. B. Du Bois and A. Philip Randolph. This is not a history of elites alone. Life changed for the masses—particularly women, children, minorities, and workers and their stories are dramatic and revealing.

The book depicts not only a heroic nation surmounting great challenges, but a democracy with a dark side of racism, anti-Semitism, provincialism, smugness, intolerance, and corruption. It is a side of America worth remembering if we are not to duplicate its flaws.

Transformation and Reaction is designed to be complemented by other readings, yet it can stand alone in providing basic information. Each chapter includes a bibliographical essay detailing supplemental primary and secondary source material. There is approximately one chapter for every week in a semester, allowing time for reviews and tests.

I hope that *Transformation and Reaction* is half as much fun to read as it was to write.

✧ ACKNOWLEDGMENTS

It is a pleasure to acknowledge those who have helped this book grow from an idea. My former student Michael Gauger edited the first draft superbly, complementing his editing skills with his thorough knowledge of American history, and indexed the book expertly, as he did for two of my previous books. Another former student, Kari Frederickson, did research, and proofread the manuscript. Doug Groen researched and edited the chapters on World War II. Keith Brown was my research assistant during the summer of 1992. My colleague David Hoeveler made suggestions for the initial proposal. Bruce Borland of HarperCollins nourished the project from its inception, and my editor, John Matthews, was a pleasure to work with. Robert A. Divine, Dimitri Lazo, and Leo P. Ribuffo critically read the book proposal, and Dennis C. Dickerson, Henry C. Dethloff, David M. Oshinsky, and Richard C. Frey read the manuscript, made fruitful suggestions, and detected potentially embarrassing errors. My wife Sharon, as always, made it possible for the work to get done, and my daughters, Leah and Hannah, made it meaningful.

Glen Jeansonne

TRANSFORMATION AND REACTION

CHAPTER ONE

AMERICA IN TRANSITION

✣ AN OVERVIEW OF THE ERA

An elderly historian once advised a graduate student, who was about to take his doctoral examinations, that if he was asked to discuss an era he knew nothing about he should reply, "It was an age of transition and the middle class was rising." Such a characterization would indeed be appropriate for almost any period in Western civilization, but it fits few eras better than the period from 1921 to 1945 in the United States, a time that was unique because it was encapsulated by the only world wars in history.

The two decades in the era were almost mirror opposites. In the 1920s wealth was exalted; in the 1930s it was resented. The 1920s were characterized by conservative politics and radical social change; in the 1930s the pattern was reversed. Hedonism prevailed in the 1920s, but a soberness pervaded the 1930s; ironically, alcohol was illegal in the former and legal in the latter.

The two decades that differ so much are inextricably intertwined, as a binge is connected with a hangover. Each was necessary to the other, and both were necessary to surmount the challenge of World War II. More change was packed into these two-and-one-half decades than into many periods twice or three times as long. Mature Americans in 1900 might have been quite comfortable in 1921; they would have found themselves in a different world in 1945. "The generation," Malcolm Cowley wrote, "belonged to a period of transition from values already fixed to values that had to be created. Its members . . .

were seceding from the old and yet could adhere to nothing new; they groped their way toward another scheme of life, as yet undefined; in the midst of their doubts and uneasy gestures of defiance they felt homesick for the certainties of childhood."

Hopes and dreams had been realized, crushed, reborn. Anyone who lived through the peaks and valleys of the era should have emerged spent and exhausted; instead, most were grateful, subdued, and realistically confident. It seemed that repeatedly the nation was poised on a precipice above a canyon of despair, made a leap of faith, and landed safely on the other side. Meeting great challenges at a time when many thought the nation in decline, Americans made their country wiser and more prosperous.

Throughout the era, change, whether cultural or political, was met with resistance. Change did not occur smoothly or evenly but in fits, with lapses and regressions. The interwar era was characterized by a society in dynamic tension between transformation and reaction. In the end the transformation occurred despite the reaction, but the reaction in part dictated the nature of the transformation. Not all of the transformation was good; the world was a far safer place in 1921 than in 1945. Not all of the reaction was bad; both reformers and conservatives were fallible.

It took courage to change, and it took courage to resist counterproductive change. Moreover, the political and cultural landscape was confused by a host of conflicting armies; it was possible to do battle as a cultural radical and a political reactionary, or as a cultural reactionary and a political radical. Some generals switched armies. Young radicals rebelled, grew up, and became old reactionaries.

The United States fought an economic war and a military war and won both, although it paid dearly in dollars and lives. The victories were difficult and uncertain and there was no guarantee that either victory would last. Over the course of the period the average American changed his or her mind, not once but repeatedly. What characterized the period was not certitude but flux, not merely change but accelerating change, which encompassed revolution and counterrevolution.

No roller coaster ride could have been more dizzying. Still, one takes only a small risk in riding a roller coaster. Americans who bet on the stock market, moved from Mississippi to Massachusetts, or landed at Normandy, took risks that defined their lives, or possibly ended them. The tension between transformation and reaction was like that between centripetal and centrifugal force. Too much of one and the nation would collapse into the center; too much of the other and it would fly apart.

The interwar years constitute neither a steady march toward democracy nor a story of inexorable oppression. Most people who lived through them experienced good times and bad times, and it is the experience of such variety that provides a rich texture to the history of the period. There were some who experienced only destitution and others who experienced little save sublime comfort. Some were impoverished in the midst of prosperity; others prospered in the depths of the Great Depression. It is also true that some who prospered were quite unhappy, and some of those who were indigent would not have sacrificed their happiness for the sad comfort of their wealthier neighbors.

To people living in the 1920s, social developments dominated the news; in the 1930s political developments dominated. The politicians of the 1930s profited by learning from the mistakes of their predecessors of the 1920s; in turn, they made mistakes. Each generation learns more from its trials and errors than from the lessons trumpeted by historians and economists. History tends to move in political and economic cycles, but this is not an iron law. The cycles are neither regular nor uniform in duration, an inconstancy that makes prediction hazardous and history interesting.

The tragedy of America in the 1920s might be that business prosperity did not continue. To some extent, the surge and the collapse were independent of business and government; it is equally true that recovery would occur in part independently of government programs. The Republicans won the presidency in 1928 for the same reason the Democrats won it in 1932: the state of the economy. Had Al Smith or Franklin Roosevelt been elected president in 1928, it is quite possible that the stock market crash would have arrived on schedule and that neither would have been reelected in 1932.

Neither the depression nor recovery was entirely inevitable. It is quite possible that under slightly different conditions, including limited regulation and reform, prosperity could have endured. It is also plausible that despite reforms, the nation might have remained in an economic trough indefinitely without the demand for goods and workers produced by World War II.

In the post–World War I era, according to Roderick Nash, "the bottom dropped out of Western belief." James Harvey Robinson wrote of the period, "Never did bitterer disappointment follow high hopes." Yet it was also a period of affirmation; the values of capitalism and democracy and the inevitability of progress were subscribed to by far more people than rejected them.

In the aftermath of the Great War transformation swept industry: the automobile, the assembly line, electricity, refrigeration, and indoor plumbing. Business management was rationalized and streamlined, forms of investment were created, great risks were taken. By 1920, fifty-four percent of the population was engaged in industry, and the value of manufactured goods was three times that of agricultural products. Industrial production and profits had soared during the war, and industry had become concentrated in large corporations capitalized by stock traded on the New York Stock Exchange. Transportation and communication, as well as government and industry, were becoming centralized.

At the same time immigration was restricted, nonconformists persecuted by the Ku Klux Klan, and a tariff barrier erected. Religion turned to social issues on a larger scale, and progressive theologians were fashionable. Simultaneously there was a fundamentalist reaction dramatically illuminated in the "monkey trial" of John Thomas Scopes. Flexibility lay with the modernists, but strength of conviction lay with the fundamentalists.

Perhaps the greatest tension resulted from urbanization, which technology facilitated. Sometimes the tension was demonstrable in a single individual such as Henry Ford, an industrial innovator and a social reactionary. The clash between urban and rural was dramatized in the 1928 presidential election when Al Smith (born into poverty in New York City) faced Herbert Hoover (born into poverty in rural Iowa).

Sexuality, which aggravated generational and religious conflict, created a rift between traditionalists and modernists. Habits such as smoking and drinking were linked to sexuality. Conservatives deplored women who were openly sexual, used cosmetics, bobbed their hair, and shortened their skirts. Birth control, more technologically feasible than before, created moral and social dilemmas. Yet the age was not so libertine as the movies and magazines might have us believe; there were clearly defined limits, and the predominant theme was sexuality without intercourse (except among engaged couples).

Before the depression the interwar writers attacked cultural sterility and materialism, insisting that a prosperous society meant neither cultural sophistication nor economic equality. H. L. Mencken satirized materialism, while Sinclair Lewis depicted the hypocrisy of small town life. Yet the very people they ridiculed bought and read their books and articles.

Nowhere were inequality, hypocrisy, and neglect more poignant than in race relations. The prosperity of the 1920s largely excluded blacks, most of whom lived in the rural South, mired in poverty and lacking educational opportunity. Blacks made great progress during the interwar period and even more during the war, but it was largely economic, not political. And economics as well as social attitudes excluded blacks from the American dream.

In foreign relations there were tensions between crusades for peace and the stark reality of a violent world. Jeannette Rankin was elected to two congressional terms 24 years apart, just in time to vote against two world wars. Women crusaded against war, and public opinion was nationalistic and cautious through most of the period. Isolationists and internationalists clashed in the late 1930s until both were overwhelmed by a world at war.

In the New Deal, which has been depicted as a domestic revolution, there was tension within and without the Roosevelt administration between traditionalists and advocates of change. Roosevelt evinced initial reluctance to change, but circumstances set the agenda and he responded. He succeeded a president who had a reputation as a progressive and who struggled valiantly and rationally to combat conditions largely beyond his control, failing because he lacked insight into his mistakes.

✣ MODERNIZATION

The most fundamental change was an exponential increase in human knowledge, precipitating modernization, the adaption of historically evolved institutions to new knowledge. Previously such increases had occurred incrementally, taking hundreds, even thousands of years. But World War I accelerated the pace of modernization. The war required reorganization of politics, rationalization of industry, consolidation of transportation, centralization of government, and rapid implementation of scientific discoveries. "Intervention in World War I shoved Americans faster and further down a road they were already traveling," John M. Cooper writes.

The greatest impetus to modernization in the United States was the rapid growth of scientific knowledge and the speed with which scientific discoveries made their impact on the masses. Science affected American jobs, life-styles, and beliefs. As knowledge changed, the basis of belief in traditional verities was shaken. After the work of Darwin, Einstein, and Freud, religious revelations, sacred texts, and social and political institutions lost much of their underlying credibility. As science introduced new truths and new standards by which to judge old truths, truth became relative, not eternal, and institutions came to be judged on how well they worked, not by abstract standards.

Science changed more rapidly than religion or politics, and existing institutions lagged behind scientific advances. Those who tried to adhere to both custom and science were pulled in different directions. Those who sided with one were likely to be ostracized or ridiculed by the partisans of the other. Most people reacted ambivalently; they could no longer believe things they wanted to believe, and they began to believe some things that destroyed their serenity. It was widely debated whether science was a tyrant or a liberator and whether the future was bright with promise or dark with foreboding.

Modernization was related to, but quite different from, a movement in the arts known as modernism. Modernists were opposed to some aspects of modernization, and they arose largely in reaction to it. Modernists applauded scientific knowledge but decried the dehumanizing aspects of the machine civilization and corporate and government bureaucratization. With modernism, the ultimate aim was integration of the emotional and the rational; its short-range result was fragmentation and destruction through emphasis on the irrational aspects of humankind, expressed through abstract art, Freudian psychiatry, rejection of materialism, and sexual experimentation. The modernists believed the prevailing Victorian culture stifled self-expression by suppressing the emotional side of human nature. Modernism was defined largely by its rebellion against the traditional in the fine and literary arts; modernist works inspired and energized some, confused and appalled others. To traditionalists, modernism was a fad; to modernists, traditionalists were hopelessly backward. The war, waged in literary journals, art galleries, and intellectual discussions, raged throughout the interwar era, the modernists appealing to the avant-garde, the traditionalists to the masses.

✣ THE VERSAILLES TREATY

Casting its shadow over the carefree rebellion of the 1920s was the catastrophe of World War I, which had left 50 million soldiers and civilians dead or injured worldwide. This slaughter was followed by a worldwide influenza outbreak in 1918 that killed four times as many people as did the war, including half a million in the United States. If the war had ended with a peace that ensured international healing, economic recuperation, and favorable auspices for future peace, Americans might have entered the 1920s less pessimistic about world affairs and domestic politics. Unfortunately, the relief that the war had ended and the satisfaction of a military victory were erased in the bitter fight to ratify the peace treaty.

President Woodrow Wilson made American participation in a new League of Nations the cornerstone of the Versailles Treaty and his vision for a peaceful world order. Wilson had expressed his war aims in his Fourteen Points, the fourteenth of which was the League, meant to adjust inequities in the treaty and enforce the peace. A majority of Americans favored Senate ratification of the treaty, including participation in the League, but a simple majority was insufficient; it would take two-thirds of the Senate to ratify. The ratification process degenerated into a political struggle between Wilson and his archenemy, Republican Henry Cabot Lodge, chair of the Foreign Relations Committee. Each hoped to assure his party's victory in the 1920 presidential election by directing the outcome of the ratification fight. Moreover, there were principles at stake. Lodge wanted to attach reservations to the treaty to assure that the United States would not carry out certain League policies, especially the dispatching of American troops without congressional approval. Wilson believed Lodge's reservations would fatally weaken the treaty and render the League ineffective.

Lodge held the upper hand because the Republicans had a two-vote majority in the Senate. Wilson appealed to the public to place pressure upon senators to ratify the treaty, trading upon his popularity and oratory. But following a national speaking tour, Wilson suffered a debilitating stroke, and the Democrats were virtually leaderless.

On November 19, 1919, the Senate voted on the treaty twice, once with Lodge's reservations, once without them. Each time it failed to muster even a simple majority. Wilson angrily refused to compromise by permitting Democrats to break ranks and vote for the treaty with mild reservations. Some Democrats broke ranks anyway and voted for the modified treaty when it came to a final vote on March 19, 1920. This time the treaty carried 49–35, still seven votes short of the two-thirds majority. Some remarked bitterly that the Constitution was flawed by its provisions requiring only a simple majority to initiate a war, but a two-thirds majority to conclude one.

✣ POLITICAL ENERVATION

Rejection of the Versailles Treaty did not mean that most Americans wanted to withdraw into a shell; it simply meant that fewer than two-thirds of the U.S. senators were willing to risk using American troops to enforce world peace. Too, there would have been a letdown in public enthusiasm for politics even if the treaty had passed, just as there has been in the aftermath of every American war. While the politicians squabbled over the treaty, a magazine poll found some Americans who believed the League of Nations was a baseball league. The war and the haggling over ratification of a treaty to end it did not literally kill the reform impulse in the United States, but they accelerated its decline and helped set the psychological tempo of the 1920s.

Faith in reform, optimism about America, and a crusading moralism animated the progressive movement that dominated the first two decades of the century. There is no easy profile of the movement, for its ranks included people from rural areas, middle-class urban dwellers, professional men, women activists, white-collar workers, and business interests. What united the groups, broadly speaking, were fears that large private concentrations of economic and political power imperiled democracy and their social status. The two most important exponents of the movement were the great presidents Theodore Roosevelt and Woodrow Wilson, who—in contrast to the presidents of the 1920s—inspired the public with their oratory, invigorated their office and American politics, and dramatized critical issues.

On the national level, the progressive movement had accomplished the direct election of U.S. senators, an income tax, and women's suffrage. On the state and local levels it had implemented, among other things, the direct primary, the initiative (whereby voters could place proposed legislation on the ballot), the referendum (whereby voters could enact laws), the recall (through which voters could remove incumbent politicians), and limited regulation of business to promote competition and protect public health. Few reforms would be enacted in the 1920s. In part, the progressive movement was a victim of its success; it had achieved many of its objectives, and much of the public was prepared to go no further. In part, the ranks of progressive politicians were thinned by age, illness, and internecine quarrels.

Few Americans supported additional reforms in the prosperous period that began about 1922, for they perceived themselves beneficiaries of economic bounty. "Nothing defeats liberalism so thoroughly as a conservative government that seems to have fulfilled its economic guarantees," Frederick Hoffman writes. Socialism and communism failed to attract large numbers of Americans because they did not want to abolish capitalism, only to share in its plenty. Reformers had to concede that America's material accomplishments were impressive. Radical writer Lincoln Steffens confessed, "The world which I tried so hard, so honestly, so dumbly, to change, has changed me." Capitalism and democracy looked like a combination that could not be beaten. Elmo Calkins, in a book entitled *Business the Civilizer*, wrote, "There is no country in the world so efficiently governed as the American Telephone and Telegraph Company or the General Electric Company."

Nonetheless, liberalism was not dead, only dormant. It was most evident on the local level, where a strong social welfare movement persisted, concerned with child labor and poor housing. The left remained active as an irritant, seldom able to enact national legislation but sometimes effective in opposition. Republican Senator George W. Norris of Nebraska, for example, led a crusade against Henry Ford's attempt to acquire and develop the Muscle Shoals dam site on the Tennessee River, owned by the federal government.

After blocking Ford's bid, Norris persuaded his colleagues twice to enact bills calling for federal operation of the Muscle Shoals power plant, only to see them vetoed. Norris did manage to retain the option for federal development of the Tennessee watershed, which materialized in the Tennessee Valley Authority of the New Deal.

In addition to Norris, Robert M. La Follette of Wisconsin kept alive the flickering reform spirit. After serving three terms in Congress and three terms as governor, La Follette was elected to the U.S. Senate in 1905 and took his seat in 1906, remaining there until his death in 1925. As governor, La Follette had won approval of a direct party primary, railroad regulation, and equitable taxation of railroads. He was among the first American governors to use university experts to suggest a political agenda and draw up legislation, a system he called the "Wisconsin idea." La Follette seemed to grow more radical the longer he remained in the Senate, opposing American entry into World War I and the Versailles Treaty. In the 1920s he devoted most of his efforts to regulating big business to ensure efficiency and fair competition. In 1924 he ran for president on the Progressive party ticket, aided by Socialists and labor unions. Although he failed to affect the outcome, he carried Wisconsin and outpolled the Democratic nominee John W. Davis in 17 western states.

The progressive strength in the 1920s was concentrated in the West, which sent to the Senate such men as Norris, Republican Hiram Johnson of California, Republican William E. Borah of Idaho, and Democrat Burton K. Wheeler of Montana. In addition, the western states led the way in electing women to office, including Jeannette Rankin of Montana, the first woman in Congress, elected as a Republican in 1916. The western states were among the first to permit women to vote and to participate in party caucuses.

Two organizations created to combat bigotry and preserve civil liberties were founded in the early 1920s, the American Civil Liberties Union and the Anti-Defamation League of B'nai B'rith; the latter focused on anti-Semitism. In addition, intellectuals such as the novelist Upton Sinclair, the philosopher John Dewey, and the civil rights leader W. E. B. Du Bois continued to agitate for social and political changes, using as their forums such liberal and radical magazines as the *Nation,* the *Masses,* the *Liberator,* and the *Crisis.*

To a larger degree than their numbers justified, anarchists, socialists, and communists made news in the post–World War I era. The most influential anarchist, Emma Goldman, a writer, social organizer, agitator, and birth control advocate, was deported to her native Russia because of her activities. Communists were particularly successful in recruiting union organizers and intellectuals. As late as 1926 the communist *New Masses* carried on its letterhead the names of such prominent writers as Sinclair, Carl Sandburg, Eugene O'Neill, and John Dos Passos. The poet Edna St. Vincent Millay wrote, "If one could not be a Christian, one had to be a Communist."

Still, the radical left's influence was limited because it could not unite behind a single leader or program, although both the Socialist and Communist parties ran presidential tickets in each election during the 1920s. Communists not only fought socialists and anarchists but were divided into feuding factions. They failed to organize strong independent labor unions (ironically, there were no unions in the Soviet Union) or to convince American blacks that the party would carve out for them an independent republic in the South. Some initial sympathizers were dismayed at the infighting and the slavish adherence to party lines dictated by Moscow. In the long run the party, whose membership did not reach the 1919 level again until the late 1930s, proved stifling to creative individuals because they were not permitted to think for themselves.

The United States had the world's highest standard of living during the 1920s, yet there were sufficient limitations to economic prosperity, social tolerance, and political freedom to justify calls for reform. Although income improved at an unprecedented rate for the upper and middle classes, millions lived in poverty, crowded into city tenements or farm shacks without running water or electricity. Millions more, many of them children, toiled in unhealthy factories for subsistence wages. At the bottom of the social and economic pyramid were blacks and other minorities, whose poverty was chronic and hopeless. Women voted in presidential elections for the first time during the decade, but jobs remained gender segregated, and women were underpaid. Jews were prohibited from buying property in some neighborhoods and from patronizing exclusive resorts, and their enrollment at some universities was limited by quotas. Anti-Semitism was common among the upper classes, expressed particularly in hostility toward recent immigrants. Catholics were also objects of prejudice and discrimination.

✦ THE CITY

Among the institutions in need of reform, none posed more challenges than the American city, whose growth was largely a by-product of the growth of industry and the decline of agriculture. In 1920, for the first time, more Americans lived in cities and towns than on farms and villages, if one accepts the Census Bureau's rather dubious definition of an urban area as a community of more than 2,500 inhabitants. Cities of substantial size, however, grew faster than small towns. In 1920 there were 68 cities of more than 100,000 inhabitants; by 1930 there were 96, with 44.6 percent of the nation's population. Urbanization, under way for generations but accelerated by the war, revolutionized American life. The urban life-style was antithetical to that of the farm; it was more complex, liberating, filled with opportunity, and undermined by vice, crime, crowding, pollution, and the loss of individual autonomy. People who lived in cities had far more choices available than rural people had in jobs, purchasing, entertainment, education, and social intercourse. However, if urbanites were less limited by their environment, they were less sure of their identity. They worked in large factories or offices, ate among strangers at restaurants, and went to theaters and stadiums filled with individuals they had never seen before. The anonymity of the city provided some freedom but encouraged social disintegration. Close ties with neighbors were rarely possible; children were no longer reared in an atmosphere suffused by emotional security. It was difficult to ensure privacy, and changes in gender relations were accelerated by mechanization and a breakdown of the sharp distinctions between masculine and feminine roles. Crime, delinquency, divorce, suicide, and mental illnesses increased. Race relations were aggravated by demographic changes that juxtaposed blacks and whites, immigrants and natives, the poor and the rich, within limited areas. On the other hand, increased specialization expanded leisure time and promoted intellectual stimulation. Cities were first to awaken to new ideas and to experiment with new ways.

Politics in the city was complex and often corrupt. Political bosses, supported by machines that thrived on patronage, had at their command enormous resources with which to perpetuate their power. The progressives had addressed problems in city government with limited reforms, but their success was ephemeral. Such antireform mayors as William Hale ("Big Bill") Thompson of Chicago, James J. ("Jimmy") Walker of New York, and James Michael Curley of Boston demonstrated the appeal of demagoguery, promises, patronage, and chicanery for perpetuating the rule of incompetents and crooks. H. L. Mencken joked that a public officeholder was "indistinguishable from . . . a child-stealer, a well-poisoner or a Sunday-school superintendent."

Many rural people viewed cities as the scourge of American society, hostility that was due in part to their coveting of urban affluence. American farmers found themselves increasingly outside the mainstream in the 1920s and 1930s. From constituting one-half of the population in 1900, farmers fell to only two-fifths by 1920, and they lagged far behind city dwellers in modern comforts. After prospering from increased foreign demand during the war, they were enticed to overexpand; consequently, they overproduced and prices declined after the war. In 1919 the average annual return on a cotton farm was more than $60 an acre; from 1920 to 1927 the return averaged about $29, and when the Great Depression struck, cotton markets collapsed, the price falling by more than half between 1929 and 1931.

✥ THE SOUTH

No section of the country felt the decline of the farm and the small town more than the predominantly rural South. Plagued by inadequate diets and poor medical care, many southerners lived in tar-paper shacks with no windows and no indoor toilets, houses that could not have survived a single northern winter. Clinging to fundamentalist religious beliefs amid convulsive social change, white southerners feared communists, labor unions, and blacks. They largely excluded blacks from voting by such devices as the white primary, poll tax, and literacy test. Black southerners were the most deprived in the most impoverished region. Denied a decent education, they were largely confined to menial agricultural jobs.

Southern sharecroppers, especially blacks, endured grinding poverty in the interwar era. Many lived in tar-paper shacks that could not have survived a single northern winter.

Southern whites of all classes united on the issue of white supremacy. Blacks were whipped into line by economic coercion and the threat or use of force; lynching was justified as necessary to intimidate black men from raping white women. Such white demagogues as Theodore Bilbo of Mississippi, Eugene Talmadge of Georgia, and Cole Blease of South Carolina thrived on white supremacy, including a defense of lynching. In his 1930 campaign for the U.S. Senate, Blease said, "Whenever the Constitution comes between me and the virtue of the white women of the South, I say to hell with the Constitution."

Yet if the reality for many in the South was grinding poverty, the region was potentially rich, with mild weather, oil and timber, and a tourist mecca, Florida. An increase in the popularity of smoking during the 1920s offered promise for southern tobacco farmers, and the automobile would create a voracious demand for petroleum. Even some of the more bigoted politicians, such as Bilbo, were liberal on economic issues.

The prosperity of the 1920s did not entirely bypass the South, but when the Great Depression struck the region suffered more than any other. As a rural section, the South was one of the last to modernize and one of the more resistant to modernizing influences. However reluctantly, the South did change, and by 1945 it had experienced more changes than any other region. No place in America escaped change in the era.

✛ CHANGE

It is not likely that the nation will ever again experience two world wars, fantastic prosperity, and numbing economic depression within a 25-year period. No one who lived through the interwar era could doubt that it offers lessons, warnings, and inspiration for future generations. No other era has held such a concentration of the flippant, the futile, the tragic, and the heroic.

BIBLIOGRAPHICAL ESSAY

NOTE: I cite books only once in the bibliographical essays, although many of them deal with more than one decade and most deal with more than one subject. I list the edition I used in my research, but many of the books have gone through numerous editions. I include books most helpful to students rather than to specialists.

General histories of America in the twentieth century that are useful for the period from 1921 to 1945 include Daniel J. Boorstin, *The Americans: The Democratic Experience* (1973), which emphasizes the growth of democracy; James MacGregor Burns, *The Workshop of Democracy* (1985), beautifully written; Eric F. Goldman, *Rendezvous with Destiny* (1952); Frank Freidel and Alan Brinkley, *America in the Twentieth Century* (1982); Arthur S. Link and William B. Catton, *American Epoch: A History of the United States Since 1900*, vol. 1, *1900–1945* (1980); George E. Mowry and Blaine A. Brownell, *The Urban Nation, 1920–1980* (1981); James T. Patterson, *America in the Twentieth Century* (1989); and David W. Noble, David A. Horowitz, and Peter N. Carroll, *Twentieth Century Limited: A History of Recent America* (1980).

The most detailed study of the interwar period is Page Smith, *Redeeming the Time*, vol. 8, *A People's History of the 1920s and the New Deal* (1987). Other studies of the era include David A. Shannon, *Between the Wars: America, 1919–1941* (1979); Michael Kurtz, *The Challenging of America, 1920–1945* (1986); and the more detailed Sean Dennis Cashman, *America in the Twenties and Thirties: The Olympian Age of Franklin Delano Roosevelt* (1989). Older works that are useful include Robert A. Divine, *The Age of Insecurity: America, 1920–1945* (1968); Donald R. McCoy, *Coming of Age: The United States During the 1920s and 1930s* (1973); Henry Morton Robinson, *Fantastic Interim* (1943); Forrest McDonald, *The United States in the 20th Century*, vol. 2, *1920–1945* (1970); Jonathan Daniels, *The Time Between the Wars: Armistice to Pearl Harbor* (1966); J. Joseph Huthmacher, *Trial by War and Depression* (1973); and Ralph K. Andrist, ed., *The American Heritage History of the 1920s and 1930s* (1970), a popular history. Isabel Leighton, ed., *The Aspirin Age, 1919–1941* (1968), is a collection of sprightly essays.

General surveys of the preceding period include John M. Cooper, Jr., *Pivotal Decades: The United States, 1900–1920* (1990); Robert H. Wiebe, *The Search for Order, 1877–1920* (1967); and Burl Noggle, *Into the Twenties: The United States from the Armistice to Normalcy* (1974). Studies of World War I and the peacemaking include Arthur Walworth, *Woodrow Wilson and His Peacemakers* (1983); Robert H. Ferrell, *Woodrow Wilson and World War I, 1917–1921* (1985); and

Lloyd G. Ambrosius, *Woodrow Wilson and the American Diplomatic Tradition: The Treaty Fight in Perspective* (1988).

Studies of reform during the era include Richard Hofstadter, *The Age of Reform: From Bryan to FDR* (1955); Arthur S. Link, *Woodrow Wilson and the Progressive Era, 1910–1917* (1954); Robert M. Crunden, *Ministers of Reform* (1982); John D. Buenker, *Urban Liberalism and Progressive Reform* (1975); James Weinstein, *The Decline of Socialism in America, 1912–1925* (1967); LeRoy Ashby, *The Spearless Leader: Senator Borah and the Progressive Movement in the 1920s* (1972); and James T. Patterson, *America's Struggle Against Poverty, 1900–1980* (1981).

On the city, see Jon C. Teaford, *The Twentieth-Century American City: Problem, Promise, and Reality* (1986); and Charles N. Glaab and Theodore Brown, *A History of Urban America* (1976). Studies of the South include C. Vann Woodward, *Origins of the New South, 1877–1913* (1951); George B. Tindall, *The Emergence of the New South* (1967); Jack Temple Kirby, *Darkness at the Dawning: Race and Reform in the Progressive South* (1967); Monroe Lee Billington, *The Political South in the Twentieth Century* (1975); and Michael O'Brien, *The Idea of the American South, 1920–1941* (1979).

C. E. Black, *The Dynamics of Modernization: A Study in Comparative History* (1966), is an outstanding study of modernization; and Daniel J. Singal, *Modernist Culture in America* (1991), is useful in understanding cultural modernism.

Biographies of leading figures of the early 1920s include David P. Thelen, *Robert M. La Follette and the Insurgent Spirit* (1976); John M. Blum, *Woodrow Wilson and the Politics of Morality* (1956); John A. Garraty, *Henry Cabot Lodge* (1954); Richard W. Leopold, *Elihu Root and the Conservative Tradition* (1954); Melvin I. Urofsky, *Louis D. Brandeis and the Progressive Tradition* (1981); and John M. Cooper, Jr., *The Warrior and the Priest* (1983), a study of Theodore Roosevelt and Wilson.

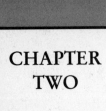

CHAPTER
TWO

THE REPUBLICAN DECADE

✧ THE ELECTION OF 1920

As the United States entered the decade of the 1920s, Woodrow Wilson was an ill, unpopular president, and the odds favored the Republicans in the November presidential election. There had been only two Democratic presidents since the Civil War, and the second of them, Wilson, would not have won except for a split in Republican ranks because of the third party candidacy of Theodore Roosevelt in 1912. Wilson's failure to secure ratification of the Versailles Treaty tainted the Democrats, but even more troublesome to them was the state of the economy. Wilson had made no plans for reconversion to a peacetime economy, and when World War I ended veterans were released so rapidly that many were unable to find jobs. The economy slackened with the reduction of wartime demand, agricultural prices plummeted, inflation soared, and the government, which had operated the railroads during the war, abruptly returned them to their owners.

Wilson wanted the election to be a referendum on the League of Nations, although the economic recession was a larger issue. The chief problem the Republicans faced was finding a suitable candidate. Theodore Roosevelt, the most popular Republican, died in January 1919. After Roosevelt's death, the front-runner was General Leonard Wood, who had commanded the Rough Riders in the Spanish-American War and later served as army chief of staff. If the nominee had been selected by popular vote, he would have been the

16

party's choice. His chief opponent was Governor Frank O. Lowden of Illinois, who had substantial support among farmers. Both major parties considered nominating Herbert Hoover, the most famous humanitarian in America, who had led international efforts to feed Belgium during the First World War and, after the armistice, had directed relief to all of Europe. Franklin D. Roosevelt, Wilson's assistant secretary of the navy, urged Democrats to nominate Hoover. "He is certainly a wonder," Roosevelt wrote, "and I wish we could make him president of the United States. There could not be a better one." Hoover, who had no political experience, announced that he was a Republican, yet made no serious effort to obtain the nomination.

Warren G. Harding of Ohio was a dark horse candidate who did not desire the nomination but agreed to run because he was persuaded that national attention would aid his reelection to the Senate. Although he was not the first choice of many delegates, a substantial number considered him an acceptable compromise candidate. As the Republican convention opened in Chicago in July, gamblers placed odds of 8 to 1 against a Harding nomination. Harding's campaign manager, Ohio lobbyist and small-time politician Harry Daugherty, worked energetically to make Harding the second choice of delegates who favored Wood or Lowden.

Harding, a newspaper publisher, was a friendly man who had never taken a stand on controversial issues, had few enemies, and was known for his ability to harmonize discordant viewpoints. He represented a key state where the balance between Democrats and Republicans might be swayed by the presence of a native son on the ticket. Harding's worst flaws were known to few in 1920, but no one considered him an outstanding senator or a first-rate intellect. He had been present on less than 50 percent of Senate roll calls, failed to vote on 35 percent of motions when he was there, and never filed an important bill, much less passed one. He expressed himself in polysyllabic platitudes that amused intellectuals. "Harding writes the worst English that I have ever encountered, outside of a college professor or two," H. L. Mencken wrote. "It is so bad that a sort of grandeur creeps into it." In a speech in Boston in May, Harding said the times called for "not heroism, but healing, not nostrums but normalcy." His use of the term "normalcy" captured the public mood; he meant that the nation should return to quiet times and not engage in domestic reform or international crusades. He popularized the word "normalcy" although he did not coin it; it had first appeared in a dictionary in 1857.

Harding was an even more vulnerable candidate because of his flawed private life. He had married a woman five years his senior, a rich divorcee, strong willed and shrewish. It was an advantageous but unhappy marriage that drove the weak-willed Harding to philandering. Harding had two mistresses, Carrie Phillips, the wife of one of his friends, and Nan Britton, a much younger woman. The Phillips affair did not become public knowledge until many years after his death, but Britton published a book in 1927, which badly damaged his reputation posthumously. Britton had become infatuated with Harding when she was only 12, and she followed him east when he became a senator.

Their affair began in 1916 when Britton was 19 and Harding 49. They continued to meet clandestinely in the White House after he became president, sometimes making love in a closet in the Oval Office while the Secret Service stood guard. She got a job in New York and occasionally traveled with Harding as his niece. Britton bore Harding a daughter and, while president, he sent her at least $100 a week for support.

Harding's habits were crude: he smoked, drank, and ate excessively, and preferred poker and golf to statesmanship. Worse, he was most at ease in the company of cronies who had little to recommend them except that they were equally crude. "Harding wasn't a bad man," Alice Roosevelt Longworth wrote, "he was just a slob."

Harding's health was another issue that could have hurt him in the campaign had it been known. He suffered from high blood pressure and had a weak heart. Although he had a playboy personality, he was a chronic worrier and on five occasions had entered a sanitarium to recover from nervous exhaustion. He was often depressed; in fact, his drinking and womanizing were in part efforts to escape depression.

Harding's wife, Florence, visited an astrologer during the campaign. The astrologer predicted that her husband would be elected president but would die before his term expired. With that in mind, Florence confessed, "I can see but one word written over the head of my husband if he is elected and that word is 'tragedy.'"

When the Republican delegates began balloting, Wood led, with Lowden close behind, yet after four ballots it became apparent that neither could muster a majority. After a brief adjournment, a group of party bosses met at the hotel suite of George Harvey, a wealthy magazine editor and prominent Republican, to break the deadlock. They considered various candidates until by the process of elimination Harding remained. Senator Boies Penrose, one of those present, said they wanted a man "who would listen" rather than tell them what to do.

The next day, the bosses slowly fed delegates to Harding. He rose gradually in the voting and was nominated on the tenth ballot. "Harding is no world-beater," a Republican senator admitted, "but he's the best of the second-raters." Harvey was blunter: "He was nominated because there was nothing against him and because the delegates wanted to go home."

The bosses nominated Senator Irvine L. Lenroot of Wisconsin for vice president, but the delegates chose the governor of Massachusetts, Calvin Coolidge, who had won fame by firmly, if belatedly, opposing a strike of policemen in Boston. Journalists depicted the nomination of Coolidge as a grass-roots rebellion against the choice of the bosses; ironically, the choice of the bosses, Lenroot, was more reform oriented than Coolidge. Also ironically, Coolidge was better known than Harding. Just prior to the vice-presidential voting, a friend of Coolidge had told a reporter, "If Calvin Coolidge were nominated for the vice presidency, I wouldn't take the presidency for a million dollars." "Why?" asked the reporter. He replied, "Because I would die in a little while. Coolidge has always been lucky politically. Everything comes to him in a most uncanny and mysterious way."

The Democratic convention, which met in San Francisco two weeks later, also deadlocked. The leading candidates were William Gibbs McAdoo, Wilson's treasury secretary, and A. Mitchell Palmer, his attorney general. After eight days and 44 ballots the delegates nominated a compromise choice, Governor James M. Cox of Ohio, also a newspaper publisher. The vice-presidential nominee was also a surprise: 38-year-old Franklin D. Roosevelt, nominated largely because delegates believed the Roosevelt name might appeal to Republican voters who fondly remembered Franklin's distant cousin, Theodore Roosevelt. FDR was well liked in both parties, but many leading politicians did not consider him a serious person. Henry Cabot Lodge called him "a well-meaning, nice young fellow, but light."

Progressives saw little to recommend either candidate. Robert La Follette refused to endorse either Harding or Cox. The chief protest candidate was Eugene V. Debs, candidate of the American Socialist party, who was running for the fourth and last time. Debs was an inmate in the federal penitentiary in Atlanta, put there for resisting the draft during World War I. His campaign literature featured his prison number.

The public did not show much interest in the campaign, and less than half of those eligible would vote. Given the unpopularity of the Democratic administration and that registered Republicans far outnumbered Democrats, the outcome appeared a foregone conclusion. One journalist berated the Democrats for fighting among themselves when whoever they nominated was likely to lose, comparing the bitter struggle between McAdoo and Palmer to two bald-headed men fighting over a hairbrush. That neither Harding nor Cox was distinguished led one reporter to write that the most hopeful aspect of the campaign was that "they both can't win."

Cox and Roosevelt campaigned aggressively, vainly attempting to make the League of Nations a viable issue. Harding became the first presidential candidate to deliver a speech over the radio, and station KDKA in Pittsburgh became the first to broadcast election returns. Otherwise, Harding remained at his home in Marion, Ohio, avoiding mistakes, leaving much of the campaigning to surrogates. He pledged to support federal aid for highways, conservation, equal pay for women, the abolition of child labor, economy in government, a high tariff, and limits on immigration.

The only real controversy of the campaign was over circulars distributed by the Ohio professor William E. Chancellor, which claimed that Harding, who had a dark complexion, was part Negro. Few took the charge seriously, but Chancellor was sufficiently credible; he had history books published by such reputable houses as Houghton Mifflin and Macmillan. Later he self-published a book making similar claims, complete with a bogus genealogy. The Justice Department under Harding bought all unsold copies, confiscated those in private hands, burned them, and destroyed the printing plates.

Harding swept the nation by a record vote. He won 404 electoral votes, the greatest total up to that time, to 127 for Cox, who carried only 11 states. His 16.2 million popular votes, to Cox's 9.1 million, represented almost 60.4 percent, one of the higher percentages in American history. Debs received 919,799 votes, the most ever by a Socialist party candidate.

✧ THE HARDING ADMINISTRATION

Pathetically aware of his limitations, Harding feared the presidency was beyond his abilities. He surrounded himself with a cabinet he called the "best minds" and tried to take their advice. The three most important members were Charles Evans Hughes, secretary of state; Herbert Hoover, secretary of commerce; and Andrew Mellon, secretary of the treasury. Hughes, a former Supreme Court justice, had been the Republican presidential nominee in 1916. Hoover was in the cabinet, over the opposition of conservatives, because Harding considered Hoover among the smartest men he had ever met. Vindicating his selection, Hoover made a previously obscure position the most creative department in the government. Mellon, the third richest American behind John D. Rockefeller and Henry Ford, was a frail, diffident man weighing barely one hundred pounds, but was so respected by businessmen that they predicted he would be the greatest secretary of the treasury since Alexander Hamilton. Mellon continued to serve under Coolidge and Hoover, the only cabinet member in history to serve three presidents in the same position.

Most of the cabinet members were Republican millionaires, many of them were businessmen, and all were supporters of business. Hoover was the most progressive of them. Harding's secretary of the interior, Albert B. Fall, was opposed by conservationists and was involved in the most prominent scandal of the administration. Daugherty, the attorney general, also disgraced the administration. Harding appointed four conservative Supreme Court justices, including former President William Howard Taft as chief justice; the others were George Sutherland, Pierce Butler, and Edward Sanford. All believed the government should protect private property and limit its regulation of business.

Harding made some appointments on the basis of personal loyalty rather than ability: Daugherty's appointment was a reward for engineering Harding's election; a casual friend, Charles R. Forbes, was appointed director of the Veterans Bureau, although his reputation for honesty was dubious. Some of Harding's cronies were known as the Ohio Gang, and he liked to socialize with them; they played poker twice a week. Alice Roosevelt Longworth described one of Harding's poker parties at the White House:

> No rumor could have exceeded the reality; the study was filled with cronies . . . the air heavy with tobacco smoke, trays with bottles containing every imaginable brand of whiskey stood about, cards and poker chips ready at hand—a general atmosphere of waistcoat unbuttoned, feet on desk, and spittoons alongside.

Harding lacked statesmanship, yet he excelled at public relations, and the part of his job he enjoyed most was meeting people. He kept the White House gate open and the curtains raised, and every day during the lunch hour he greeted any citizen who wanted to drop by to meet the president. In three

Warren G. Harding, who tried to play the tuba, was something of a middle-aged playboy who found the presidency a burden.

years he shook hands with some 250,000 people. His generosity was expressed through a pardon of Debs and other political prisoners shortly before Christmas in 1921. He got along better with the press than any previous president and held more press conferences than his predecessors. A conscientious president who wanted to be successful and popular, he worked hard, arriving at the Oval Office by 7 a.m. and frequently remaining there until midnight.

Shortly after his inauguration Harding summoned Congress into special session and urged it to enact legislation providing for a protective tariff, a tax cut, budget reductions, aid to agriculture, a subsidy for the merchant marine, an antilynching law, and creation of a Department of Public Welfare. Portions of Harding's program were enacted, but other bills died in committee, on the floor, or due to a filibuster. Although his party had a 303–133 majority in the House and a 59–37 margin in the Senate, Harding found it difficult to work with Congress. Once bills were drafted by members of the cabinet and introduced in Congress, he did not provide the leadership necessary to overcome opposition. Only when there was broad agreement would he publicly campaign for bills.

Harding's bill to provide a subsidy to shippers to maintain the merchant marine acquired during World War I was killed by a filibuster. Congress also defeated his bills to reorganize the federal bureaucracy, to outlaw lynching, and to create a Department of Public Welfare. Congress did enact the Government Reclassification Act of 1923, which established uniform qualifications and pay for positions in federal employment.

Congress agreed that a tariff should be enacted to protect farmers and manufacturers from foreign competition. Two such bills were passed, the Emergency Tariff of 1921 and, subsequently, the Fordney-McCumber Tariff. The latter was loaded down with 2,000 Senate amendments to protect special interests. Harding received authority to adjust rates to changing conditions but used his presidential discretion primarily to increase rates. The tariff, popular with business, proved little help to farmers. Other nations retaliated by raising their duties and closing their markets to American goods.

Harding knew that to implement tax reductions while reducing the national debt it would be necessary to simplify and systemize the nation's budgetary process. The Budget and Accounting Act of 1921 thus created a Bureau of the Budget and a General Accounting Office. For the first time, the federal government would operate under a unified budget, which attempted to rationalize revenue and expenditures.

Perhaps the most popular aspect of Harding's program in the short run was the reduction in taxes and in government expenditures conceived by Mellon. Because the nation was in a recession in 1921, both parties agreed that a tax cut would stimulate the economy, yet progressives and conservatives differed over the type of cut that would be most beneficial. Mellon believed that tax cuts for the wealthy would make capital available for investment; progressives, many from the South and West, preferred a broader tax cut. Existing law provided for a 4 percent tax on the first $4,000 earned and an 8 percent tax on income above that, with a surtax of 1 percent on incomes above $5,000, escalating to 65 percent on incomes in excess of $1 million. There was an excess profits tax and a corporate tax of 10 percent.

Harding, who knew little economics, was frustrated by the debate. "I can't make a damn thing out of this tax problem," he confessed. "I know somewhere there is a book that will give me the truth; but hell! I couldn't read the book." Ultimately Harding endorsed Mellon's proposal, although the law that emerged was a compromise. The general rates remained the same, but exemptions were raised and the excess profits tax was abolished. The maximum surtax was reduced to 50 percent, the corporate tax was raised to 12 percent, and for the first time a 12.5 percent tax on capital gains was imposed. This was hardly a "soak-the-poor" law; in fact, under it most working-class Americans paid no income tax.

Mellon, not satisfied with the outcome, continued to work for tax reductions at the higher income levels. With the cooperation of Harding and Charles G. Dawes, the first budget director, he was successful in reducing expenditures and retiring the federal debt, which had soared from $1.2 billion in 1914 to $23.1 billion in 1921. It fell to $21.8 billion by the end of Harding's term and to $16.5 billion by 1929.

Hoover was the most active cabinet member in working to end the recession. He organized a national conference on unemployment in 1921, collected and distributed economic statistics, helped manufacturers eliminate waste and duplication, and urged industry to cooperate through trade associations. He negotiated voluntary agreements to regulate the new radio and aviation industries. The Federal Reserve Board and the Interstate Commerce Commission also supported business by reducing interest rates and relaxing regulatory standards.

The weakest sector of the economy was agriculture. Demand declined because of changing dietary habits, a desire for fashionable, slim figures, the invention of synthetic fabrics, and less need for livestock feed because tractors and automobiles were replacing mules and horses. And many farmers, producing perishable products that all reached markets at the same time, were at the mercy of weather and insects.

Farm representatives in Congress created the Farm Bloc to work for relief. Through their efforts farmers gained a representative on the Federal Reserve Board, which subsequently provided easier credit. The Packers and Stockyards Act of 1921 prohibited price setting by interstate packers, the Capper-Volstead Act of 1922 exempted farm cooperatives from antitrust laws, and the Agricultural Credits Act of 1923 lent money to farm cooperatives. In addition, the Highway Act of 1921, administered by the Agriculture Department, provided money for farm-to-market roads, and under it federal highway expenditures increased from $19.5 million in 1920 to $88 million in 1923.

The recession was largely responsible for heavy Republican losses in the November 1922 congressional elections, but the GOP did retain small majorities in each house. Within six months prosperity had returned to many sectors of the economy, although farmers continued to suffer. The Republicans controlled Congress for the rest of the decade.

In the wake of the congressional losses, Harding became increasingly unhappy in the presidency. He was finding the job too big for him. Although he worked long hours, he wasted time on trivia, answering many letters from constituents in longhand. Told that he was dissipating his energies, he confessed, "I suppose so, but I am not fit for this office and never should have been here." Asked to describe the presidency, he exclaimed, "It is hell! No other word can describe it." On another occasion he wrote a friend, "Frankly, being president is rather an unattractive business unless one relishes the exercise of power."

By 1923 Harding was tense and morose. Always a compulsive golfer, he now tired after nine holes. His face aged, and his skin grew slack; he was bending under his burden. Most ominous, rumors began to reach him that his administration was riddled with graft and corruption. The first stories concerned Jesse Smith, who shared with his close friend Daugherty a house worth $50,000 in annual rental fees on one $12,000 government salary. Smith, who was not a government official, had an office in the Department of Justice, franked his mail on the attorney general's letterhead, traveled on departmental money, and spent his time exchanging favors for bribes.

Daugherty had taken office with assets of less than $10,000 and liabilities of $27,000. But he obtained shares in an airline that received a big government subsidy, and two years later he deposited $75,000 cash and $40,000 in bonds in his brother's bank. When they heard that their schemes were coming to light, the Daugherty brothers burned the bank records.

Daugherty and Smith were minor operators compared to Forbes and his attorney, Charles F. Cramer, at the Veterans Bureau. Forbes entertained more lavishly than anyone in Washington, on a legal income of only $10,000. His legal income, however, was merely the tip of the iceberg. Forbes and Cramer received kickbacks from two sources: builders who constructed hospitals for veterans and firms that were sold new supplies—on the pretense that supplies were damaged or obsolete—for a fraction of their value. Sheets bought for $1.37 were sold in their original packages for 27 cents for resale; simultaneously the department was buying new sheets. As sheets were unloaded, others were carried out the other end of the same warehouse to be sold. Towels that cost 34 cents were sold for 3 cents; gauze bought at $1.33 per roll was sold at an 80 percent discount. One of Forbes's cronies was in the floor wax business, so the bureau obligingly bought enough to last one hundred years, paying 98 cents a gallon for wax worth 4 cents. One expert estimated that Forbes and Cramer, who controlled a budget of half a billion dollars a year, looted $200 million.

When Harding learned of the affair, he summoned Forbes to the White House, pinned him to a wall, and called him a "yellow rat," but he permitted Forbes to resign and flee the country. Forbes, though, was convicted of fraud and bribery. Three weeks later Cramer committed suicide. Harding also confronted Smith and told him he would be arrested the next day. A few hours later Smith killed himself in Daugherty's hotel room.

It was clear that the scandals could not remain hidden much longer. Deeply troubled, Harding left Washington on a transcontinental railroad tour on June 20, 1923, planning to return on August 26. On his journey west he played bridge up to 15 hours a day until he collapsed from exhaustion. For Harding it was an escape from responsibility; for the other players it was an endurance contest. Hoover, who joined the party, said he never enjoyed bridge again.

In Tacoma, Washington, Harding boarded a steamer for an excursion to

Alaska. When his ship collided with a navy destroyer, incurring slight damage, he said, "I hope the boat sinks." At Vancouver he delivered a listless speech. At Seattle he dropped his manuscript during a long talk and became confused, but recovered. That night he suffered a mild heart attack, and as his train sped to San Francisco he contracted pneumonia. On the night of August 2 he died suddenly from a stroke.

Still a popular president, Harding received a hero's funeral. Within months, though, his reputation was shattered as scandal after scandal became public. The most serious scandal, the Teapot Dome affair, emerged after his death. Interior Secretary Fall, purportedly concerned about government oil reserves being drained by wells on adjoining private property, leased the oil at Teapot Dome, Wyoming, to oilman Harry Sinclair and oil reserves at Elk Hills, California, to Edward L. Doheny. Fall, who received $300,000 from Sinclair and $100,000 from Doheny, denied the money was a bribe. He pointed out that the oilmen had pledged to build pipelines and storage facilities for the navy, and argued that if he had not leased the oil it would have been depleted by the adjoining wells. The complex affair dragged on long into the Coolidge administration. Sinclair and Doheny were acquitted of offering bribes, but Sinclair was convicted of bribing a juror. Fall was convicted by a different jury and became the first cabinet member convicted of a crime in office.

Harding's reputation was further decimated when Britton published *The President's Daughter*, a gossipy account of their torrid affair and their child. In 1930 a film company announced plans for a movie based on the book, but movie czar Will Hays, who had been Harding's postmaster general, prevented it. The same year Gaston B. Means published *The Strange Death of President Harding*, which argued that Florence Harding had poisoned her husband to save him from impeachment. Circumstances lent a superficial plausibility to the obviously fraudulent account; the widow had refused to permit an autopsy, and she had burned her husband's papers.

❖ THE COOLIDGE YEARS

At the time of Harding's death, most politicians issued respectful condolences. However, Lodge's first words were, "My God, that means Coolidge is President!" When he was later asked what his first thought was, Coolidge replied, "I thought I could swing it."

Under most scenarios, Calvin Coolidge would not have been considered presidential timber. In terms of raw intelligence, Coolidge was brighter than much of the general population; among presidents he probably ranked near the middle. But he had assets that every politician needs; he was shrewd, cautious, and opportunistic, and he gauged the attitudes of voters as perceptively as any politician of his time. Nor was Coolidge lazy; his long afternoon naps while president were due more to poor health, particularly stomach disorders, than to lassitude.

Coolidge, notorious for his silence, was reticent probably because he was depressed. The fear of death haunted his family: His mother died when he was 12, his sister when he was 15; his stepmother died in 1920; and he lost his father and his younger son while president. As a child, his grandmother had sometimes locked him in the attic to punish him. Coolidge's silence was exaggerated, although he was as shy and laconic as Harding was gregarious. It was impossible to consider him dishonest. So frugal he quibbled about nickels, he seemed an archetypal New England Puritan. In his mind, he never left the green hills and stony soil of his native Vermont. Toward the end of his presidency he said: "Vermont is a state I love. . . . It was here that I first saw the light of day; here I received my bride; here my dead lie, pillowed on the loving breast of our everlasting hills." Coolidge retained a Vermont accent all his life, and his nasal twang was so pronounced that, it was said, he could say the word "cow" in three syllables. He remained a country person throughout his public career; until late in life he owned neither a car nor a telephone and never learned to drive.

Born in 1872 in the hamlet of Plymouth Notch, Coolidge split wood, milked cows, fed chickens and pigs, and plowed furrows on his father's farm. When he outgrew the local school, his father sent him to a boarding school at Ludlow, then to Amherst College in Massachusetts, where he received average grades. He had few close friends and rarely participated in extracurricular activities. "A drabber, more colorless boy I never knew than Calvin Coolidge when he came to Amherst," a classmate wrote. "He was a perfect enigma to us all." When he filled out a questionnaire for Amherst seniors asking what they expected to do after graduation, Coolidge wrote, "Nothing, I reckon."

Coolidge settled in nearby Northampton, where he read law. In the early 1890s he entered politics at the local level and proved remarkably adept at winning elections, losing just once in 20 times, with a straightforward approach that included few promises. Approaching a voter he would say only: "I want your vote. I need it. I shall appreciate it." For a man lacking charisma, he was strangely appealing. His only defeat was in a race for the Northampton School Board in 1905, the year he married. His bride was the intelligent, vivacious Grace Goodhue of Burlington, Vermont, as spontaneous and witty as her husband was reserved. The unlikely pairing astounded Northampton residents; even Grace's father was surprised. When Mr. Goodhue found Coolidge sitting in his living room one morning he asked if Coolidge had business in Burlington. "No," Coolidge replied, "came up to marry Grace." Despite such an improbable match, the Coolidges were a devoted couple. They never talked politics, however; Coolidge thought it an inappropriate subject for women.

The public confidence he inspired enabled Coolidge to serve in the Massachusetts legislature, then to become mayor of Northampton, president of the state Senate, and lieutenant governor. In 1918 he was elected governor. He won fame for calling out the National Guard during the Boston police strike of 1919 even though it was his negligence that had allowed the situation to deteriorate.

The guiding spirit behind Coolidge's career was Frank W. Stearns, a millionaire Boston department store owner and an Amherst alumnus. After meeting Coolidge in 1913, he devoted himself unselfishly to advancing Coolidge's career. He paid for and circulated thousands of copies of Coolidge's pamphlet, *Have Faith in Massachusetts,* to help him obtain the vice-presidential nomination in 1920.

As vice president, Coolidge became known as a quaint nonentity who spent much of his time attending banquets and delivering speeches. Asked why he attended so many dinners when he obviously did not enjoy socializing, Coolidge replied, "Got to eat somewhere." Grace Coolidge, a sparkling conversationalist, enjoyed telling stories about her husband's reputation for silence, which the press carried in an effort to make him interesting. A reporter who sat with the Coolidges at a baseball game said that Coolidge's only words through nine innings were to ask his wife, "What time is it?" When he did speak, he often uttered aphorisms and vacuous generalities. Sinclair Lewis's *Man Who Knew Coolidge* satirized Coolidge through his fictitious friend, Lowell Schmaltz, who had attended school with the future president. Schmaltz recalled: "I can remember just's well as if it was yesterday, Cal and me happened to come out of a class together and I said, 'Well, it's going to be a cold winter,' and he came back, 'Yep.' Didn't waste a lot of time arguing and discussing! He knew!"

Coolidge's superficial calmness seemed to charm the nation and reassure the business community. He rarely intervened in congressional affairs unless a crisis arose, and during his presidency there were few crises. So relatively tranquil was his tenure that near the end, when a woman asked him what had worried him most, he replied, "The White House hams," explaining that he never found out what happened to the leftovers. He usually followed the dictum he had laid down as governor, when he said, "A great many times if you let a situation alone it takes care of itself."

Coolidge was effective in implementing the program he wanted; in consonance with the times it was a program of limited government activity. However, his liabilities were substantial: he lacked vision, possessed little imagination, had no master plan for his administration, procrastinated, and did not like to take advice. When confronted with problems, he sometimes diverted the conversation to trivialities and irrelevancies. He did not understand the complexities of economics, government, or human relations, and read only superficially. He did not comprehend the modern world and was largely ignorant of the vast, pluralistic nation over which he presided.

Philosophically, Coolidge was more conservative than Harding. To Coolidge, economy in government was a sacred principle; to Harding, it had been an expediency. In his first message to Congress after Harding's death, Coolidge called for further reductions in taxes and government expenses, improved race relations, aid for black education, a constitutional amendment to restrict child labor, and a minimum wage for women. Like Harding, Coolidge did not lobby Congress for legislation, and only the budget and tax cuts were achieved. His first budget totaled only $3.3 billion, the lowest federal expenditures since the First World War. The Revenue Act of 1924 reduced income taxes to 2 percent on the first $4,000 (from 4 percent), to 4 percent on the next $4,000 (from 8 percent), and to 6 percent on the rest (from 8 percent). The maximum surtax was reduced from 50 percent to 40 percent and applied only to incomes above $500,000 (previously $200,000). Despite the tax cuts, federal revenue increased, and Mellon was able to continue his program of retiring the national debt.

Coolidge found political assets in his stand-pat philosophy and his disposal of the Harding scandals, which brought the guilty to justice without unduly embarrassing his party. Having no serious challengers for the 1924 Republican nomination, he was selected on the first ballot. He did not choose his own running mate, and the delegates nominated Frank O. Lowden, who declined, then Charles G. Dawes, who accepted. The platform advocated further cuts in taxes and spending, higher tariffs, arms limitations, and cooperation with the World Court.

The Democratic convention was hardly so tranquil as the Republican gathering; appropriately, it was held in Madison Square Garden, the site of many prizefights. The tension between transformation and reaction that animated the country was far more apparent in the Democratic party than in the Republican. The party was divided between an urban, liberal wing that opposed prohibition and a rural, conservative wing that supported it. The most divisive issue proved to be the Ku Klux Klan; a motion to condemn it in the platform failed by a single vote.

The convention deadlocked between the liberal candidate Al Smith, the governor of New York, and the conservative favorite, William G. McAdoo. McAdoo was somewhat tainted by having served as an attorney for Edward L. Doheny, one of the oil moguls involved in the Teapot Dome scandal, even though McAdoo committed no crimes. Smith was nominated by Roosevelt, making his first political appearance since he had been stricken by polio shortly after running on the Cox ticket in 1920. FDR said of Smith, "He is the Happy Warrior of the political battlefield." After listening to Roosevelt's speech, a reporter for the *New York Evening World* wrote, "No matter whether Governor Smith wins or loses, Franklin D. Roosevelt stands out as the real hero of the Democratic Convention of 1924."

The deadlock of 1920, which had also involved McAdoo, paled in comparison to the hopeless deadlock of 1924. The Democrats, who needed a two-thirds majority to nominate a candidate, exhausted themselves in balloting. Will Rogers wrote: "This thing has got to come to an end. New York invited you people here as guests, not to live." With delegates still stalemated, McAdoo offered to release his delegates to support his Indiana friend, Senator Samuel Ralston, but Ralston rejected the offer because of his poor health. Finally, on the 103d ballot, the Democrats nominated a compromise candidate, John W. Davis, a corporate attorney from West Virginia who had served as a congressman and ambassador to England. For vice president they nominated Nebraska Governor Charles W. Bryan, the younger brother of famous Democratic politician William Jennings Bryan.

Many liberals, who could find little hope in Coolidge or Davis, supported Robert M. La Follette, the candidate of the Progressive party. La Follette called for government ownership of railroads and hydroelectric power and advocated a constitutional amendment permitting Congress to override decisions of the Supreme Court. Most of La Follette's support came at Davis's expense; without his candidacy the Democrats would have posed a more serious challenge to Coolidge. Coolidge's chief strengths were that the nation was relatively prosperous and that Republicans were the majority party. Henry Ford expressed the views of many voters when he said: "The country is perfectly safe with Coolidge. Why change?"

The Republicans outspent the Democrats almost 5 to 1, and polls showed Coolidge leading throughout the campaign. The Coolidge-Dawes ticket won 15.7 million popular votes to 8.4 million votes for the Democratic ticket, which won only the South, and 4.8 million for the Progressive ticket. In the electoral college, Coolidge won 382 votes, Davis 136, and La Follette 13. The Republicans also won solid congressional majorities, although congressional candidates generally ran behind the national ticket.

Coolidge and Mellon continued to cut taxes and slash the federal budget. The Revenue Act of 1926 reduced maximum inheritance and surtax rates to 20 percent (from 40 percent), repealed the gift tax, and raised personal exemptions. The income tax was reduced to 1.5 percent on the first $4,000 (from 2 percent), to 3 percent on the next $4,000 (from 4 percent) and to 5 percent on the rest (from 6 percent). The corporate income tax was increased to 12.5 percent in 1926 (from 12 percent) and to 13.5 percent in 1927.

Although the tax reductions were popular, farmers, who continued to languish, resented Coolidge for twice vetoing bills that would have provided price supports for agriculture. The legislation, known as the McNary-Haugen plan, had been simmering since the Harding administration. It would have set a high domestic price for agricultural products. Surpluses would be bought by the federal government and resold abroad at a loss, with the government compensated by a tax on food processing. Coolidge correctly pointed out that the plan would only encourage farmers to produce more when the chief reason for low prices was overproduction. Neither the government nor farmers themselves were willing to mandate production limits. Due partly to farm unrest, the Republicans lost seats in the 1926 congressional elections but retained their majorities.

Coolidge signed a bill providing $165 million to construct federal buildings but limited spending in general. He even limited a flood control appropriation to $500 million, lower than the $1.4 billion that Congress wanted, after a flood in the Ohio and Mississippi valleys left 200 people dead and 1.5 million homeless and caused hundreds of millions of dollars in damages. (Hoover coordinated federal, local, and private relief efforts.) Business expansion continued, with new products, such as automobiles and electrical appliances, flowing from assembly lines and prompting massive investment in stocks that seemed destined to rise. The expansion was fueled by the Federal Reserve Board's reduction in the discount rate of 0.5 percent in August 1927. Some economists warned that the economy was overheating, yet Coolidge announced that it was sound.

It was widely assumed that Coolidge would run for reelection in 1928 and win easily. But Coolidge had grown ill in the White House with a stomach and heart that bothered him. More important, the death of Calvin, Jr., from an infection in 1924 had left him depressed. "When he went, the power and the glory of the presidency went with him," Coolidge said after his son died before the 1924 election. Coolidge wrote his father that 1924 would be his last campaign. While vacationing in August 1927, he issued a statement to the press tantalizing in its brevity: "I do not choose to run for President in nineteen twenty-eight." Coolidge, who enjoyed being enigmatic, consulted no one about his decision and refused to elaborate on his reasons. His wife learned of his decision from a senator; his close friend Stearns read it in a newspaper.

Coolidge has been maligned for sleeping at the switch while the economy hurtled toward the stock market crash of 1929, which neither he nor anyone else in the government saw coming. Many of what seemed his virtues in the 1920s were perceived as vices in the 1930s. There was no demand for a New Deal in the 1920s, nor was there any demand for a president who slept after 1929. Coolidge, lucky throughout his political career, continued to be lucky, for if he had won reelection in 1928, he, not Hoover, would have been blamed for the Great Depression.

Almost all groups who benefited from Coolidge prosperity voted Republican in the 1920s. Women, who voted nationally for the first time in 1920, seem to have voted for Harding and Coolidge in about the same percentages as men. However, they voted in far fewer numbers than men; throughout the 1920s about 74 percent of eligible male voters cast ballots, yet only about 46 percent of eligible women voted. More women voted in 1928 than in 1920 or 1924; they overwhelmingly voted for Hoover. Women steadily increased their participation as delegates to national party conventions. In 1920, ninety-six women were delegates to the Democratic convention, 9 percent of the total, and 26 (2 percent) were Republican delegates. By 1928 there were 156 women delegates to the Democratic convention (14 percent) and 70 to the Republican convention (6 percent). Eleven women served in the U.S. House of Representatives during the decade; 4 were widows of incumbents. There were no women senators, but 2 women, Democrats Nellie Taylor Ross of Wyoming and Miriam M. ("Ma") Ferguson of Texas, succeeded their husbands as state governors. Women's officeholding for the decade peaked in 1928, when there were 7 women in Congress, 119 state representatives, 12 state senators, 2 state treasurers, and 1 state supreme court justice.

Women were also active in clubs and pressure groups. The smallest but most militant, the National Woman's Party, led by Alice Paul, had only 8,000 members. The party made its sole objective enactment of an Equal Rights Amendment to the Constitution, which would eliminate all discrimination against women but would also eliminate laws that provided women with special protection. Many women's groups opposed the amendment, believing they would lose more from the abolition of protective legislation than they would gain from the elimination of discrimination. The ERA, introduced in the House and Senate in 1923, 1924, 1925, and 1929, was never reported out of committee favorably.

Among the leading women's organizations involved in politics were the General Federation of Women's Clubs, the largely female National Consumer's League, the League of Women Voters, the Women's Trade Union League, and an umbrella group, the Women's Joint Congressional Committee (WJCC). In 1923 the WJCC joined forces with the National Child Labor Committee to seek passage of a constitutional amendment prohibiting child labor, which passed Congress but was ratified by only four states. By 1928 women were becoming a more potent factor in national politics, and the Democratic and Republican national committees included women, including a vice chair.

As for Coolidge, he retired to Northampton and never again participated actively in politics. His health failing, sometimes he sat in a rocking chair on his front porch and watched people drive by to look at a former president. Asked if it gratified him that so many cars drove by, he replied: "Not as many as yesterday. Yesterday there were 163 of them."

BIBLIOGRAPHICAL ESSAY

General histories of the politics of the 1920s include John D. Hicks, *Republican Ascendancy, 1921–1933* (1958); William E. Leuchtenburg, *The Perils of Prosperity, 1914–1932* (1958); Ellis W. Hawley, *The Great War and the Search for a Modern Order: A History of the American People and Their Institutions, 1917–1933* (1979); Geoffrey Perrett, *America in the Twenties: A History* (1982); Arthur M. Schlesinger, Jr., *The Age of Roosevelt*, vol. 1, *The Crisis of the Old Order, 1919–1933* (1958); Paul A. Carter, *The Twenties in America* (1975); Preston W. Slosson, *The Great Crusade and After, 1914–1929* (1930); and David Burner, *The Politics of Provincialism* (1967), a study of the Democratic party.

On Harding, see Francis Russell, *The Shadow of Blooming Grove* (1968), which emphasizes his personal life; Robert K. Murray, *The Harding Era: Warren G. Harding and His Administration* (1969), which emphasizes his policies; Robert K. Murray, *The Politics of Normalcy: Government Theory and Practice in the Harding-Coolidge Era* (1973); Eugene P. Trani and David L. Wilson, *The Presidency of Warren G. Harding* (1977), an administrative history; Andrew Sinclair, *The Available Man* (1975), highly critical; and Samuel Hopkins Adams, *Incredible Era: The Life and Times of Warren Gamaliel Harding* (1939), which focuses on the scandals.

Specific accounts of the scandals include Burl Noggle, *Teapot Dome* (1962); J. Leonard Bates, *The Origins of Teapot Dome: Progressives, Parties, and Petroleum, 1909–1921* (1963); John Starr, *Teapot Dome* (1959); and Morris R. Werner, *Privileged Characters* (1935).

On Coolidge, see William A. White, *A Puritan in Babylon* (1938), sprightly but sketchy; David R. McCoy, *Calvin Coolidge: The Quiet President* (1967), a balanced study; Jules Abels, *In the Time of Silent Cal* (1969); and Claude M. Fuess, *Calvin Coolidge: The Man from Vermont* (1981). Peter R. Levin, *Seven by Chance: The Accidental Presidents* (1948), has a chapter on Coolidge. Robert K. Murray, *The 103rd Ballot: The Democrats and the Disaster in Madison Square Garden* (1976), is an account of the 1924 Democratic national convention.

The best account of women in the 1920s is Dorothy M. Brown, *Setting a Course: American Women in the 1920s* (1987); however, J. Stanley Lemons, *The Woman Citizen: Social Feminism in the 1920s* (1973), is also important. More general works include William H. Chafe, *Paradox of Change: The American Woman in the 20th Century* (1991); Mary P. Ryan, *Womanhood in America: From Colonial Times to the Present* (1979); Sara M. Evans, *Born for Liberty: A History of Women in America* (1989); Marty Gruberg, *Women in American Politics* (1968); William L. O'Neill, *Everyone Was Brave: The Rise and Fall of Feminism in America* (1969); and Susan D. Becker, *The Origin of the Equal Rights Amendment: American Feminism Between the Wars* (1981).

CHAPTER
THREE

AN AGE OF FEAR

✣ THE RED SCARE

The political conservatism of the 1920s belied the convulsive social change of the period. Change frequently precipitates fear among defenders of the status quo, and in the decade society developed defense mechanisms to combat and limit change. Indeed, the 1920s might be more aptly called the Elastic Age rather than the Jazz Age because, in the tug-of-war between transformation and reaction, the nation's institutions and tolerance were stretched almost to the breaking point.

Disappointment over failure to achieve a satisfactory peace settlement to World War I was exacerbated by the Bolshevik Revolution of November 1917, which had resulted in the withdrawal of Russia from the war, followed by the confiscation of private property and repudiation of international debts. The ultimate triumph of the Bolshevik faction was contingent on winning the civil war against counterrevolutionaries waged from 1919 to 1921. The United States, Britain, France, and Japan sent troops to occupy Russian territory; the troops dispatched by Wilson—5,000 in northern Russia and 9,000 at Vladivostok—were intended to encourage the counterrevolution, aid in the evacuation of foreign citizens, and prevent the Japanese from seizing Russian land. But the troops managed to alienate the Bolsheviks without defeating them and were withdrawn in 1920.

In 1919 millions of Americans came to fear that communists might take over the United States as they had conquered Russia. The fear was fed by a series of strikes by coal, textile, and railroad workers, a general strike in Seattle, and the strike by Boston police. Demanding mainly higher wages and union recognition, the strikers frightened businessmen and other Americans who dreaded radical change. There were some radical unions, such as the Industrial Workers of the World, and a few union leaders who were socialists, although most American unions, and their umbrella organization, the American Federation of Labor, opposed communism.

American radicals created the American Communist party in 1919, dedicated to violent revolution. A smaller faction, which planned to cooperate with liberal and leftist organizations, created the Communist Labor party. The membership of the two peaked at about 100,000, larger than the Bolshevik faction at the time of the Russian Revolution but never constituting a major threat to American democracy. Nonetheless, politicians and pressure groups exploited the fear of communism by posing as defenders of traditional values. Coolidge, for instance, wrote an article entitled "Are the Reds Stalking Our College Women?" Most prominent was Attorney General A. Mitchell Palmer, the leader in what became known as the Red Scare of 1919–1920. A Quaker who opposed violence and denounced wartime repression, Mitchell was a target of anarchist bombing campaigns against prominent Americans. Luckily, he was not around when a bomb exploded on his front porch, killing the anarchist who delivered it.

The American Legion (created in 1919), the Daughters of the American Revolution, and the Ku Klux Klan demanded action against the purveyors of violent revolution. The New York legislature responded by prohibiting five duly elected Socialists from taking their seats; other states outlawed the flying of red flags. Palmer, politically ambitious and fearful of revolution in America, cracked down with a series of raids in which anarchists, socialists, and communists were arrested. Some 249, including veteran anarchist Emma Goldman, were deported in December 1919 aboard the USS *Buford,* bound for Russia. On January 2, 1920, Palmer staged his largest raids, arresting more than 4,000 people in 33 cities.

Palmer's excessive use of force alienated many Americans, who believed that peaceful dissenters should not be harassed. After Palmer's prediction of a May 1 revolution failed to materialize, he was ridiculed in the press as a Chicken Little who warned that the sky was falling. But fear arose again in September when dynamite planted by anarchists exploded on Wall Street, killing 43 people, injuring others, and demolishing the offices of banker J. P. Morgan. By that time, however, the peak of the Red Scare had passed. Anticommunism remained an issue in American politics, ebbing, flowing, and never evaporating until the worldwide collapse of communism in the late 1980s.

✧ IMMIGRATION AND RACE CONSCIOUSNESS

Fear of communism was soon overshadowed by a vague but broad antipathy to immigrants from southern and eastern Europe, who had been pouring into America since the 1880s. These immigrants, as opposed to earlier immigrants from northwestern Europe, rarely spoke English and settled in urban ghettos. Most were Catholic or Jewish, and Protestant Americans feared they would not assimilate as well as previous immigrants. In addition, the recession of 1921 created concerns that immigrants would take jobs from American citizens.

The race consciousness that increased in the late nineteenth and early twentieth centuries also stimulated prejudice against newer immigrants. A new discipline evolved: eugenics, which involved the study of racial differences and plans for the scientific breeding of human beings. The eugenicists believed that American democracy flourished because the early immigrants had been of the Nordic or Anglo-Saxon race (the two were used interchangeably), which was superior to other races. American racists were alarmed at the dilution of Nordic stock by immigrants from southeastern Europe. If the trend continued, such writers as Madison Grant and Lothrop Stoddard argued, the inferior stock would overwhelm the Nordic, and America would cease to be a prosperous and democratic country.

Encouraged by such organizations as the American Protective League and the American Legion, racists and eugenicists developed a program for preserving Anglo-Saxon supremacy. Nordic couples were urged to raise large families, recent immigrants were encouraged to practice birth control, and limits on immigration were demanded. The American Legion proposed a total freeze on immigration for five years but settled for curtailing immigration and redirecting it from southern to northern Europe.

Southern Europeans were not the only objects of restriction: laws barred Chinese immigrants in 1882, illiterates in 1917, and anarchists in 1918. And when the Harding administration took office in 1921, it was committed to restricting immigration further. The Emergency Quota Act passed by Congress in May 1921 placed ceilings on overall immigration for the first time; total immigration was not to exceed 357,000 per year. Also, Congress applied a quota system. Each foreign nation was assigned a quota of immigrants equivalent to 3 percent of the American citizens whose ancestors had come from that nation based on the 1910 census. The Census Bureau and the Labor Department were instructed to discover the country of origin of every American, an impossible task in view of intermarriage.

The act was extended to last until 1924, when a permanent law was enacted, the National Origins Act, which reduced total immigration to 164,000 per year, based on the 1890 census. Because immigration from southeastern Europe had not peaked until after 1890, the law effectively reduced immigration from southeastern Europe by four-fifths, although immigration from northern Europe remained about the same. The act created a furor in Japan by barring Japanese immigration entirely even though it had already been reduced to a trickle. Hispanic immigration from the Western Hemisphere, on the other hand, was not restricted at the insistence of western farmers who relied on that source of labor.

✣ THE KU KLUX KLAN

Among the chief advocates of immigration restrictions were the leaders of the Ku Klux Klan. Their Imperial Wizard wrote that "an alien usually remains an alien no matter what is done to him, what veneer of education he gets, what oaths he takes, or what public attitudes he adopts." Perceiving a war in which each race fought for its survival against other races, he warned that "Americanism can only be achieved if the pioneer stock is kept pure."

Of all the forces of reaction in the 1920s, the Klan was the strongest and most effective, and it was allied with interest groups, including fundamentalist churches and political conservatives. The growth of Klan membership (from 5,000 in 1920 to 5 million in 1924) and its virtual demise only a few years later epitomize the ascendancy and defeat of reaction. Unlike the post–World War II Klan, which was on the fringes of the far right, the Klan of the 1920s represented a powerful current in the political and social mainstream. Klansmen felt threatened because they knew America was changing, and they did not like the direction of the changes.

The original Ku Klux Klan had been created immediately after the Civil War to preserve or restore white supremacy in the Reconstruction South. Its principal victims were blacks, and it attained such a bad reputation nationally

Of all the forces of reaction in the 1920s, the Ku Klux Klan was the strongest and most effective. Klan members tried to enforce social conformity in an age characterized by moral rebellion and hedonism.

and regionally that it had faded by the mid-1870s. The Klan was revived in 1915 by William J. Simmons, a former minister steeped in the myths of the Old South. Simmons was inspired not by white supremacy but by the popularity of fraternal organizations in the United States. Without having a program of action, he devised an elaborate ritual and costume based partly on the original Klan. Unlike the original Klan, he prohibited Jews, Catholics, and aliens from joining. His other innovation was the adoption of the burning cross as a symbol; the Reconstruction Klan had not burned crosses, although a popular motion picture, *The Birth of a Nation,* which romanticized the Reconstruction Klan, depicted Klansmen using flaming crosses.

Under Simmons, the Klan was a modest organization with limited appeal. That changed in 1920 when he hired professional public relations experts Edward Y. Clarke and Elizabeth Tyler to increase membership. They created possibilities for growth, particularly in areas outside the South, by expanding the list of Klan enemies to include Catholics, Jews, Bolsheviks, and immigrants, and hostility toward the newer foes soon eclipsed southern hostility toward blacks. At its peak the Klan enrolled more members in New Jersey than in Alabama, more in Oregon than in Louisiana. More than 40 percent of Klan members lived in the midwestern states of Indiana, Ohio, and Illinois; membership in Indianapolis was almost twice that in the states of South Carolina and Mississippi combined. The secret behind the Klan's growth was advertising and the sale of memberships by recruiters paid a commission. Although the message of Clarke and Tyler was vague, their promotional ability, based on simplicity, repetition, precise organization, and an appeal to self-righteous morality, was extraordinary; even President Harding became a member. The Klan used an attempted exposé by the *New York World* to expand its membership and similarly profited from an investigation by Congress in 1921.

The Klan had a positive program as well as a negative message: Klansmen were expected to attend a Protestant church, to abstain from drinking alcohol, to support their families, and to be patriotic. A Presbyterian minister said that if Jesus were still on earth he would be a Klansman. However, when Klansmen felt their values threatened, they yielded to their worst impulses, becoming increasingly intolerant, reckless, and criminal.

The chief villains in America, according to Klansmen, were Catholics. The loyalty of the typical Catholic was to the pope, not to America or to the Anglo-Saxon race, Klansmen argued. Because the church-mandated celibacy of priests and nuns was unnatural, they engaged in illicit sexual liaisons. Sometimes priests had intercourse with nuns, Klansmen claimed; if children resulted they were aborted or buried alive. Some persons falsely claiming to be former priests and nuns earned generous incomes lecturing about sex in the church.

Klansmen considered parochial schools a device to prevent Catholics from assimilating, and one of the Klan's high priorities was to require a public education for every child. Catholic schools trained children to undermine American democracy and facilitate a takeover of the United States by the pope, Klansmen said.

The Klan also circulated wild rumors about the pope and his Catholic henchmen. He was, Klansmen said, building a tunnel under the Atlantic Ocean so his legions, swelled by the Knights of Columbus, could conquer the United States militarily. Catholics supposedly kept their guns in the basements of their churches, which had tall steeples for machine gun emplacements and were built on high ground so cannon could command the area below.

A Klan lecturer told a crowd at North Manchester, Indiana, that the pope might come there at any time, perhaps on the next train from Chicago. The next day some 1,500 persons met the southbound train and apprehended the only passenger who alighted. They considered lynching him but decided, after searching his luggage, that he was a traveling salesman.

The Klan also considered Jews a threat, albeit less of a threat than Catholics because there were fewer of them. The Jew personified many of the vices Klansmen associated with modernization: chain stores, large banks, motion pictures, and sensuous music. (Klansmen pointed out that comedian Fatty Arbuckle, accused of rape and manslaughter during a wild party with an actress, was Jewish). The Klan charged that Jews refused to assimilate, planned wars to slaughter Gentiles, and induced young girls to become prostitutes. Jews were considered the evil genius behind communism and behind the desire of blacks for racial equality.

The Klan created auxiliaries for women, the Kamelias, the Queens of the Golden Mask, and the Women of the Ku Klux Klan; the last became the largest with about 500,000 members. Klansmen considered themselves protectors of Nordic women against abusive husbands and against intermarriage with blacks or Jews. They attempted to drive prostitutes out of town and patrolled country roads for teenage couples petting in parked automobiles. Some women considered the Klan a blessing because it rescued them from husbands who beat them and compelled husbands who deserted their families to provide financial support. Many women dressed their children in tiny sheets and hoods and took them to Klan meetings. However, the Klan was thoroughly patriarchical and patronized the women it protected. Klansmen denounced women who smoked or drank, and a Klan newspaper claimed that a "real man wants a real woman for a wife, one who can make an eatable biscuit and use a broom as well as play on the piano."

The Klan's fall, almost as rapid as its growth, was due to its gratuitous violence, a divisive struggle among its leaders, and their corruption. In 1921 Klansmen branded the letters "KKK" in the forehead of a black bellboy from Dallas for soliciting prostitutes and whipped a black taxi driver for flirting with white women. Forty-three Klan tar-and-featherings were reported in Texas in the first six months of 1921. And in 1922 Klansmen kidnapped, castrated, mutilated, and murdered two men from the Louisiana town of Mer Rouge who had ridiculed the Klan. That year Hiram Wesley Evans, a Texas dentist, wrested control of the Klan from Simmons, and a protracted court battle ensued.

The Klan's credibility was crippled by the moral turpitude of its Indiana

Grand Dragon, David C. Stephenson. A political power and a potential candidate for the U.S. Senate, Stephenson abducted a young woman, raped her, and was convicted of second-degree murder in her death. He threatened to expose his political cronies if sent to prison, and after he did, the Klan in Indiana evaporated like alcohol in the noonday sun; within a year of Stephenson's conviction it had declined from 350,000 to 15,000 members.

But excesses were not the sole reason for the Klan's decline. Another factor was that by accomplishing its objectives, it made itself obsolete. With the passage of immigration restrictions and the decline of American radicalism, and in a climate characterized by political conservatism, the Klan was robbed of its purpose. In its dying gasp, the Klan worked to defeat the presidential candidacy of Al Smith in 1928.

Had the Klan consisted only of fanatical, violent, night-riding perpetrators of atrocities against minorities, it would have been less formidable, less important, and less dangerous. Instead, the presence of thousands of people who were respectable and churchgoing, if naïve and misguided, made it the most successful right-wing mass political organization of twentieth-century America. In a society in flux, the Klan addressed the uncertainty and anxieties of old-stock Americans with arguments and solutions that sounded plausible, yet were unrealistic, inhumane, and irrelevant. Other forms of camaraderie gained more appeal, and the traditional verities the Klan sometimes hypocritically promoted were relegated to the past. It was typical of an America that was dying, but not without a struggle, not without a legacy.

✥ THE PLIGHT OF MINORITIES

During World War I hundreds of thousands of blacks left the rural South to take industrial jobs in northern cities. They were crowded into ghettos where they lived in inadequate housing and received poor medical care; the death rates for blacks from disease and childbirth were far higher than those for whites. In addition, for the first time, significant numbers of blacks settled in western cities, and segregation, which had not previously existed in the West, developed there.

The experience of many blacks who moved to such cities as New York, Chicago, Detroit, and Washington was mixed. Older blacks often resented the newcomers, and whites usually abandoned neighborhoods when blacks moved in. Unemployment was high and wages were low, but their standard of living was generally higher than that of blacks in the rural South, and segregation was not so severe. The black churches, predominantly Protestant, served as acculturating forces. Some small black businesses such as barbers and hairdressers earned satisfactory incomes. For example, C. J. Walker of Indianapolis, who manufactured beauty aids for black women, became one of the first American women to become a millionaire by her efforts. Blacks also obtained new political and economic importance because of their increased concentration. In 1928, Oscar DePriest of Chicago, a Republican, became the first black elected to Congress since Reconstruction; he served until 1935, when he was defeated by a black Democrat, Arthur W. Mitchell. More important, blacks' votes in northern cities provided some negotiating power.

The unrest of 1919, including strikes and the Red Scare, involved some 26 race riots in American cities, the worst in Chicago, Washington, and New York. The Chicago riot, which left 34 dead, was the most destructive. A black swimmer who crossed the racial line at a segregated beach was hit by stones thrown by white bathers and drowned. After the police failed to arrest the stone throwers, black violence erupted, and whites retaliated until local police and the National Guard restored order. In Washington white soldiers began beating blacks after rumors circulated that black men had raped white women; in New York blacks attacked whites after a false account of the shooting of a black soldier by a policeman.

The Harding administration proved less biased against blacks than the Wilson administration, and Harding appointed blacks to minor positions in the federal bureaucracy and in the diplomatic corps. In October 1921, at Birmingham, Harding became the first president since the Civil War to deliver a speech in a southern city urging amicable race relations. He refused to denounce the Klan, however, and he was woefully ignorant about black culture and accomplishments; he had never heard of the black educator Booker T. Washington. President Coolidge did urge Congress to prohibit lynching, but he was not interested in race relations, and his neglect facilitated the transfer of black allegiance to the Democratic party during the New Deal.

Repression of blacks remained strongest in the South, where they received only a rudimentary education and segregation of public facilities was strictly enforced. In *Nixon v. Herndon* (1927) and *Nixon v. Condon* (1932) the Supreme Court ruled that a state could not directly or indirectly prohibit blacks from voting in party primaries, although it did not prohibit parties from excluding blacks. The Democratic party remained entirely white in the southern states, and because the only party that accepted blacks, the GOP, had little chance of winning elections in the South, blacks were denied meaningful political participation. Moreover, southerners reinforced white supremacy by economic coercion, intimidation, and lynching as well as by state laws.

Washington, the paramount political and economic black leader until his death in 1915, said blacks had to advance economically before they could hope for political rights, and advocated cooperation with whites and vocational education as the path to progress. Washington's philosophy was challenged by the more militant W. E. B. Du Bois, the first black Ph.D. from Harvard, who became the leading black intellectual of the 1920s. A prolific writer and editor and a college teacher, Du Bois believed that black progress could best be achieved by training exceptional blacks to be leaders. Du Bois opposed capitalism and colonialism, emphasized racial pride, and advocated a worldwide movement of black people to win political liberation. A versatile intellectual with a brilliant mind but a difficult personality, he created the Niagara movement in 1905 to advance black political rights. In 1909 he and other civil rights leaders created the National Association for the Advancement of Colored People (NAACP) to work for black rights and, from 1910 to 1934, Du Bois edited its magazine, the *Crisis*.

More popular among the black masses was Marcus Garvey, a Jamaican black who created the Universal Negro Improvement Association, which claimed 4 million members by the early 1920s and became the first mass movement of American blacks. Garvey urged blacks to invest in black businesses and to patronize them exclusively, including his Black Star steamship line, created to transport blacks to the Caribbean and to Africa. Like Du Bois, he advocated a back-to-Africa movement, but he angered Du Bois by cooperating with the Klan, which also wanted blacks to return to Africa. A charismatic speaker who claimed Jesus might have been black, Garvey moved passive blacks as did no other leader of his time, yet he was incompetent as a businessman and lost the money of his investors. In 1923 he was convicted of business fraud and was incarcerated in a federal penitentiary in 1925. Two years later Coolidge pardoned him but deported Garvey, who was a British citizen. He died in Britain in 1940.

A. Philip Randolph was the only black of his generation to fuse the economic perspective of Washington with the civil rights emphasis of Du Bois. A socialist, he edited a radical black magazine. He had never ridden in a Pullman car when he became leader of the first major black union, the Brotherhood of Sleeping Car Porters, in 1925. Randolph worked for more than a decade to obtain recognition for his union from the American Federation of Labor (AFL); afterward, he became a voice for blacks within the American labor movement. His influence rose in the early 1940s, even as automobile transportation was making Pullmans obsolete. Still, Randolph's unionization of sleeping car porters set a precedent for organizing black workers at a time when many AFL unions discouraged blacks from joining.

Like blacks, Hispanics suffered poverty and discrimination in the 1920s. The promise of prosperity lured millions of Hispanics, mostly Mexicans, to the United States, most of them employed as migrant workers on western farms and ranches. About 1.4 million Mexicans went north from 1901 to 1930, and demand for Mexican labor increased as European immigration declined. Hispanic workers were unorganized, and their living conditions were often primitive; many were housed in shacks without running water or indoor toilets. Wages were so low that it was necessary for whole families to work in the fields, so migrant children seldom received any education. Most Mexican immigrants settled in Texas or California, and by 1925 Los Angeles had a larger Spanish-speaking population than any city in North America except Mexico City. Those who settled in cities usually lived apart from Anglo-Saxon residents, but some urban Mexican Americans established businesses that, in time, lifted them out of poverty. The Great Depression reversed the flow of immigration; in the 1930s more Mexicans returned to Mexico than came north because the depression had ended the labor shortage in the West.

American Indians endured perhaps the most hardships of any minority group. Thousands suffered illness or death from epidemics, homicide, starvation, or alcoholism. Infant mortality was high, unemployment perhaps the highest of any group, and life expectancy among the lower of any Americans. Government policy extended citizenship to Indians, but while attempting to stamp out Indian customs, languages, diets, and traditional clothing, it offered little in return by way of jobs or education. During the 1920s most Indians lived in dirt-floored shacks or tents with no water or plumbing and little heat. In 1928 the Institute for Government Research published the Merriam Report, which documented the wretched conditions on reservations and questioned the policy of forced assimilation.

✢ RELIGION IN TENSION

Most immigrants to the United States since 1900, whether from Europe or Latin America, were Catholics, and by the 1920s there were 23 million Catholics living in the United States, making Catholicism the largest religious denomination in the nation. Indeed, the desire of Protestant leaders to curb the influx of Catholics was a major reason for the implementation of immigration restrictions. Nevertheless, immigration increased the size and influence of the Catholic church.

Anti-Catholicism, a major theme of the 1920s, was rampant among Protestant fundamentalists and such groups as the Klan. The nomination of the Democrat Al Smith for president in 1928, the first Catholic nominee of a major party, aroused unprecedented hostility among some Protestants. Perhaps no other religious group inspired such a wave of nativism and ethnocentrism before the Great Depression submerged religious bigotry in concern for economic problems.

Catholics, like Protestants and Jews, were divided by disputes between modernists and traditionalists. Although Pope Pius X had denounced modernism in 1907, many American priests and bishops were more liberal on theological and social questions than were their European counterparts. In the 1920s most Catholics opposed birth control in theory, although increasing numbers practiced it, and there was an increase in divorces among Catholics as divorce rose in the general population.

The massive immigration beginning in the 1880s brought millions of Jews, as well as Catholics, to the United States. In 1880 there were about 280,000 Jews in the nation; by 1925 there were 4.5 million. Many of the immigrants were Orthodox Jews, adding to the mix of Jews in the nation. Orthodoxy was the most traditional of the branches of Jewry, adhering to a literal interpretation of the commandments in the Hebrew Bible. Conservative Judaism represented a middle way, whereas Reform Judaism was an attempt to update and modernize rituals. During the interwar period Reform Jews abandoned some of their more radical experiments, such as Sunday morning services, and restored some of the traditional Hebrew to temple rituals. A new branch, Reconstructionism, led by Mordecai M. Kaplan, attempted to reinterpret

Judaism by reconstructing the theology behind old practices and reformulating Judaism in modern terms.

Jews, also like Catholics, were a persecuted minority in the United States. Anti-Semitism was common among upper-class Americans in the 1920s, and Henry Ford lent the prestige of his industrial empire to the publication of anti-Semitic articles in his newspaper and in their collection, *The International Jew*. Ford also sold a notorious forgery purporting to document a worldwide Jewish conspiracy against Christians, *The Protocols of the Learned Elders of Zion*.

Although most Jewish immigrants were poor, Jews rose financially faster than any other minority. Throughout the era Jews, more liberal politically than the American population as a whole, were prominent among left-wing intellectuals, labor leaders, defenders of civil liberties, and philanthropists.

In perhaps no segment of society was the struggle between transformation and reaction so apparent as among Protestant Christians. Many Protestant denominations were polarized between liberal and conservative factions, and there was some polarization between denominations. Some liberal denominations experienced a decline in fervor if not in attendance. Tithing and family prayer were less important; there was less emphasis on heaven and hell and more on social issues; most people attended church only on Sunday mornings; and churches found it necessary to offer recreational facilities to compete with secular entertainment. Missionary zeal declined: in 1920 some 2,700 Protestant students volunteered for foreign missionary service, but only 252 volunteered in 1928. Women, constituting about 69 percent of the foreign missionaries, tended to be more religious than men, outnumbering them by about 5 to 4 in church attendance. Religion was considered more important for children than for adults, many of whom attended church for social reasons.

The churches were further affected by the dominance of business in American culture, and in the 1920s ministers attempted to make religion relevant to the milieu. Churches were judged on their productivity, and some hired efficiency experts. An article in a religious magazine stated that "the minister is a salesman." A church in New York City gave an engraved certificate of preferred stock in the kingdom of God to anyone who donated $100 to its building fund, and a college president promised that "each hour spent in wholesome, Christian self-improvement is worth $10,000." Crude devices were used to encourage church attendance. One midwestern minister staged an "auto Sunday" on which he gave a prize to the person who could squeeze the most people into a car and bring them to church; the next Sunday he offered a prize to the church member with the biggest feet (the minister himself won!). Among popular books published during the decade were *Church Publicity, Principles of Church Advertising*, and *How to Fill the Pews*. One writer encouraged pastors to publish photographs of pretty women in church bulletins to attract men to services.

Businessmen were flattered by being told that making money was a service to mankind. The president of the world's largest lumber company said he hoped God would make use of his business skills throughout eternity. "If there is a saw-mill up there in heaven—when I get there—and I hope to get there—I am going to ask the Lord to let me run it," he said. "Then, if He'll give me plenty of lumber, plenty of orders, and all the transportation I want, I'll be happy."

One of the more puzzling religious phenomena of the decade, liberals thought, was the persistence of fundamentalism, which was strongest in the South. "Heave an egg out of a Pullman and you will hit a fundamentalist almost everywhere in the United States," H. L. Mencken quipped. Mencken and other secularly oriented commentators considered fundamentalists exotic and neither respected nor understood them. Actually, it was quite easy to tell where fundamentalists stood: belief in the Bible's literal truth, in the virgin birth and deity of Jesus, in his literal resurrection and atonement for the world's sins, and in his second coming in bodily form.

The leading fundamentalist of the World War I era was Billy Sunday, a former major league baseball player who was among the first evangelists to apply modern organizational and business techniques to his crusades. Renowned more for emotional enthusiasm than for theological depth—"I don't know any more about theology than a jack-rabbit knows about Ping Pong, but I'm on my way to glory," he said—he converted audiences by the hundreds. Fiery, forceful, magnetic, he preached against smoking, dancing, adultery, fornication, and motion pictures; his most famous sermons, however, were against booze.

Even more publicized than Sunday in the mid-1920s was Aimee Semple McPherson. Born in Canada to a mother who had worked for the Salvation Army, she married Robert Semple, a Pentecostal evangelist, and went with him to China as a missionary. Widowed less than two years after the wedding, she returned to America, remarried, and became an itinerant evangelist. In 1918 she settled in Los Angeles, where she preached to huge audiences and staged faith-healing sessions. Divorcing her second husband, she constructed Angelus Temple, which seated 5,000 and cost $1.5 million, by 1923.

In May 1926, McPherson vanished while swimming in the ocean and was believed to have drowned, yet 32 days later she emerged at a Mexican village, claiming to have been kidnapped. Her disappearance, one of the leading news stories of the decade, was discredited when the kidnappers, and the cabin where they supposedly held her, could not be found. In fact, McPherson had been having an affair with the married man who operated her radio station, and they had fled Los Angeles together.

McPherson returned to her temple, bobbed and dyed her hair, and began wearing the flapper's short skirts. She drew increasingly large crowds, and her sermons continued to be dramatic; she dressed as a fireman, policeman, and mechanic and opened one sermon by roaring down the aisle on a motorcycle. But McPherson grew more unstable in the late 1920s and 1930s: she had a nervous breakdown and a face-lift, married and divorced again, broke with her mother and daughter, and was sued more than fifty times. She created a series of mission churches called Lighthouses and said she planned to establish a Salvation Navy with the motto, "Throw Out the Life Line." Although mem-

Aimee Semple McPherson was the most highly publicized evangelist of the 1920s. Her disappearance for 32 days in 1926 was one of the leading news stories of the decade.

bership increased in her denomination, called the Four-Square Gospel, the grandiose Salvation Navy never materialized, and in 1944 she died of an overdose of barbiturates, possibly a suicide.

McPherson, Sunday, and their fellow believers were alarmed because they lived in a period of transition during which their majority position became a minority one. Essentially counterrevolutionary, the fundamentalism of the 1920s provided a buffer against modernization. "Protestantism did not prevent Americans from committing sin," one woman remarked, "but it kept us from getting any fun out of it." Modernists considered fundamentalists antiquated morons; fundamentalists returned the compliment by considering modernists infidels.

Modernists, the thoughtful fundamentalist theologian J. Gresham Machen complained, had eliminated God from religion and made him merely a First Cause or even just a Source of Energy. By reducing Christianity to an ethical system, or a kind of philosophy, they had deprived the religion of its essence, Machen said. Providing an equally eloquent defense of modernism, Shailer Matthews argued that Christianity was not static but dynamic, based not upon a perfect knowledge of God but upon knowledge filtered through human experience, which changed with society. The crucial issue, he said, was whether to view history through the lens of the Bible or the Bible through the lens of history.

Modernists accused fundamentalists of being anti-intellectual and of using the Bible to fight new ideas. One fundamentalist minister, who considered the Bible the only essential book, remembered that his father, also a minister, had told him, "If it is more than the Bible it is too much; if it is less than the Bible it is not enough; if it is the same as the Bible we don't need it." He added, "Christianity is as simple as a Western Union telegram. . . . It wouldn't take an intellectual to bring a telegram to your door."

Mencken, who scorned all religion, proposed the construction of huge stadiums, where spectators could watch fundamentalists and modernists engage in mortal combat. His satire aside, the struggle between the adversaries was a serious one. "This is not a battle, it is a war from which there is no discharge," said W. B. Riley, a leading fundamentalist minister and educator.

The clash climaxed in the debate over whether the theory of evolution should be taught in schools. Fundamentalists argued that Charles Darwin's theory undermined belief in the biblical account of creation and, by implication, the credibility of the entire Bible and of Christianity. Modernists answered that academic freedom precluded restrictions on what teachers taught; moreover, any belief that suppressed evidence to preserve its tenets, as fundamentalism suppressed scientific data, was of questionable validity.

By 1925, Oklahoma and Tennessee had enacted laws prohibiting the teaching of evolution in public schools, and similar laws were under consideration in almost half the state legislatures. But the American Civil Liberties Union offered to finance the defense of any teacher who would violate an antievolution law to test the constitutionality of such legislation. A few businessmen from Dayton, Tennessee, a farm community of 1,500, asked high school teacher John Thomas Scopes to raise the issue so their town could have a trial to attract tourists and national publicity. They could hardly have anticipated the degree to which they would succeed.

Before the trial—the first to be broadcast on radio—began on July 10, 1925, more than one hundred newspapers sent reporters, the famous Mencken among them. Revivalists flocked to Dayton to preach on street corners, booksellers marketed volumes on biology, and hot dog vendors set up stands. Rarely had a theological debate been presented in a more circuslike atmosphere. It was, of course, naive to believe that the issue of biblical versus scientific truth could be resolved in a brief trial in a small Tennessee town before a country judge. The real battle, as everyone knew, was for public opinion. No more diametrically opposed partisans could have been recruited to argue the issue than William Jennings Bryan, whom the World's Christian Fundamental Association hired to help the prosecution, and Clarence Darrow, hired by the American Civil Liberties Union to lead the defense. Each was distinguished: Bryan was a famous orator, a secretary of state, and a three-time candidate for president; Darrow had been a champion of labor and was one of the most brilliant trial lawyers of his generation. Bryan, a rock of Christian belief, considered Darrow an infamous atheist; Darrow, a skeptic, considered Bryan an imbecile. Both were dogmatic and self-righteous, unwilling to concede that the other might be acting in good faith or had a right to his own beliefs. The issue, as they saw it, was not a common curriculum versus academic freedom; it was whether man descended from God or arose from an ape. Their debate was fierce, bitter, and irreconcilable. Darrow declared that his purpose was "to prevent bigots and ignoramuses from controlling the educational system of the United States." Bryan, shaking his fist at Darrow, responded that his mission was "to protect the word of God against the greatest atheist and agnostic in the United States."

On the afternoon of July 20, Darrow, frustrated that Judge John T. Raulston, a lay preacher, would not permit scientific experts to testify, asked if he could put Bryan on the stand as an authority on the Bible. Bryan foolishly agreed. Bryan testified that the world was created in 4004 B.C., that Eve was literally created from Adam's rib, that the world's languages originated at the Tower of Babel, and that an enormous fish had swallowed Jonah without digesting him. Bryan's answers, showing his lack of contemporary knowledge, proved embarrassing.

The judge and jury, viewing the issue more narrowly than did Bryan and Darrow, followed the legal precedent that juries are authorized only to determine whether a law has been violated, not whether the law is wise. Thus the verdict was never seriously in doubt although it should have been: Scopes confessed to a friend that he had been absent from class on the day he had intended to teach evolution. The jury convicted Scopes, and Raulston fined him $100. In doing so, Raulston violated the law, which specified that the jury, not the judge, was empowered to set the fine, which might range from $100 to $500. A year later the Tennessee Supreme Court used Raulston's technical mistake to sidestep the issue of the act's constitutionality, nullifying the sentence on the grounds of his error but letting the law stand. This ruling deprived opponents of the law of the opportunity to appeal to federal courts.

Mencken and other journalists proclaimed that fundamentalism had been exposed as a fraud; in his dispatches Mencken described the citizens of Dayton as "hillbillies," "peasants," and "morons." Five days after the trial Bryan died in his sleep; his enemies said he died a discredited, broken man, but his followers considered him a martyr to the cause of fundamentalism. When it was all over, few who had witnessed the spectacle or read about it had changed their minds. Two states, Mississippi and Arkansas, passed antievolution laws after the trial, as did a few cities, including Cleveland, but Oklahoma repealed its 1923 law. The Tennessee law remained on the books until 1967, but authorities, fearful that it would not survive a constitutional test, refused to prosecute anyone for violating it. And fundamentalism, though ridiculed, did not fade; like a hardy perennial it continued to blossom in the rockiest of gardens.

✧ THE DECLINE OF LABOR

Just as fundamentalists and modernists fought to gain the upper hand in churches, labor unions and employers battled over the profits of business and the ultimate control of the workforce. In this arena, the outcome was less indecisive; business was triumphant. In no other decade in the twentieth century has business been so ascendant. "America is an employer's paradise," an Australian journalist wrote in 1928.

Membership in the AFL peaked in 1920 at 5,047,000, then, in only three years, fell to 3,622,000, and to 3,442,600 by 1929. In 1920 some 19.4 percent of nonagricultural workers belonged to unions, but by 1930 the figure was down to only 10.2 percent. Moreover, organized labor was heavily concentrated in a handful of industries: coal, construction, railroads, clothing, and water transportation. There were no unions at all among clerical workers, unskilled and semiskilled factory workers, the white-collar workforce, and domestic servants.

Several factors contributed to the decline of labor during the 1920s. Technology created high productivity, and annual wages increased by 9.1 percent from 1923 to 1928; credit buying raised the purchasing power of workers beyond their immediate incomes; increasing numbers of married women workers contributed to the family income; and the variety of inexpensive items available made workers relatively satisfied. Furthermore, the migration of 1.2 million blacks to northern cities between 1915 and 1928 offered cheap competition to white union workers. Most unions excluded blacks, who were last hired and received low wages and were sometimes used as strikebreakers. Because many factory jobs required little training, workers who struck or quit could easily be replaced. Furthermore, labor leaders were less aggressive; William Green, who succeeded Samuel Gompers as president of the AFL in 1924, was known as "the Calvin Coolidge of the labor movement" because of his reluctance to shake the status quo.

The Republican presidents of the 1920s were no friends of labor, although Harding at least attempted to remain neutral. He helped to negotiate a voluntary 8-hour day to replace the 12-hour day in the steel industry and sought to avoid siding with management or labor during strikes. His attorney general, however, had no scruples about breaking strikes. When railroad workers struck in 1922 after two wage cuts, Daugherty obtained the most sweeping injunction in labor history to help break the strike.

The unrest among railroad workers led to the Railway Labor Act of 1926, the only major piece of labor legislation passed at the federal level during the 1920s. It created a federal mediation board appointed by the president, which attempted to persuade parties in labor disputes to submit to voluntary arbitration, but the law produced little success. Not until the Railway Labor Act of 1934 and the elimination of company unions during the New Deal did real progress occur in negotiating railroad labor disputes.

The United Mine Workers, too, made scant headway in the 1920s. Its nationwide strike in 1922, to protest wage cuts, turned nasty, and 19 strikebreakers and 2 strikers were killed in Herrin, Illinois. The violence resurrected the Red Scare, and public opinion turned against the strikers, who settled for preserving the status quo on wages. John L. Lewis's union, the largest in the nation in 1920, declined steadily during the decade because of overproduction in bituminous mining and the availability of cheap nonunion labor in southern mines.

Union leaders differed over whether they would gain the best deal for their members by militance or by compromise. Industrialists, favoring the latter, hoped to preempt radicalism by strategic concessions such as profit sharing, retirement programs, health plans, and labor-management committees, all implemented by company unions. John D. Rockefeller called his program "welfare capitalism." Company unions helped to make workplaces safer, but they had no real bargaining power. Relying entirely on management concessions, they could not strike, nor could they negotiate agreements over wages and hours. They did undercut independent unions, however. Independent unions declined during the decade, while membership in company unions rose from 690,000 in 1922 to 1,547,766 in 1928.

Business had, of course, friends in the federal government, including Secretary of Commerce Herbert Hoover. Leading the movement to view labor and capital as producers with a common interest, he considered war between labor and capital as wasteful as war between nations. Businessmen liked this philosophy because it tended to preserve the system in which they held the upper hand.

The Supreme Court was another ally during the 1920s, consistently favoring business and voiding more prolabor state laws than it had in the previous fifty years. It placed severe restrictions on picketing outside plants; ruled boycotts of companies illegal under most circumstances; nullified a law prohibiting injunctions against unions; and struck down a District of Columbia law setting minimum wages for women. The Court also interpreted the Clayton Anti-Trust Act of 1914, which had exempted unions from antitrust prosecution, in a way that gave few rights to labor. Further, it and other federal courts upheld the use of yellow-dog contracts, which thwarted organizing by requiring that workers agree not to join a union.

Flare-ups during 1929 presaged some of the labor violence of the 1930s. The 1929 strikes were concentrated in the southern textile industry, which was suffering from excess capacity and competition from synthetic fabrics. The workers, many of them women and children, had lower wages and longer hours than any industrial workers, and their industry was largely unorganized. Violent strikes at Elizabethtown, Tennessee, and Gastonia and Marion in North Carolina resulted in extensive property damage and deaths among strikers and police. The Gastonia strike achieved special notoriety because of the role of communists in attempting to organize the mills and because seven strikers convicted of killing a policeman jumped bail and fled to the Soviet Union.

✣ THE SACCO-VANZETTI CASE

No event of the 1920s galvanized radicals and intellectuals against the American legal system as did the trial and execution of two Italian anarchists, Nicola Sacco and Bartolomeo Vanzetti, for murder and robbery in South Braintree, Massachusetts. Sacco and Vanzetti were charged with participating in the robbery of a shoe company payroll and the murder of the paymaster and his guard on April 15, 1920. Both were radicals and atheists committed to undermining capitalism, and their defenders, including such prominent writers and intellectuals as Felix Frankfurter, John Dewey, H. L. Mencken, and John Dos Passos, claimed they were convicted because of their beliefs, not because they were guilty of criminal acts.

The case initially attracted little attention. The two were armed when arrested, and ballistics tests seemed to indicate that the revolver found on Sacco had been taken from the guard and used to shoot the guard. It even had a nick in the handle, as a witness testified the guard's gun had. Several witnesses identified the two, but other witnesses testified that they had been elsewhere when the robbery occurred.

Communists in the United States viewed the case as an opportunity to claim a capitalist conspiracy against working-class people with radical beliefs, evidence that American capitalism was rotten. The presiding judge, Webster Thayer, detested the beliefs of Sacco and Vanzetti, but thorough reviews of the court record failed to reveal any procedural errors by him. Although their defenders claimed prejudice against anarchists, it was the defense that introduced their beliefs into the record. The jury, based primarily on the ballistics evidence, convicted Sacco and Vanzetti, and Judge Thayer sentenced them to death.

The two remained in prison for seven years, during which numerous appeals were denied. Several men convicted of other crimes confessed to the murder and robbery, yet their descriptions of the robbery did not match the known facts. The Massachusetts Supreme Court upheld the convictions, and the Supreme Court ruled that it lacked jurisdiction to consider the case. Massachusetts Governor Alvin T. Fuller appointed a special commission composed of two college presidents and a retired judge to review the case, promising to commute the sentences if the panel recommended it. After conducting further ballistics tests and interviewing additional experts, the commission concluded that Sacco and Vanzetti were guilty, and they were electrocuted on August 27, 1927.

Riots erupted worldwide to protest a perceived miscarriage of justice. Several novels, a play, and dozens of poems were written to denounce the

American legal system. In the intellectual community, belief in the innocence of Sacco and Vanzetti became a dogma, and in 1977 Massachusetts Governor Michael Dukakis formally expunged their guilt from the legal record.

To many recent observers, faith in the innocence of Sacco and Vanzetti seems misplaced. Ballistics tests conducted in 1961, using more precise scientific instruments than were available in the 1920s, indicate that the gun found on Sacco was indeed the murder weapon. Several years after the trial, the men's attorney, Fred Moore, said "Sacco was probably, Vanzetti possibly guilty." The historian Francis Russell, who has written the most complete account of the case, concluded that Sacco was guilty; Vanzetti knew of Sacco's guilt but did not participate in the robbery. Russell found no evidence of an attempt to frame the men, and the liberal historian Page Smith agreed in 1987 that "the legal record did not support the charge that Sacco and Vanzetti had not received a fair trial." The historian Paul Avrich expressed doubt of the guilt of Sacco and Vanzetti in a 1991 book, but his study focused on the anarchist movement more than on the specific crime of which they were convicted.

The significance of the case does not lie in the guilt or innocence of Sacco and Vanzetti. Its significance is that it was exploited to become a trial of America, of traditional values and unconventional beliefs. Many people judged Sacco and Vanzetti innocent or guilty because they sympathized or disagreed with their political views. Each side exaggerated the virtues of its own partisans and exaggerated the vices of its opponents. More than any incident of the decade, the Sacco-Vanzetti case epitomized the age of fear.

BIBLIOGRAPHICAL ESSAY

General treatments of social history in the 1920s include Frederick Lewis Allen, *Only Yesterday* (1931); Elizabeth Stevenson, *Babbitts and Bohemians: The American 1920s* (1967); Paul Goodman and Frank O. Gatell, eds., *America in the Twenties: The Beginnings of Contemporary America* (1972); Joan Hoff-Wilson, ed., *The Twenties: The Critical Issues* (1972); and Paul A. Carter, *Another Part of the Twenties* (1977). James S. Olson, *Historical Dictionary of the 1920s* (1988), is an indispensable reference tool.

On the Red Scare, see Robert K. Murray, *Red Scare: A Study in National Hysteria, 1919–1920* (1955); and two excellent biographies, Stanley Coben, *A. Mitchell Palmer: Politician* (1963); and John Chalberg, *Emma Goldman: American Individualist* (1991).

Immigration is covered in John Higham, *Strangers in the Land: Patterns of American Nativism, 1860–1925* (1968); Oscar Handlin, *The Uprooted* (1951); and Roger Daniels, *Coming to America: A History of Immigration and Ethnicity in American Life* (1990). David H. Bennett describes hostility to immigrants and nonconformists in *The Party of Fear: From Nativist Movements to the New Right in American History* (1988).

Studies of the Ku Klux Klan include Wyn Craig Wade, *The Fiery Cross: The Ku Klux Klan in America* (1987); David M. Chalmers, *Hooded Americanism* (1968);

Arnold S. Rice, *The Ku Klux Klan in American Politics* (1962); Charles C. Alexander, *The Ku Klux Klan in the Southwest* (1965); Kenneth T. Jackson, *The Ku Klux Klan in the City, 1915–1930* (1967); and Kathleen M. Blee, *Women of the Klan: Racism and Gender in the 1920s* (1991), which focuses on Indiana.

Leonard Dinnerstein et al., *Natives and Strangers: Blacks, Indians, and Immigrants in America* (1990), is a survey of minority history. Studies of blacks include John Hope Franklin, *From Slavery to Freedom: A History of American Negroes* (1967); Herbert Aptheker, *Afro-American History: The Modern Era* (1971); David Gordon Nielson, *Black Ethos: Northern Urban Negro Life and Thought, 1890–1930* (1977); Nicholas Lemann, *The Promised Land: The Great Black Migration and How It Changed America* (1991); and William M. Tuttle, Jr., *Race Riot: Chicago in the Red Summer of 1919* (1970). Biographies of black leaders and their movements include Francis L. Broderick, *W. E. B. Du Bois: Negro Leader in a Time of Crisis* (1959); Elliott M. Rudwick, *W. E. B. Du Bois: A Study in Minority Group Leadership* (1960); Arnold Rampersad, *The Art and Imagination of W. E. B. Du Bois* (1990); Paula F. Pfeffer, *A. Philip Randolph: Pioneer of the Civil Rights Movement* (1990); Edmund D. Cronon, *Black Moses: The Story of Marcus Garvey and the Universal Negro Improvement Association* (1955); John H. Clarke, ed., *Marcus Garvey and the Vision of Africa* (1974); and Judith Stein, *The World of Marcus Garvey: Race and Class in Modern Society* (1986).

The religious history of the 1920s is rich. Among the most useful studies of Protestantism are George M. Marsden, *Fundamentalism and American Culture: The Shaping of Twentieth Century Evangelism, 1870–1925* (1980); Donald B. Meyer, *The Protestant Search for Political Realism, 1919–1941* (1960); Robert M. Miller, *American Protestantism and Social Issues, 1919–1939* (1958); Ferenc M. Szasz, *The Divided Mind of Protestant America, 1880–1939* (1982); William V. Trollinger, Jr., *God's Empire: William Riley and Midwestern Fundamentalism* (1990); and Bernard Weisberger, *They Gathered at the River: The Story of the Great Revivalists and Their Impact upon Religion in America* (1958). Biographies of leading evangelists include Robert Bahr, *Least of All Saints: The Story of Aimee Semple McPherson* (1979); two studies by Lately Thomas [pseud.], *The Vanishing Evangelist* (1959) and *Storming Heaven: The Lives and Turmoils of Minnie Kennedy and Aimee Semple McPherson* (1970); William G. McLoughlin, Jr., *Billy Sunday Was His Real Name* (1955); and Lee Thomas, *The Billy Sunday Story: The Life and Times of William Ashley Sunday* (1961).

The Scopes trial is covered in Ray Ginger, *Six Days or Forever? Tennessee v. John Thomas Scopes* (1958); and L. S. de Camp, *The Great Monkey Trial* (1968). For the role of Bryan as a spokesman for evangelism, see Robert W. Cherney, *A Righteous Cause: The Life of William Jennings Bryan* (1985); and Lawrence W. Levine, *Defender of the Faith: William Jennings Bryan, The Last Decade, 1915–1925* (1965). Norman F. Furniss, *The Fundamentalist Controversy, 1918–1931* (1954), is an account of the clash between modernists and fundamentalists.

For Catholicism, see William M. Halsey, *The Survival of American Innocence: Catholicism in an Era of Disillusionment, 1920–1940* (1980); and for Judaism, see Joseph L. Blau, *Judaism in America: From Curiosity to Third Faith* (1976). Charles H. Lippy, ed., *Twentieth-Century Shapers of American Popular Religion* (1989), is an excellent reference tool.

The best account of labor is Irving Bernstein, *The Lean Years: A History of the American Worker, 1920–1933* (1960). See also Robert H. Zieger, *American Workers, American Unions, 1920–1985* (1986); and David Brody, ed., *Industrial America in the Twentieth Century* (1967).

The best study of the Sacco-Vanzetti case is Francis Russell, *Tragedy in Dedham: The Story of the Sacco-Vanzetti Case* (1971). Other accounts include David Felix, *Protest: Sacco-Vanzetti and the Intellectuals* (1965); Louis Joughin and Edmund M. Morgan, *The Legacy of Sacco and Vanzetti* (1948); William Young and David E. Kaiser, *Postmortem: New Evidence in the Case of Sacco and Vanzetti* (1985); Herbert B. Ehrmann, *The Case That Will Not Die: Commonwealth vs. Sacco and Vanzetti* (1969); and Paul Avrich, *Sacco and Vanzetti: The Anarchist Background* (1991).

CHAPTER FOUR

AN ERA OF INDULGENCE

✣ CHANGES IN MANNERS AND MORALS

The postwar world came in," songwriter Hoagy Carmichael wrote, "with a bang of bad booze, flappers with bare legs, jangled morals and wild weekends." The 1920s, a decade unlike any Americans had known, seemed dedicated to hedonism and materialism. Victorian morality, which had emphasized restraint, silence about sex, prim and proper women, and starkly defined gender roles, yielded to a modern morality that was less disciplined and more indulgent, a morality that found love erotic and sex enjoyable. Young men and women were in the vanguard of the revolution, which was encouraged by the temporary liaisons of World War I, by the exposure of soldiers and nurses to looser continental life-styles, and by a live-for-the-moment mentality. Rebellion was not universal; it began among an elite, college students on urban campuses, and filtered to rural areas and high school students. The cult of the rebels was less apparent on farms and in small villages, and many youths retained the traditional values of their parents. By the end of the decade, however, the rebels, whose values were disseminated by the mass media, had won the cultural battle.

Personifying the youthful insurgent was the flapper, a woman who flaunted her sexuality. The term came from the fad of young college women wearing open galoshes that flapped when they walked, an image popularized by cartoonist John Held. Disdaining petticoats, corsets, and girdles, the flapper wore short skirts and short sleeve dresses made of light fabrics, bobbed her hair, and used cosmetics. She accentuated her sexuality by appearing provocative and naughty, and young men found her irresistible.

Sigmund Freud was an ally of the sexual rebels. Published in Europe in the 1890s, popularizations of Freud spread to America after the war, and Freudian psychology found more acceptance in the United States than abroad. Americans were fascinated and titillated by Freud's emphasis on sex and by his thesis that sexual repression was unhealthy and caused mental illness. The chief lesson many took from a superficial understanding of Freud was that an uninhibited sex life was the basis of mental health. The new freedom had some limits. Discussion of an openly homosexual life-style was still taboo, for example, and few professed Freudians championed it. But Freud gave the imprimatur of science to sexual experimentation, and people talked more frankly about sex than ever.

Margaret Sanger contributed to the debate over sexuality by crusading for birth control. She believed her mother had worked herself to death raising a large family and had seen a close friend die in childbirth after unsuccessfully seeking help to obtain an abortion. Sanger founded a magazine, wrote several books advocating birth control, and established the American Birth Control League, which evolved into the Planned Parenthood Federation of America, and established some 300 birth control clinics throughout the country. Fought bitterly by traditionalists, Sanger served a jail term for sending birth control information through the mail. By 1930 she had allied herself with physicians and was making substantial headway. Meanwhile, with condoms, spermicides, and diaphragms becoming available, an increasing number of couples practiced birth control.

The sexual revolution was also abetted by the institution of dating, which by 1930 had replaced calling. Victorian ladies, when they came of age, were permitted to invite young men to their homes, where they would spend an evening in the parlor or on the front porch in the presence of chaperones. In the 1920s, urban life created new limits and opportunities. City dwellings often lacked parlors and porches, so young men invited women out to a movie or a restaurant or for a drive.

Dating shifted the initiative from women to men. Because it was assumed that the man worked and the woman did not, he paid. A date became an act of consumption in which the woman was selling her company: the higher the price she commanded and the more dates she had, the more popular she was considered. Placing a premium on a woman's looks and personality, dating became competitive; it became important for women to have numerous dates and for men to be seen with attractive women.

Couples who dated were expected to neck and pet. In the lingo of the time, necking involved caresses above the neck; petting involved caresses below the neck, including genital stimulation short of intercourse. Men came to expect petting in return for spending money on a date. One young man complained, "When a boy takes a girl out and spends $1.20 on her (like I did the other night) he expects a little petting in return (which I didn't get)."

Movies and magazines also encouraged sexual liberties. Watching stars such as Greta Garbo taught women how to kiss, to hold a cigarette or a drink. Mass magazines were accused of inciting lust. Founded in 1919, *True Story* had 300,000 readers by 1923, almost 2 million by 1926, and carried articles with titles such as "Indolent Kisses" and "What I Told My Daughter the Night Before Her Marriage."

Promiscuity, nevertheless, was not so widespread as the magazines of the decade might suggest. A survey taken in the early 1930s reveals that about one-fourth of the women and about one-half of the men had sex before marriage; among women, three-fourths confined intercourse to their future spouse. The attitudes toward sexuality changed more profoundly than the practice. Those who did indulge in premarital sex were no longer considered outcasts by their peers. The new belief that sex was meant to be enjoyable had more extensive repercussions among married than among unmarried couples.

In another change, smoking, a habit believed to have been confined to prostitutes and bohemians, spread among women in the 1920s; Grace Coolidge became the first president's wife to smoke in the White House. Between 1918 and 1928 the annual sale of cigarettes doubled, in large part because of women. Advertisers depicted pretty women asking men to blow smoke their way; Lucky Strike encouraged women to "reach for a Lucky instead of a sweet." Taking a loftier tone, the American Tobacco Company, aiming at women intent on achieving gender equality, labeled cigarettes "torches of freedom" and staged a march of women smokers in the 1928 Easter parade down Fifth Avenue in New York.

Women also began to drink more frequently in male company. Nice girls, who previously would not have sipped gin, enjoyed getting drunk, and the hip flask became part of every school dance and football game. "In order to be collegiate, one must drink," the handbook of the University of Chicago stated. That drinking was illegal made it a more formidable weapon in the arsenal of youthful rebellion. Like smoking, it became a manifestation of sexuality.

Sexual restraint had been an important factor in preserving social cohesion, and some believed that society would come apart if looser standards prevailed. Blamed on sexual libertines, the rate of divorces to marriages rose from about 1 in 10 to 1 in 6 during the 1920s, and two-thirds of the divorces were initiated by women. The chief factor, though, was not promiscuity but divorce's loss of stigma; people were no longer willing to endure unhappy marriages.

Traditionalists fought the tide of change by proposing laws, regulations, and curfews. A Utah legislator introduced a bill calling for the imprisonment of women caught wearing skirts higher than 3 inches above the ankle; the Virginia legislature considered prohibiting dresses that exposed more than 3 inches of a woman's throat; and the Ohio legislature considered a sweeping bill to outlaw any "garment which unduly displays or accentuates the lines of the female figure." Many colleges prohibited women from smoking, such as Northwestern, which could expel violators. Other colleges confined smoking to off-campus areas or denied diplomas to women who smoked. Most colleges imposed curfews, and some forbade students from owning automobiles and women from riding in them, rules designed to make sex logistically difficult.

Women held a central place in the cultural wars of the 1920s, enlisted on both sides, as advocates of change and as disciples of tradition. The most sweeping change was that women became less passive in all aspects of life. They were liberated not only from sexual taboos but from laborious house-work due to advances in food preparation, electrical appliances, and smaller houses.

Women, even married women, worked outside the home in increasing numbers; by the end of the decade, 10.6 million women older than 15 did such work, up from 8.3 million ten years earlier, and some 11 percent of white married women and some 37 percent of black married women were employed. Some 20 percent worked as domestics, 33 percent worked in clerical positions, and 30 percent worked in factories. Their incentive for taking jobs was usually financial necessity rather than personal fulfillment. Most people considered work a stopgap for a woman, something to do until she settled down and raised a family. And the chief objective of the typical flapper, for all her rebelliousness, was to get a man, marry him, and raise children.

Fields opened up for women, but most jobs remained segregated by gender. Women vitually took over the occupations of typist, stenographer, librarian, nurse, elementary school teacher, and telephone operator. Women fared poorly in the professions, though; the percentage of women doctors declined from about 6 percent in 1920 to 4.4 percent in 1930, and the number of women dentists, architects, and chemists declined. In 1930 only 2 percent of attorneys were women, and percentages declined for women among college students and among Ph.D.'s. Hard-pressed to meet the many demands on their time, women were expected to keep themselves attractive if they were to keep their husbands. They were confused by expert advice on how to raise children, told that too much attention would thwart a child's development but that too little was also harmful. John B. Watson, the most famous child psychologist, told women they should prepare to send their children into the world as independent persons by the age of 2. "Never hug and kiss them, never let them sit in your lap," he wrote. "If you must, kiss them once on the forehead when they say good night. Shake hands with them in the morning. . . . Coddled children become mother's boys."

✣ PROHIBITION

Drinking and attempts to circumscribe it have long histories in the United States. Opposition to alcohol gained widespread support in the 1840s, declined after the Civil War, and peaked during World War I. Advocates of prohibition, one of the best remembered symbols of the 1920s, considered alcohol dangerous to health, destructive to the family, and injurious to the productivity of workers. The evils of demon rum were also connected with aliens, immigrants, Catholics, city dwellers, blacks, and prostitutes.

The fight to outlaw alcohol was led by the Woman's Christian Temperance Union and the Anti-Saloon League, allied with Protestant churches and aided by fundamentalist evangelists such as Billy Sunday, who claimed that drinking violated biblical laws. Many Catholics also supported prohibition, but in smaller percentages than Protestants. Women often led the fight against alcohol consumption, and the prohibition movement was strongest in the West, where they first voted. Many advocates of women's suffrage also campaigned for prohibition, which was an objective of the progressive movement.

The prohibition campaign began on the state and county level. Maine was the first state to outlaw alcohol, and Oklahoma entered the union as a dry state; by 1914, twenty-three states were totally dry and 75 percent of Americans lived in dry counties. Prohibition gained millions of adherents during World War I because it seemed wasteful to use grain for making alcoholic beverages when it could be used for food and for war industries. Many also believed that soldiers would perform better if they were denied alcohol.

The Lever Act of 1917 prohibited the use of foodstuffs in the manufacture of distilled liquors and barred their importation. On December 18, 1917, Congress approved the Eighteenth Amendment to the Constitution, outlawing the manufacture, sale, or transportation of intoxicating beverages. Ratified in January 1919, it went into effect on January 16, 1920. The Volstead Act of 1919 defined "intoxicating" as any beverage that was more than 0.5 percent alcohol; this included wine and beer as well as distilled liquors.

Advocates of prohibition did not expect to stop all drinking, but they believed that most people would respect the Constitution that discouraged it. Expecting to punish only manufacturers and sellers of booze, not ordinary drinkers, they did not make mere possession of alcohol a crime. Even ministers, fearing that strict enforcement would make the law too unpopular, did not support use of force against consumers of alcohol. Initially, consumption declined substantially, but by the late 1920s the sale of alcohol had become so profitable that enforcement became a practical impossibility.

There were simply too many ways that anyone determined to drink could obtain an alcoholic beverage. There were 18,700 miles of border through which alcohol could be smuggled, and the Coast Guard and border patrols had insufficient staff to cope with the problem. Enforcement officials, underpaid, were susceptible to bribes, and local judges and juries often punished bootleggers with a small fine. In Louisiana, where drinking was a cherished tradition, a weekly newspaper reported that a jury had acquitted a man accused of bootlegging and the judge had ordered his whiskey returned to him.

Those who could not afford expensive smuggled liquor could get it on a prescription from a doctor or make it. Hardware stores sold all the equipment necessary to construct a still, and the Department of Agriculture obligingly published a pamphlet describing how to make home brew. Near-beer (with little or no alcohol) was available, and sometimes the dispenser added a squirt of alcohol before serving it. Too, many people purchased wort, a mixture that could be turned into beer simply by adding yeast and letting it ferment.

In every large city speakeasies that served drinks operated almost openly;

prohibition agent Izzie Einstein found one only 35 seconds after arriving in New Orleans. Chicago boasted 10,000 drinking establishments, Detroit 20,000, New York 32,000. The prices of drinks were high, and the quality was bad, but booze could be obtained. Some speakeasies served poisonous industrial alcohol, with flavoring added to disguise it as expensive distilled liquor. Bootleggers sold Jamaica Jake, which was 90 percent alcohol and paralyzed thousands of people; Jackass Brandy, which caused internal bleeding; and a concoction called Soda Pop Moon, a combination of Coca Cola and rubbing alcohol strained through a loaf of bread. People drank antifreeze, wood alcohol, hair tonic, and patent medicines containing alcohol. Farmhands in the Midwest drank fluids drawn from the bottoms of silos, where silage had rotted and fermented for several years. Moonshiners plied a trade so lucrative that they seldom paused to wash their tubs and vats. In many of the vats, prohibition agents found dead rats, cats, mice, and cockroaches that had been attracted by the odor, fallen in, and drowned.

Prohibition proved a bonanza for organized crime in almost every large city where a gang, by intimidating or murdering competitors, gained a monopoly on the liquor trade. Nationwide, bootlegging was a $2 billion business annually at a time when the federal budget was only $4–6 billion. The most notorious bootlegger was Al Capone, who dominated Chicago and its suburb, Cicero. In 1927, Capone grossed $60 million from beer and distilled liquor, compared with $25 million from gambling, $10 million from prostitution, and $10 million from the protection racket.

Capone became a local celebrity, giving away food and coal to the poor, donating money to charity, and investing in legitimate businesses. (He refused to invest in stocks, however, because he claimed that Wall Street was crooked.) On St. Valentine's Day of 1929, Capone's men, disguised as police officers, murdered six members of a rival gang, a massacre so brutal that few people laughed about Capone any longer. In 1931 he was convicted of income tax evasion after repeatedly beating more serious charges and was imprisoned.

Herbert Hoover was the only president to make a serious effort to enforce prohibition, increasing the penalties, transferring enforcement from the Treasury to the Justice Department, and placing prohibition agents under the Civil Service. He also appointed a commission headed by former Attorney General George W. Wickersham to study federal law enforcement, especially prohibition. The commission reported that prohibition violations were overwhelming the federal justice system. As early as 1924 one-half of all inmates in federal prisons were prohibition violators, yet they represented only a fraction of those who were flouting the law.

Ultimately, most reformers became convinced that prohibition was unenforceable. Women, progressives, labor unions, and industrialists concluded that the experiment had proved a failure. Just as World War I had proved conducive to enacting prohibition, so the Great Depression proved its death knell. The clinching argument was that the return of the legitimate liquor industry would create jobs for the people, furnish revenue for the government, and aid recovery.

By 1932 the Republican and Democratic platforms advocated repeal or alteration of the prohibition amendment; the only real difference was in the degree of "wetness" of the platforms and the candidates. Franklin Roosevelt, whose wife and mother were abstainers, became the rallying point for repeal, although FDR was ambivalent about prohibition. After Roosevelt defeated Hoover in 1932, the lame duck Congress that met before his inauguration enacted the Twenty-first Amendment, which repealed the Eighteenth. It was ratified in December 1933, bringing a virtual end to the prohibition era.

But eight states and many counties remained dry, and not everyone considered prohibition a failure. Defenders pointed out that alcoholic consumption, automobile accidents, and such diseases as cirrhosis of the liver had declined under prohibition. Alcoholism, they reminded America, took a heavy toll on family life, and they helped found Alcoholics Anonymous in 1935. Defenders of prohibition also argued that drinking was not the only stimulant to organized crime; urbanization, the automobile, the availability of guns, and increasing criminal sophistication exacerbated the problem. Repeal did not solve the problems of America any more than prohibition had solved them. In the end, compulsive drinkers drank to escape anxiety, and in no decade did they seek escape so desperately, and so unsuccessfully, as in the 1920s.

✢ THE AUTOMOBILE

It was in the 1920s that America began its love-hate relationship with the automobile. Car ownership became part of the American dream. There were 8,000 automobiles registered in the United States in 1900, about 8 million in 1920, and almost 23 million by 1930. By 1925, there were 20 percent more cars than telephones, and although only 12 percent of farm families had running water, 60 percent had cars. A farm wife explained that her family owned a car but not a bathtub because "you can't go to town in a bathbub." Never had so many people so quickly become users of a machine that revolutionized their lives. The automobile captured the imaginations and pocketbooks of most Americans, although the noisy vehicles that clanked along dusty roads and frightened horses disturbed some traditionalists, who appealed to lawmakers to limit use of the machine. In the pioneering period of automobiling, Tennessee passed a law that required a motorist to advertise his intention of going upon the road one week in advance. Vermont enforced an ordinance compelling drivers to hire a person to walk one-eighth of a mile ahead of the car, bearing a red flag. A law introduced in the Illinois legislature stated: "On approaching a corner where he cannot command a view of the road ahead, the automobilist must stop not less than one hundred yards from the turn, toot his horn, fire a revolver, halloo, and send up three bombs at intervals of five minutes."

The automotive industry, which paid some of the highest wages in America, stimulated the economy more than any other industry. By 1928 the manufacture of automobiles was the nation's largest industry; by 1929 it employed 1 person in every 10. The industry consumed 85 percent of the rubber imported, 19 percent of the iron and steel made in the United States, 67 percent of the plate glass, and 27 percent of the lead, and automobiles consumed almost all the gasoline.

In addition, the automobile transformed the city and the farm. Cities, previously compact by necessity, could sprawl, faciliting the growth of suburbs, branch offices, and shopping centers. School buses helped eliminate the one-room school in favor of large consolidated schools, and churches and businesses were forced to follow the highways. Wasteland became prime real estate when a major highway cut through it. Automobiles alleviated some of the isolation and loneliness that made rural life bleak, and threshers, tractors, and reapers eliminated backbreaking hand labor on farms. Millions of Americans began to vacation by automobile, ending the monopoly of leisure travel by the rich. Tourism soared in such previously isolated states as Florida and California; motels, tourist courts, and campgrounds sprang up to serve vacationers.

Nevertheless, some uses of the automobile particularly alarmed ministers, parents, and the police. One juvenile court judge termed the automobile "a house of prostitution on wheels," explaining that one-third of the girls brought before him for sex crimes had committed their offense in cars. The automobile made chaperoning dates impossible, and parking to pet became the most popular form of dating. A New York police officer complained in 1927 that "conditions have been getting worse, with all sorts of couples kissing and hugging in automobiles and the girls openly smoking cigarettes." Motels, which Federal Bureau of Investigation (FBI) Director J. Edgar Hoover called "little more than camouflaged brothels," also facilitated premarital sex. A survey by sociologists found that 75 percent of the patrons of tourist camps in Dallas were not tourists but local couples; one cabin had been rented 16 times in a single night.

Crime, too, became easier because of the automobile: bank robbery, bootlegging, kidnapping, insurance fraud, and car theft. Drunken driving became another scourge, causing millions of accidents. On the other hand, automobiles aided law enforcement by enabling officers to cover more territory, especially when dispatched by radio. And ambulances could transfer victims of accidents and illnesses to hospitals.

Henry Ford became the high priest of the automobile industry. An old-fashioned moralist but a revolutionary industrialist, he combined the warring forces of tradition and modernization. Ford unleashed some forces he did not understand, and he did not approve of some aspects of the revolution he helped to precipitate.

Founding the Ford Motor Company in 1903 with a capital investment of $28,000, Ford was the first to conceive of the motorcar as a product for the masses, not the elite. By the early 1920s Ford had captured 60 percent of the American market. His secret was that he produced only one model, in only one color (black), but it was cheap and dependable. His strategy was to undersell competitors by reducing his price each year; in 1914 the Model T sold for

$450; by 1924 it sold for $290. But Ford, voted the third greatest figure in human history (Jesus was first and Napoleon second), gradually fell behind the times, and by 1927 the Model T was being outsold by the Chevrolet produced by the General Motors Corporation. Ford's answer was to shut down production entirely while designing the Model A. When it appeared in 1928, he overtook General Motors and regained his heroic glamor. He even received a fan letter from the gangster Clyde Barrow, who wrote that he drove Fords exclusively when he could get away with one.

The automobile made a fluid society more mobile; more than any other invention of the era, it accelerated the pace of life. It proved especially liberating to women and to young people, offering them unprecedented freedom to travel. Even the patriarchal Ford was compelled to design his Model A to suit women, who demanded that cars be comfortable and stylish as well as cheap and dependable.

✢ THE DOMINANCE OF BUSINESS

It has been said that the buildings constructed by a civilization reflect its priorities. In the Middle Ages, for instance, Europeans constructed great cathedrals. In the 1920s the most conspicuous edifices in America were towering office buildings, for business paid the piper and called the tune.

The war had damaged Europe and left America untouched except to stimulate its industry, consolidate its banking, and accelerate scientific development. In the 1920s American industry became the most efficient in the world due to mass production, technical proficiency, increased productivity per worker, managerial professionalism, and the application of the assembly line technique that Ford pioneered. Relatively new industries such as cigarette manufacturing expanded, and new products appeared; besides autos, there were radios, rayon, cosmetics, telephones, and electrical appliances.

Many of these products were bought in huge chain stores, which applied economies of scale to retailing. Chain stores sold groceries, drugs, cosmetics, 5- and 10-cent items, and hardware. Most successful were chain department stores that sold a variety of products, such as Sears, Roebuck, and J. C. Penney's, which also sold nationwide through catalogs.

The demand that fueled the economic boom of the 1920s was generated by mass advertising that made up 80 percent of all mail and 60 percent of all newspaper space. Advertisers learned to lure buyers with sex, eternal youth, envy, and the desire to conform. One ad told of a poor man who had been stopped short of executive success by "faulty elimination"; the solution was to eat Post Bran Flakes. And in 1929, Charles Atlas, "the world's most perfectly developed man," began to advertise his testimonial, "I was a 98-pound weakling" until using the technique of "dynamic tension" (isometric exercise).

Profits, wages, and stocks rose consistently, the value of investments appreciated, and incomes increased for most people. Still, richer Americans benefited the most, and not all people shared in the prosperity. Wages rose

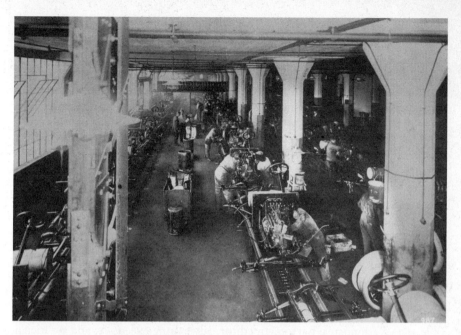

The movable assembly line was an innovation of Henry Ford, who introduced it to the automotive industry. The automobile transformed American life and the assembly line transformed industry.

less than business profits, ultimately circumscribing purchasing power and causing a business decline. And even during the height of the boom, coal mining, textile manufacturing, shipbuilding, shoe and leather manufacturing, and the farm sector languished.

To most middle-class Americans, however, the rich were to be emulated, not resented. No calling was higher than business. "At the head of the list of all professions is that of salesmanship," one business advocate wrote. A business historian added, "No greater calamity could befall this nation than that its business geniuses should resign their positions to direct symphony orchestras and little theaters." Businessmen were said to have sounder judgment than artists or intellectuals; it was considered more difficult to write an advertisement than to write a sonnet.

Business, it was believed, also had much to teach government. Certainly, a business background proved crucial to success in government for men such as Harding, Coolidge, Mellon, and Hoover. Harding wrote a popular article in 1920 entitled "Less Government in Business and More Business in Government." Hoover, who had taken over unprofitable mines and made them pay, considered himself an efficiency expert. As a government official he had the opportunity to reorganize on a larger scale. "He is engineering our material civilization as a whole," a contemporary wrote.

If business were left alone, much as these men suggested, businessmen believed that their profession would eliminate social evils and elevate humanity. The pursuit of wealth was thought to be ennobling; an individual's worth was determined by the wages one could command, and the more money one had, the more good one could do. Even ministers became businessmen so they could do more good, business advocates explained.

Businessmen and ministers believed that God had ordained the capitalist system and that material success was proof of His favor. A wildcatter who almost always struck oil attributed his success to his tithing of money. "I couldn't miss," he said, "because I was in partnership with the Big Fellow and He made geology." The Metropolitan Casualty Insurance Company published a tract, *Moses, Persuader of Men*, which depicted Moses as the first successful salesman: "He sold his people a vast tract of real estate—The Promised Land—through his eloquence, and kept it sold through forty years of deferred delivery." Jesus, who, as one writer noted, "spent far more time in marketplaces than in synagogues," was said to have presided over business groups. The Last Supper was interpreted as the first Rotary Club luncheon, and a minister claimed that Christ was "the first president of Lions International. I quote you from the Bible: He was 'Lion of the tribe of Judah.'"

"Proving" that Christ was a businessman was also the objective of Bruce Barton, the writer most effective at melding religion with the business culture. The son of a minister, Barton, an editor, advertising executive, and politician, wrote four religious books, including *The Man Nobody Knows* (1924), a biography of Jesus that was the number one best-seller for two years. Barton, who considered Jesus the most successful businessman in history, wanted to make his story relevant to Americans and persuade them to follow his example. The "proof" that Jesus was a businessman was his reply to the doctors in the temple, "Wist ye not that I must be about my father's business?"

Businessmen in the 1920s could boast of substantial accomplishments, but business grew overconfident, arrogant. In their zeal and greed the irresponsible elements in the business community claimed too much, sought too much, and, by rampant speculation in stocks, destroyed themselves. A force for modernization at the beginning of the 1920s, business had, by the end of the decade, hardened into defense of the status quo.

BIBLIOGRAPHICAL ESSAY

For the revolution in manners and morals see Stanley Coben, *Rebellion Against Victorianism: The Impetus for Cultural Change in 1920s America* (1991); Beth L. Bailey, *From Front Porch to Back Seat: Courtship in Twentieth-Century America* (1988); Paula S. Fass, *The Damned and the Beautiful: American Youth in the 1920s* (1972); John D'Emilio and Estelle B. Freedman, *Intimate Matters: A History of Sexuality in America* (1988); and two books of essays, Ronald L. Davis, ed., *The Social and Cultural Life of the 1920s* (1972), and George E. Mowry, ed., *The Twenties: Fords, Flappers, and Fanatics* (1963).

Studies of women that include sections on the 1920s are Glenna Matthews, *"Just a Housewife": The Rise and Fall of Domesticity in America* (1987); Alice Kessler-Harris, *Out to Work: A History of Wage-Earning Women in the United States*

(1982); Lois Scharf and Joan M. Jensen, eds., *Decades of Discontent: The Women's Movement, 1920–1940* (1983); and Robyn Muncy, *Creating a Female Dominion in American Reform, 1890–1935* (1991). Among the books on birth control are Linda Gordon, *Woman's Body, Woman's Right: Birth Control in America* (1990); David M. Kennedy, *Birth Control in America: The Career of Margaret Sanger* (1970); and James Reed, *The Birth Control Movement and American Society: From Private Vice to Public Virtue* (1978).

Prohibition is covered in Andrew Sinclair, *Prohibition: The Era of Excess* (1962), which considers prohibition a total failure; Norman H. Clark, *Deliver Us from Evil: An Interpretation of American Prohibition* (1976), which considers it a partial success; and Herbert Asbury, *The Great Illusion: An Informal History of Prohibition* (1950), a colorful account. Other studies include Joseph R. Gusfeld, *Symbolic Crusade: Status Politics and the American Temperance Movement* (1963); Thomas M. Coffey, *The Long Thirst: Prohibition in America, 1920–1933* (1975); Sean Dennis Cashman, *Prohibition: The Lie of the Land* (1981); and Charles Merz, *The Dry Decade* (1930). The key organization that agitated for prohibition is the subject of E. Austin Kerr, *Organized for Prohibition: A New History of the Anti-Saloon League* (1985). Books on organized crime spawned partly by prohibition include Humber S. Nelli, *The Business of Crime* (1976); and John Landesco, *Organized Crime in Chicago* (1968). John Kobler, *Capone* (1971), is a biography of the most infamous criminal.

Among books about the automobile that discuss the 1920s are James J. Flink, *The Car Culture* (1987); Frank Donovan, *Wheels for a Nation* (1965); and two books by John B. Rae, *The American Automobile Industry* (1984), and *The American Automobile: A Brief History* (1965). The relationship between women and cars is discussed in Virginia Scharf, *Taking the Wheel: Women and the Coming of the Motor Age* (1991). Among the many studies of Henry Ford are Keith Sward, *The Legend of Henry Ford* (1948); and Reynold Wik, *Henry Ford and Grass-Roots America* (1972).

There are numerous books about business that include the 1920s. Among them are Thomas C. Cochran, *American Business in the Twentieth Century* (1972); Joseph G. Knapp, *The Advance of American Cooperative Enterprise, 1920–1945* (1973); James Truslow Adams, *Our Business Civilization* (1929); and two books by Alfred D. Chandler, Jr., *The Visible Hand: The Managerial Revolution in American Business* (1977), and *Strategy and Structure: Chapters in the History of the American Industrial Enterprise* (1991). Books that emphasize the impact of business in the 1920s include George Soule, *Prosperity Decade: From War to Depression, 1917–1929* (1947); and James W. Prothro, *Dollar Decade: Business Ideas in the 1920s* (1954). On advertising, see Stuart Ewen, *Captains of Consciousness: Advertising and the Social Roots of the Consumer Culture* (1976); Roland Marchand, *Advertising the American Dream: Making Way for Modernity, 1920–1940* (1985); and Stephen Fox, *The Mirror Makers: A History of American Advertising and Its Creators* (1984). For contemporaneous attitudes toward business and religion, see Bruce Barton, *The Man Nobody Knows: A Discovery of the Real Jesus* (1924).

CHAPTER FIVE

POPULAR CULTURE IN THE 1920S

✣ THE BUSINESS OF LEISURE

In the 1920s the United States, an affluent nation where people enjoyed abundant leisure, became the entertainment capital of the world. Shorter workdays, weekend holidays, and annual vacations created a demand for entertainment to fill leisure time. Restlessness increased because of the monotony of industrial jobs, and Americans were willing to pay billions to avoid boredom. For centuries, humankind had alternated between work and rest; now play acquired new attractiveness, attitudes toward leisure changed to accept fun, and the Puritan work ethic declined. Too, the resulting popular culture nationalized a people who had been sharply defined by regional traits. For the first time, Americans heard the same songs and news, danced the same dances, watched the same stars in movies and sports, read the same publications, and followed the same fads.

✣ AMERICAN CONTRIBUTIONS TO MUSIC

Some of the most memorable popular music in American history was composed during the 1920s. The most important musical development was jazz, America's chief original contribution to the art. Jazz emerged from the blues, a major genre created by rural and urban working-class blacks that became popular in the South, California, and the Midwest. Blues lyrics emphasized the drudgery of farm and factory work and the struggles of the poor to find meaning in love and labor.

Originally jazz was unwritten and improvised yet intricate and sophisticated. It was an antidote to conformity, boredom, and tradition; it soothed and excited. Emphasizing beat and accent rather than melody, jazz was designed to be listened to and danced to, not to be sung or hummed, and it was an urban art form that thrived in crowded places. "Jazz is the result of the energy stored up in America," George Gershwin wrote, and a journalist explained, "I like to think that it is a perfect expression of the American city, with its restless bustle and motion, its multitude of unrelated details, and its underlying rhythmic progress toward a vague somewhere."

Jazz was born in New Orleans among black musicians who worked the opulent houses of prostitution in Storyville, the red light district. When the United States entered the war in 1917 the War Department closed Storyville because New Orleans was a port of debarkation for troops en route to France. The unemployed musicians migrated to St. Louis and Chicago, then to New York and the West Coast. Most of these early performers were talented, self-taught musicians raised in poverty in the slums; among the pioneers were Joe ("King") Oliver, Ferdinand ("Jelly Roll") Morton, and Louis Armstrong, who played in Oliver's band and ultimately became America's leading jazz musician.

Among whites, the rise of big bands ensured the popularity of jazz. Paul Whiteman became the best known of the big band leaders, although his orchestra played music that was more structured than the spontaneous efforts of the early black musicians. Whiteman, who had played in the San Francisco and Denver symphony orchestras before turning to popular music, led the favorite dance band of the era, yet a black band leader and composer, Fletcher Henderson, was more influential among fellow musicians.

In the struggle between transformation and reaction, jazz was in the forefront of change; the poet Langston Hughes called it "the tom-tom of revolt." Traditionalists deplored its lack of structure, its uninhibited quality, and the dominant influence of black musicians. One writer described jazz as "music in the nude," and a professor argued that "if we permit our boys and girls to be exposed indefinitely to this pernicious influence, the harm that will result may tear to pieces our whole social fabric." A clergyman claimed that "in 1921–22 jazz had caused the downfall of 1,000 girls in Chicago alone." Another opponent complained that 70 percent of the prostitutes in New York and an even higher percentage in Los Angeles had been corrupted by jazz. Some moralists wanted to outlaw jazz with a constitutional amendment.

Popular melodic music in the 1920s was concentrated in Tin Pan Alley, an area of clubs, restaurants, ballrooms, and composing offices in Manhattan, where the sound of tinny upright pianos sounded like the banging of tin pans. The king of the area was Irving Berlin, perhaps the greatest composer of popular music America has ever produced, who wrote songs for Broadway, the musical revues, and motion pictures, as well as Tin Pan Alley. He scored an instant hit in 1911 with "Alexander's Ragtime Band" and by 1920 had written about 100 songs. He went on to compose more than 800, including "God Bless America," "White Christmas," and "Easter Parade." Among the other talented composers were George Gershwin, whose "Rhapsody in Blue" was the most acclaimed song of the decade, and Cole Porter, who became prominent near the end of the 1920s. (Porter was distinguished by his ability to compose music without the aid of an instrument.) Perhaps most versatile was George M. Cohan, a songwriter, singer, actor, playwright, and theater manager born to a theatrical family. Lighthearted love was the most frequent theme of the major composers, but there were also popular nonsense songs such as "Yes, We Have No Bananas."

Popular singers of such hits included Al Jolson and Rudy Vallee. Jolson's life paralleled the role he played in the movie *The Jazz Singer*. His father, a rabbi, wanted him to become a cantor, but Jolson turned to popular music and made more hit records than any singer of his time, popularizing such songs as "My Mammy," "April Showers," "California Here I Come," "I'm Sitting on Top of the World," and "Back in Your Own Backyard." Vallee, whose popularity peaked near the end of the decade, created his first band, the Yale Collegians, while a student, then formed the Connecticut Yankees, who played a long stand at the Heigh Ho Club in New York. His soft crooning was the antithesis of forceful jazz.

The 1920s was a golden age for Broadway musicals. More than 400 opened on the Great White Way in the period, twice as many as opened in the 1930s. Gershwin, Berlin, and Cohan wrote for Broadway, although the leading composer was Jerome Kern, a pioneer in modernizing the musical theater. During the 1920s Kern wrote ten complete musicals, including some of the biggest hits of the decade: *Sally, Sunny,* and *Sweet Adeline.* He also scored *Show Boat,* the first musical in which the music, dance, and dialogue were integral to the plot. (Previously plots had been simplistic devices used to introduce songs.) Kern's lyricist was Oscar Hammerstein II, one of the greatest songwriters of his time, who later collaborated with Richard Rodgers. Rodgers wrote 15 scores for Broadway and London shows from 1925 to 1930, collaborating with Lorenz Hart before linking up with Hammerstein.

In addition to musical comedies, the musical revue provided a bevy of hit songs. Unlike plays, revues were not tied to a plot; they emphasized wit, satire, scantily clad dancers, topical humor, and lavish sets. The major revues of the decade were the "Ziegfeld Follies," "George White's Scandals," and "Earl Carroll's Vanities."

When Americans were not listening to jazz or humming Tin Pan Alley tunes, they were likely to be dancing. The dances of the decade were as frenetic and uninhibited as the music. The first dance craze was the shimmy, popularized by Mae West, in which the dancer stood in one place and, with little movement of the feet, shook the shoulders, torso, and pelvis. It was created by black stevedores who worked in Charleston's harbor and moved north when they took jobs in industry during World War I. In 1923 the shimmy was supplanted by the Charleston. Characterized by rapid movements of the feet, the dance was popularized by the hit song of the same name. In 1926 the Black Bottom superseded the Charleston; the phrase referred to the muddy bottom of the Suwannee River because the movements of the dance suggested the dragging of feet through mud. More sedate ballroom dancing continued to be popular, and Arthur Murray, who had launched his first studio in 1919, became a millionaire by teaching couples to dance. Some absorbed the lessons too well, participating in dance marathons (one of the leading fads), exhausting themselves, and risking their health to win small prizes.

Like jazz, dancing had its critics. Clergymen deplored the exhibitionism of the Charleston and claimed it was sending its practitioners to hell. Some cities passed laws to regulate dancing. A Cleveland ordinance stated: "Dancers are not permitted to take either exceptionally long or short steps. . . . Don't dance from the waist up; dance from the waist down. Flirting, spooning, and rowdy conduct of any kind is absolutely prohibited." A law passed by the city council in Oshkosh, Wisconsin, must have been difficult to enforce. It prohibited partners from "looking into each other's eyes while dancing."

❖ RADIO

Without radio, jazz might have remained in New Orleans and the hit makers of Tin Pan Alley limited to selling sheet music. Initially broadcasts were confined to ships and the military, and individuals who bought radios did so as a novelty. But the industry, consisting of only two commercial radio stations in the United States in 1921, exploded the next year, when 500 stations were launched. The Radio Corporation of America (RCA), which began the first station to promote the sale of radios, organized the first national network, NBC, in 1926. CBS followed in 1928 and MBC (Mutual) in 1930.

Although music dominated the airwaves, radio began to vary its programs. In 1920 presidential election returns were broadcast; in 1924 the Democratic and Republican conventions were broadcast; in 1928 candidates campaigned by radio. In 1921 the first World Series was broadcast, and coverage of sporting events attracted some of the largest radio audiences in the decade. Soon there were comedy shows hosted by such performers as Jack Benny and Fred Allen; dramatic programs such as "Buck Rogers" and "The Lone Ranger," variety shows; soap operas; and quiz contests. Radio covered news events more quickly and more dramatically than any previous medium, and most stations broadcast a few minutes of national news each hour. Lowell Thomas became the best-known newscaster of the 1920s.

The sale of radios increased from $10 million in 1921 to $178 million in 1925 and to $843 million in 1929. By 1930 one-half of all American families had radios, and there were more receiving sets in the United States than in all other countries combined. Before long, advertisers recognized the potential of radio, and by 1928 Ford was paying a thousand dollars a minute for a chain of stations to advertise his cars.

At first there were so few stations that they could broadcast at any frequency without overlapping with another station. As stations multiplied, however, Hoover worked out voluntary agreements to transmit at different frequencies. In 1927 the Radio Act formalized the federal government's oversight over broadcasting and created the five-member Federal Radio Commission to license stations; it was succeeded by the Federal Communications Commission in 1934.

✣ THE MOTION PICTURE INDUSTRY

Movies' roots can be traced to 1889, when Thomas Edison developed the kinetoscope, and to 1896, when Thomas Armat invented the vitascope, which projected motion pictures on a wall or screen. By 1908 some 10,000 nickelodeons were showing short films throughout the country. A breakthrough came when producers realized that there was a market for longer films, and between 1910 and 1927, the silent screen industry expanded. There were 20,000 theaters in 1920, when movies were the fifth largest industry in America, and some 28,000 by 1929, among them palaces such as the Roxy in New York, which seated 6,200, had 125 ushers, and boasted a 110-person orchestra. Attending the theater involved a full evening, beginning with a newsreel, followed by a short comedy, previews, an episode in a serial, and the feature presentation. By the mid-1920s, major studios, notably Metro-Goldwyn-Mayer, Warner Brothers, Columbia, RKO, and United Artists, were churning out enough films to enable theater owners to change their offerings every other day.

If the early industry excelled in one genre, it was comedy, whose craftsmen raised pantomime to a level that has not been equaled. Producer Mack Sennett assembled the greatest stable of comedy talent in Hollywood history, and his Keystone Kops films elevated slapstick to an art. Other leading comedians were Harold Lloyd, Buster Keaton, W. C. Fields and the team of Stan Laurel and Oliver Hardy. Perhaps the best comedy genius of all time was Charlie Chaplin, creator of an unforgettable character, the Little Tramp.

The young industry, featuring brilliant producers and directors such as D. W. Griffith and Cecil B. deMille, developed other genres such as westerns, love stories, and biblical epics. But early in the 1920s producers discovered that sex sold tickets and the depiction of demure stars such as Mary Pickford yielded to sexpots, including Mae West, Rudolph Valentino, Gloria Swanson, Clara Bow, Greta Garbo, and Jean Harlow. Movies were given suggestive titles: *Married Flirts, Sinners in Silk, Rouged Lips,* and *The Queen of Sin.* The advertisement for *Flaming Youth* invited people to see "neckers, petters, white kisses, red kisses, pleasure-mad daughters, sensation-craving mothers, by an author who didn't dare sign his name; the truth, bold, naked, sensational." Concentrating in Hollywood, California—which became the center of the industry because of its accommodating weather and varied topography for sets—actors and actresses emulated their screen roles, abusing alcohol, drugs, and sex. Worried about its image and fearing censorship, the industry hired

Charlie Chaplin was the greatest comic genius of the silent screen. His medium and radio helped create a national culture in the 1920s.

Will Hays, Harding's postmaster general, to assure that movies had a moral ending and to ration on-screen sex and violence.

The silent screen era began to wane in 1926, when Warner Brothers introduced sound, first in several short films, then in *The Jazz Singer* (1927). The first commercially successful feature film with sound, *The Jazz Singer* had only 491 spoken words and six songs lip-synced by Jolson; more a "singie" than a "talkie," it employed subtitles for most of the dialogue. Despite its modest advances, the film inaugurated a trend, and before the end of the decade the era of the silent screen was over.

✣ SPECTATOR SPORTS

The 1920s were a golden age for spectator sports. Urban Americans no longer had the opportunity to participate in many sports, but they had the time and money to watch them, and the concentration of masses in cities created crowds sufficient to make professional sports profitable. Spectator sports also benefited from radio, the demand for heroes, mass journalism, and colorful sportswriters such as Grantland Rice and Ring Lardner. More important, sports appealed to fans largely because it was one of the last refuges of individualism and pure competition.

The most popular professional sport was baseball. By 1924 some 27 million spectators were watching games, and attendance doubled between 1921 and 1930. Baseball grew despite the Black Sox scandal of 1919, in which eight members of the Chicago White Sox were accused of deliberately losing the World Series to the underdog Cincinnati Reds after having been bribed by gamblers. Club owners brought in a tough federal judge, Kenesaw Mountain Landis, as commissioner to restore baseball's honor. Although seven of the players accused of accepting bribes were acquitted and the case against the eighth was dismissed, Landis banned the players for life.

Of all the superb players in the 1920s, none had a greater impact than Babe Ruth. He specialized in the game's most exciting play, the home run, which was facilitated by rule changes and a livelier ball in the 1920s. Far from an ideal role model, Ruth had excessive appetites for food, drink, sex, and gambling and, at 6 feet 2 inches and 215 pounds with a beer belly and spindly legs, did not look like an athlete. He was good enough to break in as a pitcher with the Boston Red Sox, however, and eventually moved to the outfield, for a hitter with his power had to play and bat in every game. The Red Sox owner, strapped for cash, sold Ruth to the New York Yankees in 1920, and Ruth helped his new team set an attendance record in his first year. He and the Yankees enjoyed a sparkling season in 1927, when he led a "murderer's row" lineup that sent New York to the World Series title and to acclaim as perhaps the best team ever.

College football challenged professional baseball for the loyalty of fans, attracting about 17 million in 1924. The sport was a boon to colleges, which used the game to gain recognition and attract alumni contributions. To cash in, Yale, Stanford, California, Ohio State, Michigan, and Illinois constructed huge stadiums.

An early football hero, the Indian athlete Jim Thorpe, became president of the first professional league in 1920, but it was halfback Red Grange of Illinois, the Galloping Ghost, who sent pulses racing. Small, swift, elusive, he was the greatest runner of his time. In the first game played in the new Illinois stadium against Michigan in 1924, Grange returned the opening kickoff 95 yards for a touchdown. Still in the first quarter, he scored on runs of 65, 55, and 45 yards before being taken out because Illinois was so far ahead. He returned in the second half to score a fifth touchdown and complete several long passes—gaining 402 yards in total offense, one of the more amazing gridiron performances in history—and Illinois won easily, 39–14. After completing his junior year in 1925, Grange signed a professional contract that guaranteed $12,000 a game; he then played ten games in 17 days on a national tour.

The greatest coach of the era was Knute Rockne, a Norwegian immigrant who had played end for Notre Dame, then turned down a science fellowship to become coach for the obscure midwestern college. Rockne's teams were characterized by unselfish teamwork and total dedication, values that Americans romanticized but saw fading in their society. His teams won by speed, deception, cleverness, and finesse rather than brute force. Rockne was among the first to use the forward pass and the single-wing formation, which helped popularize football by making it more offensively oriented. Rockne also had the ability to inspire his teams to play at their peak; his halftime pep talks were legendary. His death in a plane crash on March 31, 1931, shocked the nation.

The greatest single sporting event of the 1920s was the rematch between boxing legend Jack Dempsey and Gene Tunney in 1927. Their first fight in 1926, a stunner in which Dempsey lost his heavyweight title, grossed $1.9 million; the second grossed $2.5 million, the largest purses in history. Some 60 million fans heard the second fight on radio, the biggest radio audience for a single event up to that time. In the seventh round Dempsey knocked Tunney down, and the referee delayed the count until Dempsey retired to a neutral corner, giving Tunney 15 seconds to recover. (In a previous fight Dempsey had stood above a fallen fighter and pounded him as he got up; the referee had been instructed not to permit a repetition.) Tunney, who had never been knocked down before, knocked Dempsey down in the next round, and as Dempsey tired, the champion battered him badly and won a unanimous decision.

Tunney wanted a third fight, with a projected $3 million purse, but Dempsey feared another battering might blind him. Neither was at his peak when they fought; their better years were behind them. Even when Dempsey was in his prime, the faster Tunney, who relied on defensive tactics, was probably a better fighter, certainly a more sophisticated one. In athletics as in industry, raw power was yielding to technique, design, and careful planning. Future champions would emulate Tunney more than the strong but slow Dempsey.

Other popular sports were golf, tennis, and swimming, participant as well as spectator sports; by 1924 some 2 million Americans golfed and perhaps 500,000 played tennis. Amateur Bobby Jones dominated golf in the 1920s, winning the U.S. Amateur championship in 1924, 1925, 1927, 1928, and 1930, the U.S. Open in 1923, 1926, 1929, and 1930, and the British Open in 1926, 1927, and 1930. Among the leading professional golfers of the era were Gene Sarazen and Walter Hagen.

Tennis was dominated by William ("Big Bill") Tilden, who defeated William ("Little Bill") Johnston for the U.S. championship in 1920, then went undefeated between 1921 and 1928. Helen Wills was equally dominant in women's tennis, winning three U.S. singles championships and eight

Wimbledon singles titles. Between 1927 and 1932, in fact, she did not lose a set in her singles matches. Tilden and Wills helped inspire tens of thousands of children to begin playing tennis, a sport once confined to the elite.

Much the same was true of swimming, thanks to Johnny Weismuller, who set world records, then played Tarzan in the movies, and Gertrude Ederle. A gold medal winner in the 1924 Olympics at 17, she became the first woman to swim the English Channel, beating the time of the five men who had swum it, in 1926, a year when she held 18 world records. Her feats belied the stereotype of women as the "weaker sex."

Black athletes, who were barred from major league baseball and were rare in other professional sports, also made strides in the 1920s, particularly in football, basketball, and track and field. In 1924 in the long jump, DeHart Hubbard became the first American black to win an Olympic gold medal, paving the way for the eventual domination of track by blacks. Although it had a long way to go, sports was becoming increasingly democratic.

✣ LINDBERGH, HERO OF THE AGE

Of all the heroes of the 1920s, none soared higher or farther than Charles A. Lindbergh, the first person to fly the Atlantic Ocean solo. His flight from New York to Paris in May 1927 set off a celebration greater than the one that greeted the armistice ending World War I. That the greatest hero of the age was a stunt pilot and that more newspaper space was devoted to Lindbergh's flight than to any other event of the decade signify the values of the era. In the wake of the Harding scandals and the Scopes trial, after enduring corrupt politicians and failed faiths, Americans were hungry for heroes and anxious to replenish their idealism. Lindbergh, conqueror of one of the last frontiers, filled the need.

Born in Detroit, raised in rural Minnesota, Lindbergh had a passion to fly. Son of a five-term Minnesota congressman, he dropped out of college after three semesters to enroll in flying school, then joined the army, where he perfected his flying skills. Subsequently he did stunt flying and became an airmail pilot based in St. Louis.

Lindbergh was intrigued by the challenge of Raymond Orteig, a French owner of two New York hotels, who offered a $25,000 prize to anyone who would fly nonstop from New York to Paris. The Atlantic had been flown by dirigibles, and by army pilots from Newfoundland to Ireland, but the entire ocean remained one of the last challenges to flyers. Four men perished in the attempt to win Orteig's prize. At the time Lindbergh took off, three pilots were awaiting better weather in New York to attempt the feat; in Paris other pilots were preparing to try. Lindbergh beat them all.

Financed by St. Louis businessmen, Lindbergh designed and built a single-engine monoplane, the *Spirit of St. Louis,* with abundant fuel reserves. Because every pound he saved meant an extra quart of gasoline, he eliminated

No hero of the 1920s soared higher or farther than Charles A. Lindbergh. Lindbergh's solo flight from New York to Paris in the *Spirit of St. Louis* in 1927 garnered more news coverage than any other event of the 1920s and helped popularize air travel.

all excess weight, flying without a navigator or radio operator, jettisoning a radio (saving 90 pounds), carrying no parachute (saving 20 pounds), and even tearing extra pages from his notebook.

On the night of May 20, Lindbergh took off in the rain, his gasoline-heavy plane barely clearing the runway. He had been unable to sleep the previous night and faced more than 30 hours without sleep and hazardous weather. As he disappeared into the darkness, Will Rogers soberly reported on his radio show: "No attempt at jokes today. A slim, tall, bashful, smiling American boy is somewhere over the middle of the Atlantic Ocean, where no lone human being has ever ventured before."

Sometimes flying just a few feet over the waves, Lindbergh remained on course despite crude navigation devices. Then he was spotted over Ireland, over England, over the French coast. One hundred thousand people met him at the airport in Paris after the 33-hour, 29-minute flight, carried him on their shoulders, and snatched pieces of his plane as souvenirs. The first thing Lindbergh did was to call his mother; his reponse to his sudden fame was modest reticence. But the celebration for the man who had "flown like a poem into the heart of America," as the *New York Post* wrote, was just beginning.

Lindbergh met the king of Belgium and the king of England. President Coolidge sent a cruiser to bring him back to Washington, where the elite of the political and social worlds waited. Politicians pinned enough medals on him to sink a battleship, including the Congressional Medal of Honor and the Distinguished Flying Cross. He was offered millions to star in movies, to endorse products, yet his modest refusals only heightened his acclaim. He did receive $200,000 for writing a book, *We*, about him and his plane, and he embarked on a flying tour of all 48 states financed by the Daniel Guggenheim Foundation.

If anyone thought the adulation excessive, no important person said so at the time. Certainly Lindbergh, after initially relishing the publicity, deplored his loss of privacy. He knew he could never duplicate the feat he had achieved at 25; when one is on top of the world there is no way to go but down. While Lindbergh's fame did not erode, many later chapters in his story had unhappy endings.

In 1929, Lindbergh married Anne Morrow, a diplomat's daughter who became his co-pilot and navigator and wrote books about their flights to Latin America, Africa, and China. In 1930 she bore a son, Charles, at their country estate in New Jersey. In March 1932 the 19-month-old baby was kidnapped from his bedroom and later found dead even though Lindbergh had paid a ransom. Evidence incriminated a German American, Bruno Richard Hauptmann. The bills were traced to him; some $13,000 of ransom money were found at his house; the wood in the ladder used to reach the baby's bedroom had been removed from his attic; and the kidnapper had left behind a tool used to construct the ladder. Hauptmann was tried, convicted, and electrocuted in 1936, although some doubted his guilt. A few months before the execution the Lindberghs fled to England to escape the press and to build a home for their growing family. America did not forget the Lindberghs, and when Charles returned in 1939 he was still a popular figure. He remained a public figure until World War II, but he became unpopular when he predicted that Germany would win.

✣ POPULAR LITERATURE

The public's insatiable curiosity about Lindbergh reflected its appetite for simplistic stories about heroes, juxtaposing hazards and courage, good and evil. Few Americans read serious books, and the most popular writers of the era were not F. Scott Fitzgerald, Ernest Hemingway, or H. L. Mencken, but Geneva ("Gene") Stratton-Porter, Harold Bell Wright, Zane Grey, and Edgar Rice Burroughs. Fitzgerald never ranked among the best-selling authors of the 1920s, and Hemingway did not make the top ten until 1940. Over the same period that Fitzgerald's *This Side of Paradise* sold 50,000 copies, Wright's *The Re-Creation of Brian Kent* sold nearly a million. And in 1932 a survey of the best-selling novels of the century in *Publisher's Weekly* revealed that Stratton-Porter held the first four positions and Wright the fifth.

Stratton-Porter made a fortune by appealing to traditional values: optimism, love of nature, victory over adversity, and nostalgia. Four novels published before 1920 each sold more than 1 million copies; she made the top-ten list with newer novels in 1918, 1919, 1921, and 1925. Rivaling her as a dispenser of wholesome optimism, Wright, a former minister who preached the values of clean living, hard work, and the inevitable triumph of good, wrote *The Winning of Barbara Worth* (1911), which had half a million copies in print within a month of its publication. After *Barbara Worth,* Wright produced a novel every other year for two decades; his first 12 books sold an average of 750,000 copies each.

Grey, a former dentist, blended violence, heroism, and romance in a frontier setting, glorifying courage, persistence, and self-reliance. Author of more than fifty western novels that provided the basis for dozens of motion pictures, Grey, from 1917 to 1924, was never off the national list of the top-ten best-sellers, ranking first in 1918 and 1920. He might have been the most-read American novelist of the 1920s—the total sale of his books was more than 20 million. As for Burroughs, he burst upon the literary scene in 1914 with publication of *Tarzan of the Apes,* a runaway best-seller and perhaps the best-selling novel of the decade. For a nation nervous about urbanization, industrialization, and bureaucratization, the adventures of a white man in Africa revived the spirit of the frontier and individualism. Burroughs wrote more than 40 other novels, most of them about Tarzan, which inspired cartoons, films, and comic books.

Although most Americans were too busy or too impatient to read serious literature, the masses devoured periodicals such as newspapers, whose ownership was increasingly concentrated in the hands of a few chains, the largest owned by William Randolph Hearst. There were nearly 2,000 fewer newspapers in 1929 than in 1914, but total circulation increased. Some large cities had supported as many as a dozen newspapers in the nineteenth century; by the 1920s most had one or two. In 1919 the *New York Daily News* became the first tabloid newspaper and its success inspired dozens of imitators. The tabloids sensationalized and simplified news; they included a large sports section, comic strips, and puzzles. Tabloid circulation soon exceeded that of established dailies.

The reading of magazines increased, and magazines that appealed to entire families had the largest circulations: the *Saturday Evening Post,* the *Ladies' Home Journal, Collier's,* and *Literary Digest.* Magazine advertising was so profitable that a typical issue of the *Saturday Evening Post* included 100 pages of ads. More fiction was read than nonfiction, and short story magazines specialized in specific genres, including sports, romance, mysteries, and westerns. Confession magazines had higher circulations than serious journals such as *Atlantic, Harper's* and *American Mercury.*

The public became obsessed with trifles, and editors and publishers fed the appetite by exaggerating news events beyond their true significance. In 1925 the entire country became preoccupied with the fate of Floyd Collins, an explorer trapped in a Kentucky cave-in. Journalists slithered down to interview him, tens of thousands waited at the cave entrance, a choir sang hymns, a minister preached a sermon, and the National Guard kept order. After 17 days of digging, rescuers found Collins dead and the nation grieved. A month later the press barely covered the deaths of 53 men in a North Carolina cave-in.

Murder trials received extensive coverage. Clarence Darrow defended Nathan Leopold and Richard Loeb, prodigies who had killed a small boy, Bobby Franks, in Chicago simply to see if they could get away with it. They did not, but Darrow secured them life imprisonment instead of the death penalty, becoming one of the first attorneys to use insanity as a defense. The Hall-Mills case involved the murder of a New Jersey minister and his lover; the accused included the minister's wife and her two brothers, and the trial was inspired by an investigation undertaken by the *New York Mirror*. After the defendants were acquitted, they sued the *Mirror* and settled out of court. Less lucky were Ruth Snyder and her lover Judd Gray, a traveling corset salesman, who were convicted of fatally bludgeoning Snyder's husband in a New York suburb after failing to poison him with spiked prune juice. They were electrocuted in 1928.

✧ FADS AND NATIONAL CULTURE

In 1923 the Chinese game of Mah-Jongg became a national fad, only to be replaced in 1924 by a mania for crossword puzzles. The most exotic fad of the decade, though, began in 1925 when Alvin ("Shipwreck") Kelly popularized flagpole sitting. Beginning in St. Louis and peaking in Baltimore, Kelly traveled from city to city perching on his posterior at high elevations, sleeping with his thumbs anchored into a wooden seat. During one sleet storm he used a hatchet to chip ice from his body. A young woman who became enamored of Kelly was hoisted up to meet him; when he descended they were married. Setting records became a matter of civic pride, with the mayor of Baltimore praising a young boy who had set a flagpole-sitting record for exhibiting "grit and stamina so essential to success in the great struggles of life."

From Lindbergh to Kelly, Americans sought heroes in popular culture— more, for instance, knew that Rockne was the Notre Dame football coach than knew that Charles Curtis was U.S. vice president—and, as the popularity of simplistic literature indicated, they were anxious to preserve old verities amidst the chaos of change. "If changing conditions were eroding the old certainties, that was only more reason to grasp them more tightly," Roderick Nash observed. In the struggle between transformation and reaction, time was on the side of transformation, but the masses sided with reaction.

BIBLIOGRAPHICAL ESSAY

For music in the 1920s, see Arnold Shaw, *The Jazz Age: Popular Music in the 1920s* (1987), a delightful account; Marshall Stearns, *The Story of Jazz* (1956); and

Nicholas Tawa, *Serenading the Reluctant Eagle: American Musical Life, 1925–1945* (1984). Ethan Mordden, *That Jazz! An Idiosyncratic Social History of the American Twenties* (1978), is an informal account of popular culture, as is Barbara H. Solomon, ed., *Ain't We Got Fun? Essays, Lyrics, and Stories of the Twenties* (1980). Russell Lynes, *The Lively Audience: A History of the Visual and Performing Arts in America, 1890–1950* (1985), is comprehensive. On popular dances, see Tony Thomas, *That's Dancing* (1984).

The best book on radio is Erik Barnouw, *A Tower in Babel: A History of Broadcasting in the United States*, vol. 1, *To 1933* (1966). Gleason L. Archer, *History of Radio to 1926* (1971), covers technology, as does Hugh Aitken, *The Continuous Wave: Technology and American Radio, 1900–1932* (1985). Thomas Grandin, *The Political Use of the Radio* (1971), covers the entire world; Philip T. Rosen, *The Modern Stentors: Radio Broadcasting and the Federal Government, 1920–1933* (1980), describes regulation; and Frank Buxton and Bill Owen, *The Big Broadcast, 1920–1950* (1972), is a colorful account. Biographies of the most famous radio newscaster include Alexander Kendrick, *Prime Time: The Life of Edward R. Murrow* (1969); and Robert Lichello, *Edward R. Murrow: Broadcaster of Courage* (1972).

The best study of the movie industry is Robert Sklar, *Movie-Made America: A Cultural History of American Movies* (1971). Also see Lewis Jacobs, *The Rise of the American Film* (1967); Gerald Mast, *A Short History of the Movies* (1986); and Philip French, *The Movie Moguls: An Informal History of the Hollywood Tycoons* (1971). On the development of the cartoon, see Robert Field, *The Art of Walt Disney* (1943). The lives of two leading comedians are chronicled in David Robinson, *Chaplin: His Life and Art* (1985); Isabel Quigley, *Charlie Chaplin: Early Comedies* (1968); and Rudi Blesh, *Keaton* (1966).

Spectator sports are described in Harold Seymour, *Baseball: The Golden Age* (1971); Marshall Smelser, *The Life That Ruth Built: A Biography* (1975); John R. Tunis, *The American Way in Sport* (1958); and Randy Roberts, *Jack Dempsey: The Manassa Mauler* (1979).

The best book on Lindbergh is Walter R. Ross, *The Last Hero: Charles A. Lindbergh* (1976). Bruce L. Larson, *Lindbergh of Minnesota: A Political Biography* (1973), is also useful.

On popular culture in the 1920s, see Robert S. Lynd and Helen M. Lynd, *Middletown: A Study in Contemporary American Culture* (1929), a classic sociological case study; Roderick Nash, *The Nervous Generation: American Thought, 1917–1930* (1970); and Charles Merz, *The Great American Bandwagon* (1928).

CHAPTER SIX

LITERATURE AND ART IN THE 1920S

✤ NEW DIRECTIONS IN LITERATURE

In the 1920s literature and art enjoyed their greatest flowering in America since the time of Emerson, Thoreau, Hawthorne, and Melville. The blossoming, born of alienation, was casual and accidental, as if someone intending to compose a grocery list had ended up writing the great American novel. Nevertheless, Americans, ashamed of their literature at the beginning of the decade, boasted of it after 1929.

The artistic geniuses of the era enlisted on the side of modernism against the Victorian values that had dominated America from about 1830 to 1920. Victorians, protected by a benevolent God, lived in a universe of moral certainty and valued restraint and order. Modernists believed that all order was temporary and that discovery was continuous. Einstein, after all, had shown early in the century that space and time were not absolute. Victorian self-control was stultifying, and human instinct and emotion had to be liberated. Therefore, modernists sought to inject passion into art, applying such techniques as stream-of-consciousness in literature and experimenting with abstraction in painting. The revolt against traditionalists was carried furthest and most successfully in literature. The best writers of the 1920s, whom Gertrude Stein termed the "lost generation," rebelled against American society, which was not conducive to art; against Puritanism, which was repressive; and against the bland, tedious cultural landscape that characterized the

Midwest and the small town. Rejecting political reform in favor of private pleasures, they lived for art and made a fetish of being disorderly. Many of these marvelously naughty and incredibly witty writers lived like the characters in their novels. They were obsessed with sex: they wrote about it, talked about it, thought about it, did it. Growing cynical before ceasing to be naïve, some sacrificed life to art—a boon for their readers but a calamity for their selves, drowning themselves in drink or escaping in suicide.

However unhappy, the leaders of the lost generation succeeded because they were frank, willing to experiment, and unafraid of failure. They fled the Midwest for Greenwich Village, then continued to France and Italy and England, only to discover that the themes they were seeking lay in their native land. Another irony they discovered was that unremarkable places and people—such as their publishers and readers, whom they scorned as morons—can furnish the raw material for remarkable fiction. For all the redundancy of their criticism of Puritanism and small town hypocrisy, for all their pessimism, they produced a profound ferment in American literature.

The representative figure of the decade was F. Scott Fitzgerald, who amused, tantalized, and taunted with the brilliance of a dying star. Born in Minnesota, Fitzgerald attended Princeton, dropped out to enlist in the army during World War I, and, near his training camp in Alabama, met and fell in love with Zelda Sayre, a beautiful rich woman. Determined to become a writer, Fitzgerald persevered through 122 rejections before publishing *This Side of Paradise* in 1920. The book, a literary thunderbolt, made Fitzgerald rich and famous and enabled him to marry Sayre. *This Side of Paradise* described the collegiate experience in terms that appalled moralists and delighted young people. Fitzgerald was no mere chronicler of youthful rebellion; he and Zelda lived it, dancing the Charleston on restaurant tables, disrobing at a concert, plunging into a fountain fully clothed. Zelda once turned in a false fire alarm in an exclusive hotel; when firemen arrived and asked about the source of the blaze, she pointed to her breasts and shouted, "Here!"

The Fitzgeralds burned themselves out in an endless round of parties. For a time they lived in France, where Fitzgerald wrote his greatest book, *The Great Gatsby,* the story of a poor man who lost a rich woman, became a wealthy bootlegger, and sought to win her over again. (Like Fitzgerald's other novels, its themes were love and money. Fascinated by the rich, Fitzgerald could not decide whether to detest them or to emulate them.) Returning to America, the Fitzgeralds continued a gay but desperate life, Fitzgerald writing short stories to sustain their extravagant life-style. He became an alcoholic, while Zelda suffered a nervous breakdown and was sent to a mental institution. Fitzgerald's productivity suffered, he ultimately became a Hollywood screenwriter and died of a heart attack in 1940. He was only 44.

The genre that belittled the Midwest and debunked the middle class was launched by a pair of midwestern writers, Sherwood Anderson and Sinclair Lewis, and sustained by numerous imitators. Anderson, after suffering a nervous breakdown, deserted business and his wife for literature. Success came with *Winesburg, Ohio* (1919), a novel comprised of interrelated short stories.

A brilliant short story writer whose work was considered shocking for its frank treatment of sex, he could not sustain narrative sufficiently to create memorable novels. Yet no major writer enjoyed a more productive decade than Lewis. In a series of merciless satires he lampooned the village in *Main Street* (1920), the businessman in *Babbitt* (1922), medical science in *Arrowsmith* (1925), religious fundamentalism in *Elmer Gantry* (1927), politics in *The Man Who Knew Coolidge* (1928) and big business in *Dodsworth* (1929). Lewis exposed the hypocrisy, materialism, and shallowness of American society; some critics, however, misinterpreted his caricatures as realism. Becoming the first American writer to win the Nobel Prize for literature (1930), he continued to write prolifically in succeeding decades but enjoyed his greatest success in the 1920s.

The mentor of many successful writers was Theodore Dreiser, the outstanding American naturalist. Dreiser, whose most productive years were behind him, published his finest novel, *An American Tragedy,* in 1925, his first major book since 1915. Fatalistic, critical of materialism, the novel is an indictment of an unprincipled man who murdered his poor lover to marry a rich woman, was tried for murder, and executed. Dreiser wrote in awkward, cumbrous prose. Refusing to employ literary tricks, he built carefully to smoldering conclusions, his characters often trapped by forces beyond their control. Dreiser's life was unhappy; he was a binge drinker and sufficiently alienated to join the Communist party.

Maybe the most neurotic of all the great writers, yet the most influential, was Ernest Hemingway. Born in Illinois, he grew up hunting and fishing in upper Michigan, came to love the outdoors, and set his early short stories in the Michigan woods. Initially a journalist, he drove an ambulance during World War I, was wounded, and fell in love briefly with an American nurse. Hemingway returned to the United States, still a journalist, then joined the expatriate colony in Paris in the early 1920s; his first major novel, *The Sun Also Rises* (1926), was the story of American writers in Paris. Hemingway developed a clean, spare style, employed few adjectives, made the dialogue carry the story, and let the reader infer the thoughts of the characters. Called tough and realistic, he dealt with love, death, and stoicism in the face of tragedy. Hemingway's second major novel, *A Farewell to Arms* (1929), reflected his experience in the war, juxtaposing violence and love. As he grew older, Hemingway remained rooted in violence, enjoying bullfighting and big game hunting; he needed to prove his manhood and feed a voracious ego. He received a Nobel Prize in 1954 yet committed suicide in 1961.

The American writers' colony in Paris in the 1920s revolved around Stein, who shared with her brother Leo an apartment that became a meeting place for intellectuals. Wealthy, she supported artists and writers and tutored writers, doing her writing after her guests departed. She was more important for her influence on others than for her own work. Her most significant book was *The Autobiography of Alice B. Toklas* (1933), the story of her companion, secretary, and lover. After its publication, Stein embarked on a lecture tour in America.

John Dos Passos, like Hemingway, was influenced by the war and traveled in Europe. Unlike Hemingway, he was a social critic who sympathized with political radicals and became an activist, participating in the defense of Sacco and Vanzetti. An established writer by the end of the 1920s, he wrote his most enduring books in the early 1930s, a decade in which he moved politically from the left to the right. Dos Passos's major works in the 1920s included *Three Soldiers* (1921), an antiwar novel, and *Manhattan Transfer* (1925), a portrait of the disorder, confusion, and intensity of New York City.

The leading women writers of the 1920s created characters who were more complex and richly textured than the heroines in Fitzgerald's novels. Edith Wharton depicted the dissipation of New York socialites from her vantage point as a former debutante. Two of Wharton's 47 novels dealt with the war; a third, *The Age of Innocence,* won the Pulitzer Prize in 1920. Willa Cather set many of her novels on the prairie frontier. Her portraits of rural Americans are more serious and sympathetic than those of Lewis. Among her major 1920s novels were *One of Ours,* which won the Pulitzer Prize in 1922; *The Professor's House* (1925), about a professor who took on the attributes of his dwelling; and *Death Comes for the Archbishop* (1927).

Ironically, the purportedly bland Midwest and the much-maligned South produced more and better writers than any other regions. In a 1917 essay that compared the South to a cultural desert, Mencken wrote, "Down there, a poet is almost as rare as an oboe player, a drypoint etcher or a metaphysician." As for "critics, musical composers, painters, sculptors, architects, there is not even a bad one between the Potomac mud-flats and the Gulf." The joke was on Mencken, for within a few years the South exploded in a literary renaissance.

The South produced the great woman writer Ellen Glasgow. Her Dorinda Oakley, the protagonist in *Barren Ground* (1925), is the most fully developed female character of the decade. Oakley is a courageous woman who overcomes adversity and earns a living from farming the barren ground of her family homestead in Virginia. Subtly inspiring, she is a figure of heroic endurance, perhaps the most memorable character drawn from the common people in the novels of the 1920s. Glasgow wrote:

> While the soil endured, while the seasons bloomed and dropped, while the ancient, beneficent ritual of sowing and reaping moved in the fields, she knew that she could never despair of contentment. . . . At middle age, she faced the future without romantic glamour, but she faced it with integrity of vision.

Glasgow's heroines tenaciously won against the odds. Glasgow, too, achieved victories; she was among the first southern women to write realistically about the working class. In 1941 her last novel, *In This Our Life,* won the Pulitzer Prize.

The fame that long eluded Glasgow rushed in hurriedly on North Carolina's Thomas Wolfe with publication of *Look Homeward, Angel* in 1929. Wolfe's novels, based on his life, perfected the genre of autobiographical

Edith Wharton, who won the Pulitzer Prize in 1920, published 47 novels. She and other women writers created more complex female characters than did the male novelists of the 1920s.

fiction. A compulsive writer, he created huge piles of manuscripts that required prudent editing, and he shone brightly but briefly. Wolfe wrote three more novels, two of them published posthumously. Asked to rate the writers of his generation, William Faulkner ranked Wolfe first because he "made the best failure. . . . My admiration of Wolfe is that he tried his best to get it all said; he was willing to throw away style, coherence, all the rules of preciseness, to try to put all the experience of the human heart on the head of a pin."

H. L. Mencken was the most influential journalist of the 1920s. His hyperbolic style and acerbic wit entertained sophisticated readers.

Some critics ranked William Faulkner first. Born in Oxford, Mississippi, Faulkner lived most of his life there and set his most memorable fiction in a fictitious Mississippi county. He experimented with several styles before finding his groove in describing the seamy underside of life in the South. His stories involving incest, rape, murder, prostitution, drug addiction, and alcoholism belong between realism and Gothic horror. Winner of the 1950 Nobel

Prize, he employed the stream-of-consciousness technique more successfully than any American, shifting perspectives, mixing chronology, weaving bewilderingly complex story lines. Faulkner's most productive period ran from the late 1920s to the mid-1930s; novels from this period include *Soldier's Pay* (1926), *Sartoris* (1929), *The Sound and the Fury* (1929), *As I Lay Dying* (1930), and *Sanctuary* (1931).

Although not comparable with Faulkner as individuals, southern writers known as the Fugitives, or the Agrarians, collectively exerted an enormous influence. As students and teachers at Vanderbilt University, they founded a poetry magazine, the *Fugitive,* which published complex, obscure poetry characterized by attention to detail and precise language. Later they turned to regional themes, publishing essays, novels, short stories, criticism, and epic poems. Four members of the group became prominent: John Crowe Ransom, Donald Davidson, Allen Tate, and Robert Penn Warren. In 1930 they, with eight other southerners, published *I'll Take My Stand,* a defense of southern culture. They argued that agrarian society such as that of the Old South was superior to the modern, industrial state. The Agrarians agreed with the modernists that America was culturally sterile, but for the opposite reason. Modernists felt oppressed by history; Agrarians feared the neglect of history. They, too, were pessimistic, not because America was inhospitable to nonconformity and experimentation, but because it failed to preserve the past. The values they cherished were antithetical both to industrial society and to a bohemian life-style.

Just as literature flourished among white southerners, it thrived in Harlem, which had the greatest urban concentration of blacks in the world. The 1920s were the age of the Harlem Renaissance, when black writers and artists discovered African themes and black culture. Impressively versatile, the Renaissance fostered jazz and blues—particularly at the Cotton Club, where Duke Ellington played and Ethel Waters sang—and made Harlem the literary capital of black America.

James Weldon Johnson, who succeeded as a high school principal, civil rights activist, poet, consular official, and Tin Pan Alley songwriter, wrote, among many works, a novel, *Autobiography of an Ex-Colored Man* (1912); a book of poetry, *God's Trombone* (1927); and a social history, *Black Manhattan* (1930). Langston Hughes published poems, plays, fiction, and nonfiction, spanning the gamut of artistic achievement. Such virtuosity was celebrated by Alain Locke's anthology, *The New Negro* (1925), which included poems, essays, stories, and pictures.

Among writers, Claude McKay and Countee Cullen were opposites in style and temperament. McKay, an angry poet and best-selling novelist, denounced racism, applauded Marxism, and explored the seamy side of black life. The Jamaican-born writer's work was characterized by rebellion and resentment. Cullen, on the other hand, was a lyric poet who published five books between 1925 and 1935. Writing in conventional rhyme and meter, rarely experimenting, he insisted that his chief obligation was to his craft, not his race.

Complaining about Cullen's priorities, W. E. B. Du Bois argued that blacks should write novels and poems that depicted themselves heroically and served to liberate the race. Few writers were as prolific as Du Bois, who wrote 18 books, including two novels.

Black culture also prospered in the novels, short stories, and essays of Zora Neale Hurston and in the stories, poems, and plays of Jean Toomer. Hurston, who studied anthropology with Franz Boas at Barnard College, made it her life's work to document black culture. Toomer, a grandson of former Louisiana Governor P. B. S. Pinchback, wrote *Cane* (1923), which included stories, poems, and a play and was featured in *The New Negro.*

Whites, too, promoted black culture. In Harlem, where cafes, speakeasies, lounges, rib joints, and supper clubs catered to a largely white clientele, whites mingled with blacks as they did nowhere else in America. And on Broadway, more than 20 black musicals opened from 1922 to 1929; singer Paul Robeson thrilled audiences; and Eugene O'Neill wrote plays with black themes.

✧ THE THEATER AND JOURNALISM

It is doubtful that any playwright experienced a more productive decade than Eugene O'Neill. From 1919 to 1934 he wrote 25 plays, almost two per year, opening four in 1924. Considered America's greatest dramatist, he won three Pulitzers in the 1920s and a fourth in 1957, as well as a Nobel Prize in 1936.

Born into a theatrical family, O'Neill had an unhappy childhood; he lived a life of dissipation until finding himself as a playwright with the Provincetown Players, an experimental group in Massachusetts. His personal experience providing the inspiration for some of his plays, he probed the dark recesses of the human psyche. Most of his plays are tragedies, and few have happy endings.

His first Pulitzer was for *Beyond the Horizon* (1920); the same year his *The Emperor Jones,* based upon a legend about a black dictator on a Caribbean island, achieved more popular success. The following year O'Neill won a Pulitzer for *Anna Christie,* whose protagonist was a reformed prostitute. In 1924 he produced *All God's Chillun Got Wings,* about interracial marriage, and *Desire Under the Elms,* which included incest. One critic called *Desire Under the Elms* the greatest play yet written by an American. In the late 1920s O'Neill, who loved to experiment and to keep audiences guessing, wrote longer and more complex plays, testing the patience, tolerance, and endurance of theatergoers. In *Strange Interlude* (1928), for instance, characters revealed their unspoken thoughts to the audience in asides within dialogues.

The Southern Renaissance produced a major playwright in Paul Green, who won the Pultizer Prize for *In Abraham's Bosum* (1926) and published three volumes of one-act plays in 1928. His greatest drama was *The Lost Colony* (1937), a play about Sir Walter Raleigh's lost colony performed at the site on Roanoke Island, North Carolina.

The most influential journalist of the 1920s was perhaps H. L. Mencken. An acerbic wit who melded unusual comparisons and elliptical phrases into a hyperbolic style, he denounced women, fundamentalists, democracy, and prohibition. "Love is the illusion that one woman differs from another," he wrote. To the question, "If you find so much to complain of in the United States, why do you live here?" Mencken replied, "Why do men go to zoos?" If democracy had any redeeming quality, he continued, "it is the merit and virtue of being continuously amusing, of offering the plain people a ribald and endless show." And he wrote that "the American people constitute the most timorous, sniveling, poltroonish, ignominious mob of serfs and goosesteppers ever gathered under one flag in Christendom since the end of the Middle Ages." Although he fought cultural conservatism, Mencken was an elitist and a political conservative, more critical of the New Deal than of the Republican administrations of the 1920s. His unparalleled gift for social parody aside, he was a serious reporter who wrote and edited newspapers, magazines, and books, and loved words. His book, *The American Language* (1919), is valuable for its study of the genealogy and derivation of language.

✣ POETRY

The achievements of America's poets nearly equaled the new directions of its novelists in the 1920s. Two major poets, Ezra Pound and T. S. Eliot, were expatriates, while two others, Robert Frost and Carl Sandburg, remained home and wrote regional poetry, Frost focusing on New England and Sandburg on the Midwest.

Pound, like Gertrude Stein, was more important for influencing others than for his own works. His ambition was to learn more about poetry than anyone living; he succeeded. He lived in Italy, where he remained during World War II and supported fascism, and also in England and France. Fluent in six languages, incorporating material from ancient and modern sources, he was the most erudite of America's poets and critics. His major work, *Cantos*, written over 30 years, was collected in 1986.

Pound acted as editor and literary adviser to Eliot, who took up residence in London and eventually British citizenship. Like Pound, Eliot was a disciplined poet who used figurative language and drew symbols from mythology and history. His first poems were bleak and pessimistic, including "The Love Song of J. Alfred Prufrock" (1917), "The Waste Land" (1922), and "The Hollow Men" (1927). In 1928 he joined the Anglican Church, and his later poems and plays were oriented toward Christianity. He won a Nobel Prize in 1948.

Frost is sometimes considered the quintessential American poet, but his rustic simplicity and kindly philosophizing mask a tragic vision. He won four Pulitzer prizes and by 1961, when he recited a poem at the inauguration of John F. Kennedy, had become America's best-known poet. Using colloquial language, he evoked bleak New England images in such famous poems as

"Stopping by Woods on a Snowy Evening" (1923). This poem hints darkly of responsibility, but Frost neglected his family for his art; he became estranged from his wife and children and endured family deaths, including a suicide.

Equally American in themes was the poetry of Sandburg, a midwesterner who wrote for and about the common people and specialized in depicting the raw, tough atmosphere of the urban worker. Once a journalist, he sympathized with radicals and reformers. Winning two Pulitzer prizes for his poetry and another for his multivolume biography of Abraham Lincoln, he became one of the more widely read poets in the country.

Highly ambitious, Hart Crane wrote the greatest epic poem with an American theme, *The Bridge* (1930), which used the Brooklyn Bridge as a metaphor for the United States. Crane's poetry was more positive than his life; he rejected cultural pessimism, yet in his quest for inspiration and his struggle with his bisexuality, he drank heavily, ruined his health, and committed suicide in 1932.

Wallace Stevens belied the notion that a poet must live a bohemian life. A lawyer and insurance executive, he had an outwardly conventional life but a deep commitment to intellect. Stevens believed art had the power to regenerate the spirit, and he explored the relationship between reality and imagination. His poetry, characterized by wit, elegant phrases, and musical cadences, was a celebration of life. Stevens received two National Book Awards and a Pulitzer Prize in the 1950s.

Edna St. Vincent Millay, who cut a dashing figure in Greenwich Village, won a Pulitzer Prize in 1923 for her collection *The Harp-Weaver and Other Poems.* A stanza from the first poem in her *A Few Figs from Thistles* (1920) is the most-quoted verse of the decade:

> My candle burns at both ends,
>   It will not last the night;
> But ah, my foes, and oh, my friends—
>   It gives a lovely light.

Marianne Moore, another major poet who lived in Greenwich Village, wrote of commonplace subjects such as animals, baseball, and art objects in descriptive verse that incorporated quotations. Although her poems were overlooked in her own day, she also contributed to new directions in American literature as a major critic, and she edited the literary magazine *Dial* from 1925 to 1929. The era produced other important poets such as E. E. Cummings, who disdained capitalization and punctuation; Vachel Lindsay, who wrote poems to be chanted, such as *The Congo* (1914); Edgar Lee Masters, whose *Spoon River Anthology* (1915) explored the lives and passions of small town America; and Edwin Arlington Robinson, who collected three Pulitzers during the 1920s. Robinson created a mythical village, Tilbury Town, based on his hometown, Gardiner, Maine, and put bleak words into the mouths of his characters.

✢ THE WRITING OF HISTORY

Historians in the 1920s emphasized conflict, the taming of the frontier, economics, imperialism, race, the corporations, and the labor movement. Although the trend in academia was toward scholarly monographs, the great historians of the era wrote interpretive works that challenged conventional beliefs and opened controversies that endured for generations. James Harvey Robinson pioneered in writing history that attempted to explain the present as well as to record the past, to go beyond what happened and to explain why it happened. As in literature, some of the major historians were natives of the Midwest, including Frederick Jackson Turner, Charles A. Beard, and Vernon Louis Parrington.

In a paper he read at a meeting of the American Historical Association in 1893, Turner suggested that the frontier created democracy. Turner, who believed historians had overlooked the influence of the West in favor of orientation toward Europe, said the availability of free land shaped the American character and institutions. His reputation rests upon this provocative and influential thesis. Excelling as a teacher but procrastinating as a writer, Turner wrote only four books in a 45-year career and never completed books he signed contracts to write.

In contrast to Turner, Beard was a controversial personality and prolific writer, publishing nearly fifty books before his death. Among his more important works were *An Economic Interpretation of the Constitution* (1913) and *Economic Origins of Jeffersonian Democracy* (1915). In his book about the Constitution, he refused to view the founding fathers with awe, believing their politics was based on self-interest. Beard theorized that the founding fathers had been less interested in establishing democracy than in thwarting it and had supported ratification because they held securities that would appreciate under a strong government. This interpretation appealed to alienated intellectuals but angered others, who believed he impugned the motives of the founders. Harding's newspaper, the Marion *Star,* headlined an article about Beard's book "Scavengers, Hyena-Like, Desecrate the Graves of the Dead Patriots We Revere."

A celebrated teacher at Columbia from 1904 to 1917 (during which time he wrote 11 books) Beard resigned to protest the firing of professors who had opposed World War I, bought a dairy farm in Connecticut, and continued to write. With his wife, Mary, he wrote *The Rise of American Civilization* (1927), the best general history of the United States up to that time.

Parrington was an obscure scholar until the first two volumes of his three-volume *Main Currents in American Thought* appeared in 1927. Using a biographical-critical approach, he described the development of the idea of democracy in the lives and work of intellectuals from 1620 to the late nineteenth century. Parrington taught in Kansas and Oklahoma, including a three-year stint as football coach at Oklahoma, and finished his career at the University of Washington. Sympathizing with reformers and dissenters, he preferred agrarian to industrial society and local to central authority, described the interplay between literary ideas and politics, and showed how social forces shape ideas. He died suddenly in 1929, before reaping the rewards of his success.

Among other major scholars of American history were Carl Becker, a specialist in the history of ideas, and Arthur M. Schlesinger, concerned with social and cultural history. Becker challenged the idea that historians could write objectively about the past when their interpretations were influenced by the values of contemporary society. Objectivity remained an ideal for writers such as Schlesinger, whose major enterprise was to co-edit the 12-volume *History of American Life* series beginning in 1923. Professional historians and their debates, though, mattered little to lay readers. There was a significant market for popular history, and amateurs, many of them from the worlds of literature or journalism, had the lion's share. One of the most successful members of this group, magazine editor Frederick Lewis Allen, sold more than 1 million copies of his chronicle of the 1920s, *Only Yesterday* (1931). It ranked second in sale of nonfiction in 1932.

Historic preservation attracted many Americans who did not share the alienation of intellectuals. "For every American who deprecated the influence of Puritans and pioneers on the national character, there was at least one other concerned about saving an old New England home or a frontier village," Roderick Nash wrote. Among the accomplishments of preservationists were the restoration of Old Deerfield Village in Massachusetts and Monticello, Thomas Jefferson's home in Virginia. John D. Rockefeller restored Williamsburg, Virginia's colonial capital, and Henry Ford restored Greenfield Village in Michigan.

✧ PHILOSOPHY AND EDUCATION

Philosophy reflected the skepticism of the age. Einstein's theories destroyed Newtonian physics, and Darwin's theories undermined religious beliefs that had provided comfort and certainty to the Victorian world. "Several thousand years of effort directed at giving meaning to life and rules for conduct were down the drain," Nash wrote.

John Dewey, the most eminent philosopher of the 1920s, argued that philosophers had asked the wrong questions. Instead of idle speculation, metaphysics, and abstract logic that served to rationalize the status quo, he thought, they should concentrate on solving practical problems. Like the pragmatist William James (who died in 1910), Dewey believed that actions should be judged by their consequences. Theories were not meaningful unless they had practical applications; experience was a better guide than logic.

Dewey published widely, devoting much of his thought to education, and is considered the founder of progressive education. Opposing memorization and believing that teachers should guide rather than dictate, Dewey argued that schools should accommodate changing times. They should be miniature communities that taught critical thinking and combined theory and practice, a liberal and a technical education.

Education improved in the 1920s. High school enrollment increased from 2.2 million to 4.4 million, graduates from 311,000 to 667,000. At the beginning of the decade there were more illiterates than college graduates, yet the overall rate of illiteracy declined from 6 percent to 4.3 percent by 1930 and from 23 percent to 16.4 percent among blacks. Many small schools were consolidated, permitting teachers, most of whom were women, to specialize, and they taught less Greek and Latin and more vocational subjects.

During the 1920s college enrollment grew from 589,000 (4.7 percent of the college age population) to 1,101,000 (7.2 percent, of which 43.7 percent were women), and the number of Ph.D.'s awarded rose from 560 in 1920 to 2,071 in 1930. Most college students, however, were concerned chiefly with extracurricular activities and were poorly informed; some freshmen at the University of Maine believed that Martin Luther was the son of Moses (who was described as a Roman emperor). College teaching became increasingly professionalized, and pressure to publish grew. Black colleges and women's schools continued to hire mostly white males. Jewish professors moved from the East to the Midwest to avoid quotas and prejudice at older universities.

✣ ANTHROPOLOGY AND SOCIOLOGY

Franz Boas, the most influential anthropologist of the era, helped to break down the distinctions between civilization and savagery. His *The Mind of Primitive Man* (1911) concluded that primitive peoples were capable of abstract logic and art, that there was no reason to assume the superiority of European culture, and that a culture must be judged on its ability to adapt to its environment.

One of Boas's students, Margaret Mead, began fieldwork in the South Pacific in 1925 and in 1928 published *Coming of Age in Samoa,* a milestone in the comparative study of cultures. Concluding that Samoan children were happier than American children, she presented alternatives to the conventional American views of child rearing, gender roles, and sexuality.

The most important sociological study of the decade was *Middletown* (1929), in which Robert Lynd and Helen Lynd used Muncie, Indiana, as a case study of a midwestern town. Using sampling techniques and extensive interviews, *Middletown* was more scientific than previous local studies, and it produced a wealth of information on attitudes and life-styles.

✣ THE VISUAL ARTS

Interest in American art boomed during the 1920s, and artists, still painting in the shadow of Europe, began to demand high prices. Between 1921 and 1930 some 60 art museums were founded and 13 others opened, including

New York's Museum of Modern Art, in 1929. Rising with the interest in art was a debate about what constituted art, a debate of unprecedented vigor.

The Ash Can school that flourished before World War I prepared the public for rude shocks, painting scenes that reflected the gritty reality of urban life: children playing on dirty sidewalks, laundry hung behind tenements, homeless men sleeping under bridges. Academic critics who considered these inappropriate subjects condemned the school, which included painters such as John Sloan, George Bellows, George Luks, William Glackens, and their mentor, Robert Henri.

Increasingly painters depicted urban life, and their work grew experimental. Joseph Stella, who came to the United States from Italy at 19, found New York a rich environment, painting the *Brooklyn Bridge* (1922) and a series entitled *New York Interpreted* that featured innovative use of light and shadow. Edward Hopper specialized in bleak city images—a lonely diner in an all-night restaurant, a tired usher in an empty movie theater—that stood in stark contrast to the bustling scenes of the Ash Can school.

The more popular realists were the Regionalists, Thomas Hart Benton, Grant Wood, and John Stewart Curry. Benton was born in Missouri, the great nephew of the state's first senator. After studying in Paris for three years, he returned to paint the life of the Missouri Valley: farmers, workers, wheat fields, riverboats, square dancers, and politicians. Benton, who believed art should be comprehensible to the masses, enjoyed popular and critical acclaim. Wood, born in Iowa, spent much of his life painting in Cedar Rapids. Like Benton, he documented the life of the common people; his *American Gothic* (1930), depicting a staid, pious farm couple, strong, stern, and graceless, symbolizes the stark Midwest. Curry, the youngest of the Regionalists, painted scenes in his native state; his best-known painting is *Baptism in Kansas* (1928). In addition, he traveled with a circus to paint animals and performers.

The Regionalists, who also painted murals, remained popular through World War II. They were, however, exceptions in the art world dominated by nonrepresentational styles pioneered in Europe. Modernist painters sought release from representation of the external world and deliberately distorted reality, sometimes breaking it up into cubes and triangles creating visual dissonance, to convey their feelings or invoke a mood. Even painters who retained a regional emphasis began to revolt against the representational tradition of landscape painting. Georgia O'Keeffe, for instance, interpreted western deserts by enlarging details so that objects lost their recognizable quality.

The chief stimulus to modern art was the Armory Show of 1913, held in the Sixty-ninth Regiment Armory in Manhattan. American art was shown, but European modernists such as Renoir, Monet, Cézanne, Van Gogh, Gauguin, and Picasso were the stars. The show galvanized the professional art world, although most ordinary people continued to prefer representational art and some critics agreed. The *New York Times* termed some paintings "pathological" and "hideous," and the *New York Herald* summed up the exhibit as "some of the most stupidly ugly pictures in the world." Nonetheless, modernism gradually conquered American tastes.

In the 1920s modernism in art existed in a symbiotic but angry relationship with modern industrialization; in the confrontation between transformation and reaction it was progressive in an artistic sense, yet often reactionary in its resistance to technological advance. Many modernists emphasized the human costs of industrial society; they often depicted machines, yet they did not really like them. Their work was filled with rage against old standards, which they considered inhibiting, and against new realities, which they considered dehumanizing.

Alfred Stieglitz, who founded a school of photography called the Photo-Secessionists, believed the camera had made representational art obsolete. Among the first to recognize the potential and the limitations of the camera, he strove to win recognition for photography as an art form. Stieglitz, who married O'Keeffe, emphasized "straight" or "honest" photography and disdained tinkering with prints or negatives to produce an artificial effect. His protégé, Edward Steichen, one of the first to experiment with color photography, pioneered aerial reconnaisance during World War I and recorded the story of naval aviation on film. After the war he became director of the Photography Department of the Museum of Modern Art; one of his first purchases was a collection of photographs by Stieglitz.

Paul Strand, also a Photo-Secessionist, was concerned with the content of photography as well as its artistic quality. He shared concern for the dignity of the working man with Lewis W. Hine. Concerned less with art than with delivering a message, Hine focused on social problems such as child labor, depicting immigrants at Ellis Island, factory workers, and inhabitants of tenements.

American sculpture was influenced by modernist techniques and nonrepresentational experiments, but the public continued to prefer conventional forms. The best-known sculptor was Gutzon Borglum, who carved busts into the sides of mountains in Georgia and South Dakota, Confederate heroes in the former and presidents Washington, Lincoln, Jefferson, and Theodore Roosevelt in the latter.

In architecture, the most striking development was the erection of towering skyscrapers of steel and glass, symbolizing the triumph of industrial capitalism: the Woolworth Building, the Chrysler Building, and the Empire State Building in Manhattan, and the Tribune Tower in Chicago. German refugees Walter Gropius and Ludwig Mies van der Rohe led the Functionalists, who emulated Louis Sullivan in his belief that "form follows function." Considering ornamentation decadent, they designed buildings with austere lines.

Frank Lloyd Wright, a student of Sullivan, remained the most influential architect. A bold innovator with a fertile imagination, he designed stores, factories, museums, colleges, office buildings, and houses that have the stamp of individuality. An advocate of urban planning, Wright believed that buildings should develop from the inside out so architecture would help integrate the individual and the environment.

✤ THE END OF THE 1920S

From literature to architecture, the dominant motifs of the 1920s were experiment and innovation. Like all experimental activities, some succeeded, others failed. For all the superficial wickedness and rebellion of the 1920s, the decade was characterized by an innocence that collapsed with the stock market in 1929.

The 1920s was America's decade of adolescence. When it ended, America had grown up, sober and resigned. Like everyone who looks back at adolescence from adulthood, the rebels of the 1920s did so with a sense of regret, of wasted opportunities and dissipated energies. But they also looked back wistfully, as the decade had been fun at times, and they could not have matured without it.

There is something magical about youth and something sad about losing it; our failure to recognize its joys while they are ours is part of the magic. Growing up is a painful process of trial and error, for nations as for individuals. The crucible of depression and war would mature America. Like previous generations, the rebels of the 1920s would find redemption in suffering.

BIBLIOGRAPHICAL ESSAY

The best synthesis about the literature of the 1920s is Frederick Hoffman, *The Twenties: American Writing in the Postwar Decade* (1965). Other valuable works include Maxwell Geismar, *Writers in Crisis: The American Novel Between Two Wars* (1942), which has chapters on representative writers; Elliott Emory, ed., *American Literature: A Prentice Hall Anthology*, vol. 2 (1991); Daniel Joseph Singal, *The War Within: From Victorian to Modernist Thought in the South, 1919–1945* (1982); Humphrey Carpenter, *Geniuses Together: American Writers in Paris in the 1920s* (1988); Malcolm Cowley, *Exile's Return: A Literary Odyssey of the 1920s* (1934), the impressions of an expatriate; and two studies by contemporaries, Edmund Wilson, *The Twenties* (1975); and Floyd Dell, *Intellectual Vagabondage* (1926).

For black writers, see Nathan I. Huggins, *Harlem Renaissance* (1971); Addison Gayle, Jr., *The Way of the New World: The Black Novel in America* (1976); and Edward Margolies, *Native Sons: A Critical Study of Twentieth Century Black American Authors* (1968).

Many fine biographies of writers exist, among them Carl Bode, *Mencken* (1986); Janet Hobhouse, *Everybody Who Was Anybody: A Biography of Gertrude Stein* (1989); Andre Le Vot, *F. Scott Fitzgerald* (1983); Kenneth S. Lynn, *Hemingway* (1987); David H. Donald, *Look Homeward: A Life of Thomas Wolfe* (1987); Arthur Gelb and Barbara Gelb, *O'Neill* (1973); Kim Townsend, *Sherwood Anderson* (1987); R. W. B. Lewis, *Edith Wharton: A Biography* (1975); Stephen B. Oates, *William Faulkner: The Man and the Artist* (1987); and Virginia S. Carr, *Dos Passos: A Life* (1984).

For history, see Richard Hofstadter, *The Progressive Historians: Turner, Beard, Parrington* (1968). For philosophy, see Morton G. White, *Social Thought in*

America: The Revolt Against Formalism (1949); and Neil Coughlan, *Young John Dewey: An Essay in American Intellectual History* (1975).

Art histories encompassing the 1920s include Milton W. Brown, *American Painting from the Armory Show to the Depression* (1955); Lloyd Goodrich and John Bauer, *American Art of Our Century* (1961); William S. Lieberman, ed., *Art of the Twenties* (1979); and Abraham A. Davidson, *Early American Modernist Painting, 1910–1935* (1981). For photography, see Beaumont Newhall, *Photography, 1839–1937* (1937); and for sculpture, see Andrew C. Ritchie, *Sculpture of the Twentieth Century* (1952).

For architecture, see Nikolaus Pevsner, *Pioneers of Modern Design* (1949); Vincent Scully, *American Architecture and Urbanism* (1969); Frank Lloyd Wright, *An Autobiography* (1932); and Brendan Gill, *Many Masks: A Life of Frank Lloyd Wright* (1987).

CHAPTER SEVEN

A RESTRAINED DIPLOMACY

✣ AMERICAN STATESMEN AND ISOLATIONISM

Although the 1920s are described as a period of isolationism, or with-drawal from world affairs, the United States, which emerged from World War I as the planet's greatest economic and military power, was more involved in international events than in any previous peacetime decade. It is true that many Americans considered involvement in World War I a mistake and wanted to avoid participation in future wars. Ernest Hemingway, for one, wrote, "We were fools to be sucked in once in a European war and we should never be sucked in again." Isolation, however, was relative, not absolute, in the 1920s, when domestic problems took prece-dence over foreign affairs. Isolationism was in fact stronger in the early 1930s, the years just after the stock market crash. During the 1920s, as American statesmen tried to avoid the mistakes of the war era, isolationists differed from internationalists over means, not ends. Isolationists believed the most effective way to avoid war was to avoid involvement with other nations except to trade with them. Internationalists believed that collective solutions to world prob-lems might preempt war. Most isolationists were not opposed to involvement in Latin America, and most internationalists did not seek alliances. There were isolationists in influential positions, including William E. Borah of Idaho, who became chair of the Senate Foreign Relations Committee after the death of the moderate isolationist Henry Cabot Lodge in November 1924. William

Randolph Hearst, the nation's leading newspaper publisher, opposed collective security, as did Robert McCormick, publisher of the *Chicago Tribune,* the largest midwestern daily. Other prominent isolationists were William Jennings Bryan, who supported a constitutional amendment requiring a popular referendum to declare war, and Henry Ford.

Nonetheless, the key element in American foreign policy was nationalism, not isolationism, and it differed little from that of other countries. Europe was in turmoil over ethnic rivalries. The Soviet Union glorified its past, and Joseph Stalin emphasized "Socialism in One Country." Benito Mussolini came to power in 1922 promising to restore Italy to the greatness of the Roman Empire. In Germany, the Nazi party rode a crest of nationalism. In the Far East, Japanese nationalism was rising, only to clash with Chinese nationalism.

The United States was not entirely innocent of imperial pretensions, yet these were restrained for a nation with its potential might. America's overseas possessions, consisting primarily of small islands of limited economic value, was minuscule compared to those of the British or the French. The existing order served the United States well, for on the whole, American policy was oriented toward order and stability instead of economic or political equality. Statesmen were prepared to make concessions to revisionist powers, but these reforms were designed to preserve the status quo so it would not be overturned convulsively. Still, the United States stirred resentment among smaller nations simply by virtue of its size and power and by its ability to influence their destinies, deliberately or unintentionally.

By 1919 the United States, a debtor nation just five years earlier, was a creditor, led the world in exports, and was second to Britain in imports. American products and technology dominated world markets; American movies, novels, and music were ubiquitous; and thousands of Americans went abroad to teach, to convert other peoples to Christianity, and to work. The government played little role in promoting the export of goods and culture. Interests of the government and of corporations overlapped but were not identical: economic investments were concentrated in Canada and Latin America, whereas the chief concerns of diplomats lay in Europe and Asia.

The American presidents and secretaries of state usually responded to events rather than anticipated them, and the United States did not produce a notable diplomat. Warren Harding, for instance, was ignorant of world politics. He asked the journalist Arthur S. Draper, who had talked with European leaders, to remain after a press conference, then said: "I don't know anything about this European stuff. You and Jud [Judson Welliver] get together and he can tell me later; he handles these matters for me." On another occasion Harding astounded a reporter who asked about a highly protectionist tariff bill by stating, "We should adopt a protective tariff of such a character as will help the struggling industries of Europe to get on their feet." In foreign policy Harding delegated authority and referred questions to his austere and dignified secretary of state, Charles Evans Hughes. Hughes, who had been an attorney, a Supreme Court justice, and the Republican presidential candidate in 1916, was more knowledgeable than Harding, but his experience had not been in foreign affairs. He possessed a keen if unimaginative mind and was legalistic in his approach to world problems.

Calvin Coolidge was not interested in foreign policy and did not even mention foreign affairs in his autobiography. After Hughes left office in 1924, Coolidge appointed Frank B. Kellogg to replace him. Kellogg, a lawyer and former senator who had served as ambassador to England, was a mediocre diplomat, nearly 70, past his prime; unlike Hughes, he deferred to the president.

Herbert Hoover had traveled more than any president and was more intelligent and knowledgeable than Harding or Coolidge. He appointed Henry L. Stimson secretary of state. Stimson, also a lawyer, had served as secretary of war under William Howard Taft and governor general of the Philippines under Coolidge. Abler than his predecessors, he acted cautiously despite being temperamental.

The United States, after failing to ratify the Versailles Treaty, remained at war with Germany until Congress passed a joint resolution ending hostilities and Harding signed it on July 2, 1921. Harding, Coolidge, and Hoover never advocated membership in the League of Nations, and Hughes placed letters from the League in an inactive file. (When the policy was ridiculed in the *New York Times,* Hughes began to respond with noncommittal replies.) Harding, Coolidge, and Hoover did advocate American membership in the Permanent Court of International Justice (the World Court), which was independent of the League. In 1926, Congress voted for membership but attached reservations that were not acceptable to the other members, and Coolidge dropped the matter.

The Republican presidents continued Wilson's policy of refusing to recognize the Soviet Union on the grounds that it had repudiated its foreign debts, failed to respect private property, denied freedom of religion, and disseminated propaganda to overthrow the American government. The United States, however, did not attempt to restrain trade, and by 1928 one-fourth of all foreign investment in the Soviet Union was American. One-third of the tractors exported by Ford went to the Soviets, and some 85 percent of the tractors used by Russian farmers were Ford built. In 1929, Henry Ford signed a contract to help Russians produce cars and trucks, and the American entrepreneurs Julius Hammer and Armand Hammer invested heavily in the Soviet Union. In addition, from 1921 to 1923 Hoover, as commerce secretary, coordinated public and private relief efforts that sent $78 million worth of food to the famine-stricken Soviets and saved some 10 million from starvation.

❖ WAR DEBTS AND REPARATIONS

During and after World War I the United States, with money from war bond sales at home—bonds the government had to repay—loaned about $10.5 billion to the Allies and to other European nations. Europeans argued that the United States should cancel their debts because it had suffered neither the heavy casualties nor the property damages they had incurred. The war was fought for common objectives, they maintained, and American money might compensate for European contributions.

The American government did demonstrate flexibility: between 1923 and 1930 the United States renegotiated interest rates and, by reducing the rate from an average of 5 percent to an average of 2.1 percent, eliminated more than half the debt. Cancellation of the debts, though, was unacceptable to Americans because it would have made the debts the responsibility of American taxpayers. They pointed out that the Europeans were using American money to purchase weapons, and that the European Allies were receiving reparations from Germany in payment for damages inflicted by its army. An Allied commission had set reparations at $33 billion plus interest, payable in annual installments. The French, who were to receive 52 percent of the money, saw reparations as a way to weaken Germany while rebuilding their economy. But Germany soon fell behind and defaulted in December 1922, and French and Belgian troops occupied Germany's industrialized Ruhr Valley to compel payment. Germans resorted to passive resistance, and their currency collapsed. Before World War I, one American dollar was worth about 4.2 German marks; by 1924 it took 4 trillion German marks to equal one American dollar. Inflation destroyed the savings of the middle class, causing resentment of the German and French governments and provoking demands for an authoritarian regime to exact revenge.

In 1923 the League created a commission to restructure reparations, headed by American banker Charles G. Dawes. In 1924 the commission completed a plan that reduced reparations and provided Germany with a $200 million loan (half from the United States) to stabilize its currency. After Germany accepted the plan the occupation ended, payments resumed, and Dawes received the Nobel Peace Prize. Germany soon fell behind, and in 1929 another commission, headed by the American Owen D. Young, reduced reparations. The Young plan set reparations at $8 billion plus 5.5 percent annual interest and established a graduated scale of payments ending in 1988. Unfortunately, the Great Depression wrecked the plan. In 1932, President Hoover called for a one-year moratorium on all intergovernmental debts and reparations, hoping this action would enable creditors to collect private debts, thus saving American banks that had invested in European securities. In June 1932, Germany's creditors met at Lausanne, Switzerland, and agreed to forgive nine-tenths of reparations owed them if the United States would cancel the war debts. The United States refused, but after 1932 few reparations or debts were paid because of the depression.

✤ THE PEACE MOVEMENT AND DISARMAMENT

During the 1920s a movement for peace and disarmament flourished in America. Ernest Hemingway, John Dos Passos, and William Faulkner wrote antiwar novels, and historians wrote that America had been duped into intervening in World War I. After winning suffrage, many women devoted themselves to the peace movement. Some two-thirds of the peace activists were women, and they formed the Women's International League for Peace and Freedom, the National Committee on the Cause and Cure of War, the Women's Peace Society, and the Women's Peace Union. Jane Addams, leader of the Women's International League, won the Nobel Peace Prize in 1931, and the Women's Peace Union introduced a constitutional amendment to outlaw war in each Congress from 1926 to 1939. The amendment died in committee. Jeannette Rankin, a former congresswoman, was employed by the Women's International League, the Women's Peace Union, and the largest group, the National Council for the Cause and Prevention of War, led by Frederick J. Libby.

The movement influenced the issuance of invitations to a disarmament conference that met in Washington from November 12, 1921, to February 6, 1922. Persuaded by activists, Borah, a supporter of disarmament, introduced a Senate resolution asking the secretary of state to convene a conference to limit naval arms. Many believed limitations could prevent expenditures requiring tax increases. (The cost of constructing a battleship had risen from $5 million in 1900 to $40 million in 1920.) Britain had an aging fleet that would be expensive to replace, and Japan knew it could not compete with American wealth in a naval race. Limiting naval competition necessitated the settlement of issues in the Far East, a key area of competition. At the suggestion of Britain, Hughes invited all nations with an interest in the Far East to participate in the conference.

Hughes opened the conference by proposing a plan to scrap and limit naval arms. Public opinion rallied behind the plan, but the opposition of France forced delegates to limit their agreements to battleships and battle cruisers. Three treaties, benefiting each signatory, emerged from the deliberations; each complemented the others, and concessions in one were repaid by concessions in others. The Four Power Treaty bound the United States, Britain, Japan, and France to respect each other's possessions in the Pacific and to consult if disputes arose. The Nine Power Treaty signed by all nations attending tried to limit competition among foreign powers in China. Many nations had exploited the weakness of China by seizing its territory and establishing trade monopolies within their spheres of influence. The treaty's solution was to open all areas to international trade. Under the major accord, the Five Power Treaty, the parties agreed not to fortify their Pacific colonies—a concession to Japan—and, more important, to limit naval armaments. The signers would scrap some battleships and construct none for ten years. Overall tonnage ceilings were established, with each nation assigned a ratio. For each 5 capital ships permitted to the United States and Britain, Japan could have 3 and France and Italy could have 1.67 each. Aircraft carriers were included in the ceiling ratios, but no limits were set on the number of planes, submarines, destroyers, or cruisers. The inability to agree on limits on smaller vessels was a major shortcoming, as was the failure to invite Germany and the Soviet Union to participate. The United States made the greatest sacrifices by scrapping the most ships and agreeing not to fortify the Philippine Islands or Guam. Anxious to economize, Congress would have been reluctant to authorize additional naval construction or Pacific fortifications anyway.

The agreements, although not guaranteeing peace, were the critical diplomatic achievements of the interwar era; the Five Power Treaty was the first major pact limiting arms in the history of the modern world. Subsequent attempts to limit arms were less successful. In 1927, Coolidge initiated a conference that met in Geneva to place limits on smaller warships. France and Italy refused to participate, however, and the conference bogged down in technical details. The United States and Britain clashed over the size and armament of cruisers; Britain, with numerous refueling bases, wanted large numbers of small cruisers with limited range; the United States, lacking bases to refuel, wanted a smaller number of large cruisers with a longer range. The conference adjourned without an agreement.

Afterward, American peace leaders turned to a project under consideration for some time: making war illegal under international law. Peace activists believed that even in the absence of sanctions, world opinion would restrain aggressors if they knew they might be tried in an international court for war crimes. Borah introduced an antiwar resolution in the Senate in 1923, and nothing came of it. Then, in 1927, James T. Shotwell, an official with the Carnegie Endowment for International Peace, asked French Foreign Minister Aristide Briand to propose a bilateral treaty outlawing war between France and the United States. Kellogg, opposing the plan because its effect would have been to ally the United States with France, responded with a counterproposal inviting all nations to adhere to a pact. Briand, outmaneuvered, agreed, and the Pact of Paris or Kellogg-Briand Treaty was signed in August 1928, gaining the Nobel Peace Prize for Kellogg. Some 64 nations signed, including future aggressors. Many people observed that the treaty was hopelessly idealistic because there was no way to enforce it; one senator called it an "international kiss." Advocates knew it was not the final solution to achieving world peace but believed they had improved the odds against war.

Hoover initiated two attempts to limit arms, the London Conference of 1930 and the Geneva Conference of 1932. At London, the United States, Britain, and Japan agreed to apply the 5:5:3 ratio to smaller ships, with the United States agreeing to delay building to its limits in the immediate future. In addition, the Japanese were granted parity in submarines, the moratorium on capital ship construction was extended to 1936, and rules for submarine warfare were codified. But the last attempt to disarm, at Geneva, was a total failure. Hoover proposed the abolition of all offensive weapons, reduction of total weaponry by about 30 percent, and limitation of armies to 100,000 for each 65 million in population, the approximate size of the German army. His plans were doomed when, during a recess, Adolf Hitler's militaristic Nazi party won a plurality in the German parliamentary election.

✢ A PARTIAL WITHDRAWAL FROM LATIN AMERICA

In dealing with the republics of Latin America, the United States faced the dilemma of any great power that must deal with smaller neighbors. The United States preferred friendly, democratic governments to the south, but most of the Latin American republics were authoritarian and unstable, threatening American business interests and, occasionally, American lives. If the United States refused to intervene, dictators were virtually certain to triumph. If the United States chose to intervene, it would be perceived as a bully and the governments it installed might become no less autocratic than their predecessors. Moreover, the United States learned that going in was easier than getting out. Pulling out precipitously might abdicate responsibility by jeopardizing improvements, although remaining involved served the long-range interests of neither the United States nor the smaller nations. The former found the occupation expensive, unpopular, antidemocratic, and paternalistic; the latter became dependent and anti-American.

When Harding took office, the United States had troops in Panama, Cuba, Santo Domingo, Haiti, and Nicaragua. By the end of the Hoover administration, almost all of the troops had been withdrawn. The Harding, Coolidge, and Hoover administrations mark a transition from the interventionism of Theodore Roosevelt, William Howard Taft, and Woodrow Wilson to the disengagement of the New Deal.

The most pressing controversy involved Mexico. The Mexican Constitution of 1917 stated that the natural resources of Mexico were the property of its people and that property owned by foreigners was subject to expropriation. This provision angered American businessmen who had purchased properties in Mexico; by 1920, Americans owned 40 percent of Mexican land and almost 60 percent of Mexican oil reserves. Harding and Coolidge refused to recognize the government of Alvaro Obregón, who enforced the Constitution, and they demanded repeal of the laws against foreign ownership. (In addition, the Obregón government had seized property of the Catholic church and suppressed religious schools.) In 1923 the two governments concluded an executive settlement known as the Bucareli Agreement, which provided that land developed before 1917 would not be subject to confiscation. Land obtained after that could be expropriated, with compensation in Mexican bonds. American property owners remained unhappy, yet the United States recognized the Obregón government and facilitated the flow of loans to Mexico.

Obregón's successor, Plutarco Elías Calles, effectively repudiated the agreement, producing a crisis. Calles signed legislation limiting foreign ownership of property purchased before 1917 to 50 years and specifying that foreigners who owned Mexican land could not appeal to their governments. To avert a Mexican–United States war, in 1927 Coolidge dispatched Dwight Morrow, a banker and former college classmate, to Mexico to reach an accord. Morrow, who was deferential to the Mexicans, secured a compromise that saved face for both nations, and he mediated a settlement between government and church. Calles, in turn, persuaded the Mexican Supreme Court to declare the new land law unconstitutional because it was retroactive.

A crisis arose in Nicaragua in 1925, after Coolidge withdrew troops that had occupied the country since 1912. Civil war erupted, and four presidents were sworn into office within 13 months. Coolidge returned the troops in 1926 and the next year sent Stimson to mediate a settlement. The agreement was not accepted by all Nicaraguans, and the troops remained to supervise elections in 1928, 1930, and 1932. The last troops were withdrawn shortly after FDR took office.

Hoover carried the policy of military disengagement further than his predecessors. Indeed, he began the Good Neighbor policy usually associated with Roosevelt. In 1929, as president-elect, he toured Latin America and said in Honduras, "We have a desire to maintain not only the cordial relations of governments with each other but the relations of good neighbors." And in 1930 Hoover published a 1928 memorandum drafted by Undersecretary of State J. Reuben Clark, stating that the United States would intervene militarily only if a hemispheric nation were threatened by takeover by a hostile power. Hoover refused to intervene during revolutions and began the phased withdrawal of all troops completed by Roosevelt.

✧ CHINA AND JAPAN

The major foreign crisis of the Hoover administration came in response to Japanese aggression against China in Manchuria, a semiautonomous northern province. Japan had expanded into Manchuria after World War I to exploit the latter's timber, coal, and iron. A competition among the Soviet Union, China, and Japan ensued, and Japan gained the upper hand by wresting control of the major railways. Favoring aggressive activity, the Japanese army defied Japan's civilian government and cowed the prime minister.

By the early 1930s, when almost 90 percent of Japanese foreign investments were in Manchuria, Japan saw its colony jeopardized by the rise of Chinese nationalism. China had been in turmoil since the overthrow of the Manchu dynasty in 1911 and subsequent civil wars between Sun Yat-sen and regional warlords. Sun's successor, Chiang Kai-shek, leader of his Kuomintang, or nationalist, party, appeared on the brink of adding Manchuria to his conquests, a prospect that alarmed the Japanese.

On September 18, 1931, the Japanese army fabricated an incident to justify consolidating its control over Manchuria. Setting off an explosion on the Japanese-operated South Manchurian Railway near Mukden, the army blamed the Chinese for sabotage. (Actually, it is doubtful that the railroad was even damaged; minutes later the Mukden Express passed over the section of track, miraculously leaping the gap, according to Japanese reports. At the Tokyo War Crimes Trials in 1946 Japanese leaders admitted that the Chinese had played no part in the incident.) In retaliation, the Japanese seized Mukden and much of the surrounding territory, in violation of international law. They compounded their aggression by bombing civilians in Shanghai, where many foreign citizens lived. The League Covenant mandated that the world organization defend Chinese territory, yet the League equivocated. After some hesitation it dispatched a team to investigate, led by Britain's Earl of Lytton.

Stimson and Hoover failed to respond for nearly four months while the cabinet debated options. No one seriously advocated military intervention;

American forces were too weak, and American interests were not directly at stake. The *Philadelphia Record* summed up the public's attitude: "The American people don't give a hoot in a rain barrel who controls North China." Stimson favored economic sanctions, but Hoover refused, fearing they might lead to war. Instead, he suggested mobilizing world opinion by refusing to recognize Japanese conquests. On January 2, 1932, Stimson, informing although not consulting the League Council, addressed notes to Japan and China stating that the United States would not recognize conquests or treaties imposed by force or those violating international law. This policy of moral condemnation unsupported by sanctions, known as the Stimson Doctrine, did not deter the Japanese.

In February 1932, the Japanese declared the independence from China of the puppet state of Manchukuo, headed by the heir to the Manchu dynasty, who was controlled by Japan. The League and the United States refused to recognize Manchukuo, and Stimson wrote a letter, read by Borah in the Senate, declaring Japanese activities violations of the Nine Power and the Kellogg-Briand treaties. Japanese aggression, the letter hinted, might compel the United States to revoke its promise not to fortify the Philippines and Guam.

The Lytton Commission completed its investigation in 1933, and in February 1934, the League adopted its conclusions branding Japan an aggressor but took no further actions. Japan withdrew from the League. The organization had failed its first test to thwart aggression, an ominous precedent, and the potential aggressors in Europe took note. The policy of the United States was equally ineffectual.

Preoccupied by the Great Depression, the United States, possessor of the most powerful armed forces in the world at the end of World War I, had permitted its army and navy to atrophy. Not a single warship was constructed during the Hoover administration, and the United States failed to build up to the limits permitted by the Washington and London naval treaties. The army totaled a mere 136,000 troops, and the air force, despite the advocacy of General Billy Mitchell, was virtually impotent. Mitchell, who led the army's aviators during World War I, advocated air power throughout the 1920s and proved its potential when his planes sank obsolete battleships during practice runs. Because Mitchell stridently opposed his superiors' neglect of air power, he was court-martialed and convicted of insubordination. Mitchell resigned from the army and died in 1936. In 1942, shortly after the Japanese bombing of Pearl Harbor had vindicated him, Congress removed the stigma of his court-martial and promoted him posthumously.

Hoover, a Quaker, was no pacifist, yet he believed that world opinion alone might deter aggression. Grappling with unemployment, he was reluctant to spend money on arms. Making domestic problems a priority was understandable, but his reluctance to act sent the wrong message to aggressors.

In the 1932 presidential election neither Hoover nor FDR said much about foreign policy. Roosevelt, who had supported League membership as a vice-presidential candidate in 1920, now opposed it. Ironically, the world was a more dangerous place in 1932 than in 1920, a fact the United States ignored at its peril.

BIBLIOGRAPHICAL ESSAY

The best treatment of American foreign policy in the 1920s is Warren I. Cohen, *Empire Without Tears: American Foreign Relations, 1921–1933* (1987), which is particularly strong on economics. Foster Rhea Dulles, *America's Rise to World Power, 1898–1954* (1963), is an excellent survey. See also Selig Adler, *The Uncertain Giant, 1921–1941* (1965); and L. Ethan Ellis, *Republican Foreign Policy, 1921–1933* (1968). Betty Glad, *Charles Evans Hughes and the Illusions of Innocence: A Study in American Diplomacy* (1966); and Dexter Perkins, *Charles Evans Hughes and American Democratic Statesmanship* (1956), are studies of the first secretary of state during the decade; the others are examined in Robert H. Ferrell, *The American Secretaries of State and Their Diplomacy: Frank B. Kellogg, Henry L. Stimson* (1963); L. Ethan Ellis, *Frank B. Kellogg and American Foreign Relations, 1925–1929* (1961); and Robert H. Ferrell, *American Diplomacy in the Great Depression: Hoover Foreign Policy, 1929–1933* (1957). The relationship between foreign policy and economics is explored in Herbert Feis, *The Diplomacy of the Dollar: First Era, 1919–1932* (1950); Carl P. Parrini, *Heir to Empire: United States Economic Diplomacy, 1916–1923* (1969); and Joan Hoff-Wilson, *American Business and Foreign Policy* (1971).

Relations with the Soviet Union are the subject of Peter G. Filene, *Americans and the Soviet Experiment, 1917–1933* (1967); Edward M. Bennett, *Recognition of Russia: An American Foreign Policy Dilemma* (1970); Joan Hoff-Wilson, *Ideology and Economics: U.S. Relations with the Soviet Union, 1918–1933* (1967); Benjamin M. Weissman, *Herbert Hoover and Famine Relief to Soviet Russia, 1921–1923* (1974); and Robert J. Maddox, *The Unknown War with Russia: Wilson's Siberian Intervention* (1977). Relations with the League of Nations are examined in Denna F. Fleming, *The United States and World Organization, 1920–1933* (1938). Two of the major figures of the era are discussed in Robert J. Maddox, *William E. Borah and American Foreign Policy* (1969); and Alfred F. Hurley, *Billy Mitchell: Crusader for Air Power* (1964).

General treatments of disarmament include Charles DeBenedetti, *Origins of the Modern American Peace Movement, 1915–1929* (1978); Warren I. Cohen, *The American Revisionists: The Lessons of Intervention in World War I* (1967); Roger Dingman, *Power in the Pacific: The Origins of Naval Arms Limitation, 1914–1922* (1976); and Harriet H. Alonso, *The Women's Peace Union and the Outlawry of War, 1921–1942* (1989). The Washington Naval Conference is the subject of John Chalmers Vinson, *The Parchment Peace: The United States Senate and the Washington Conference, 1921–1922* (1955); and Thomas H. Buckley, *The United States and the Washington Conference* (1970). The Kellogg-Briand Treaty is explained in Robert H. Ferrell, *Peace in Their Time: The Origins of the Kellogg-Briand Pact* (1969); and John Chalmers Vinson, *William E. Borah and the Outlawry of War* (1957).

United States policy toward Latin America is explored in Joseph S. Tulchin, *The Aftermath of War: World War I and U.S. Policy Toward Latin America* (1971); Robert N. Seidel, *Progressive Pan Americanism: Development and United States*

Policy Toward South America, 1906–1931 (1973); Alexander DeConde, *Herbert Hoover's Latin American Policy* (1951); Dana C. Munro, *The United States and the Caribbean Republics, 1921–1933* (1974); Hans Schmidt, *The United States Occupation of Haiti, 1915–1934* (1971); and Kenneth J. Grieb, *The United States and Huerta* (1969).

American policy in the Pacific is discussed in Akira Iriye, *After Imperialism: The Search for a New Order in the Far East, 1921–1931* (1965); Richard D. Burns and Edward M. Bennett, eds., *Diplomats in Crisis: United States–Chinese–Japanese Relations, 1919–1941* (1974); Gerald E. Wheeler, *Prelude to Pearl Harbor: The United States Navy and the Far East, 1921–1931* (1963); and Armin Rappaport, *Henry L. Stimson and Japan, 1931–1933* (1963).

CHAPTER EIGHT

HERBERT HOOVER AND THE GREAT DEPRESSION

✤ THE ELECTION OF 1928

After Coolidge withdrew from presidential contention, Herbert Hoover became the leading candidate for the Republican nomination in 1928. Progressives and businessmen were impressed with his accomplishments, intellect, sincerity, and good intentions; conservatives and professional politicians doubted his political experience and partisan zeal. Hoover had no political machine but did not need one; he had a favorable press and an enviable reputation.

Hoover won the nomination with 837 of 1,089 votes on the first ballot at the convention in Kansas City, Missouri. He left the selection of a vice-presidential candidate to the delegates and they chose Senator Charles Curtis of Kansas. The platform called for curbing labor injunctions, outlawing lynching, reducing expenditures, protecting industry with a tariff, and reorganizing the government. The party also emphasized Hoover's accomplishments as secretary of commerce and claimed credit for prosperity. In his acceptance speech Hoover stated: "We in America today are nearer to the final triumph over poverty than ever before in the history of any land. The poorhouse is vanishing from among us.... We shall soon with the help of God be in sight of the day when poverty will be banished from this nation."

One of the best-prepared presidential candidates in some respects, Hoover was ill prepared in others. His accomplishments as an engineer, humanitarian, and cabinet officer were remarkable. Principled but not inflexible, imaginative, hard working, he had a blueprint for reform. On the other hand, he had never run for office; he did not cut deals, play favorites, exploit friendships, deliver flag-waving speeches, flatter the masses, or make extravagant promises. In private he was genial, gracious, generous to a fault, and sentimental, a lively conversationalist, a raconteur. It was a side the public rarely saw after he became president.

Hoover's background inspired confidence. Born in 1874 in West Branch, Iowa, he was the first president from west of the Mississippi. He was orphaned in childhood, and his character was shaped by poverty, a rural environment, and a Quaker upbringing. Only Lincoln's birthplace was more humble than Hoover's, which was so small it became a hot dog stand. Raised in Oregon by relatives, Hoover did not attend high school but enrolled in the inaugural class of Stanford University and became its outstanding undergraduate. His prominence was not due to his grades but to his ability to organize the students and earn money, and to his desire to help others. Hoover made friends who lasted a lifetime. Majoring in geological engineering, he fell in love with Lou Henry, Stanford's first female geology major, the only woman he dated and whom he married.

Graduating in 1895 during a depression, Hoover went to work as a miner and subsequently accepted a job with a prominent engineer, who in turn recommended him to an English consulting company that sent him to Australia to organize gold mining at $600 a month. In 1899, he went to China to manage the firm's mines at $20,000 a year. He earned a reputation for good judgment and the ability to deal with difficult people. For 13 years he managed international mining operations, becoming a millionaire by his 30s.

When World War I began, Hoover, from London, helped thousands of Americans stranded in Europe to return home, financing some travel with his own money. He then launched an independent effort to feed Belgium, which Germany occupied and Britain blockaded. It was one of the great humanitarian endeavors in history. When America entered the war, he became food administrator for President Wilson and afterward he fed Europe. When Harding invited Hoover to join the cabinet in 1921, conservatives were dubious, yet Harding was adamant about the offer. Hoover's eight years in the Commerce Department were among the most creative in memory.

The great Mississippi flood of 1927 contributed to Hoover's rise. The secretary of commerce supervised rescue work, refugee care, and rehabilitation and gained an increased appreciation for the plight of southern sharecroppers and tenants. He was instrumental in drafting and enacting the Mississippi Flood Control Act of 1928.

Hoover's Democratic opponent in 1928, Al Smith, was another rags-to-riches story: Smith was born poor in the shadow of the Brooklyn Bridge, as quintessentially urban as Hoover was rural. For example, Smith, in 1928, thought Wisconsin was east of Lake Michigan, and traveling through the prairies asked, "What do people do out here?" And his East Side accent, with his nervousness, made Smith, a witty speaker with a prodigious memory, ineffective on radio.

Like Coolidge, Smith was a folk hero, and, like Hoover, he had ability. He arose through the ranks of Tammany Hall to serve as a state assemblyman, sheriff of New York, and president of the Board of Aldermen. Few excelled his record; he championed equal pay for women teachers, better care for the handicapped, and adequate appropriations for public education. He also reorganized and consolidated government and improved state welfare. A humanitarian, he was neither a conservative nor a conventional liberal. A friend of business, a supporter of the tariff, he voted against women's suffrage. Sympathetic to workers, he admired individual initiative. He wanted to return liquor control to the states and sponsor a national referendum on repeal of prohibition.

The first Catholic nominated by a major party, Smith found his chances hurt by prejudice. Rumors that the Pope would control the president saddened him, as he was a firm believer in separation of church and state. An old man from Delaware warned, "If this man Smith is elected, the Pope is going to come over here with all his wives and concubines and live in the White House and run the country."

Smith's mild antipathy to prohibition cost him support in the Democratic but Protestant South. Also, farmers, despite suffering under the Republicans, resented the urban candidate. The record of prosperity and the belief that it would continue were potent weapons in the Republican arsenal. Moreover, almost any candidate of the GOP, the majority party, would have won. Hoover polled 21.4 million popular and 444 electoral votes to Smith's 15 million and 87. Hoover split the South and won the border states. Smith, who carried only eight states, did best in the cities. The turnout was enormous: 70 percent of those eligible to vote. The Republicans increased their majority in the House by 30 seats, for a margin of 100, and gained seven seats in the Senate, for a margin of 17.

✢ THE BEGINNING OF THE HOOVER ADMINISTRATION

Hoover intended to provide stronger leadership than Coolidge, although he cautioned admirers that he was no magician. "I have no dread of the ordinary work of the presidency," he said. "What I do fear is the result of the exaggerated idea the people have conceived of me. . . . If some unprecedented calamity should come upon the nation . . . I would be sacrificed to the unreasoning disappointment of a people who expected too much."

Nonetheless, Hoover expected much of himself, and his plan for reform was comprehensive. He worked seven-day weeks and never complained. Friends pointed out that he was the first president to have a telephone on his desk. They admired his dedication: he retired the presidential yacht, closed the White House stables, and exercised by tossing a medicine ball. He kept only Coolidge's treasury secretary, Mellon, and labor secretary, James J. Davis.

Hoover supported civil rights. He commuted the sentence of a black man convicted of murdering a white woman, addressed Congress on lynching, entertained blacks in the White House, appointed more blacks to middle-level jobs than Harding and Coolidge combined, implemented a program to reduce black illiteracy, and devised a plan to give sharecroppers money to purchase land. In addition, Hoover undertook prison reform, planned improvements in child care and protection, improved the condition of Indians, restricted oil drilling on public lands, increased the budget of the National Park Service 46 percent in two years, added 2 million acres to national forests, and planned inland waterways and a St. Lawrence Seaway. He made distinguished appointments to the Supreme Court: Charles Evans Hughes, Owen Roberts, and Benjamin Cardozo.

Hoover also encountered failures. Brusque, impatient, unable to flatter, unwilling to prod, he was not adept at passing laws, and his most impressive accomplishments were implemented by executive order. He did not use patronage effectively, and one of his nominees to the Court, John J. Parker, opposed by labor and by blacks, was rejected by the Senate. Hoover neglected politics, did not work well with the press, and failed to publicize his accomplishments.

∻ THE BULL MARKET AND THE STOCK MARKET CRASH

Hoover's deficiencies might have been minor flaws in ordinary times, but after the first six months of his term, times were no longer ordinary. When the stock market collapsed in a heap, his reputation fell with it.

The crash was preceded by a bull market, which followed a speculative land boom in Florida in 1925 and 1926. Land values soared far above their potential worth, only to decline after the market became saturated. The collapse of the boom, though, taught speculators nothing.

The rise in stock values that began in the mid-1920s was at first realistic, based on genuine value, earning potential, and dividend return. However, dividends made one rich only slowly; it was much easier to buy stocks and resell them. The bull market was predicated on faith. As long as people believed prices would rise, the belief and the demand it generated would sustain a rise. Easy credit made speculation convenient.

There were probably not even a million speculators nationwide. Still, they soaked up capital and dominated the news and culture. Few people were prudent. Bankers entered the stock market, speculating with their depositors' money. Corporations found it more profitable to loan money to brokers than to invest in productivity. Brokers, the agents for buyers and sellers, sometimes loaned money to buyers; at times only a small percentage of the cost of the shares was needed as collateral. The loan would be repaid when the stock rose. This practice, called buying on margin, worked as long as stocks went up. If they went down, the loan still had to be repaid.

Booms always end; the choice was between a deliberate decline at an early point and a cataclysmic crash later. Hoover said he considered values inflated and speculation intemperate and disposed of some of his stocks. He asked newspapers and magazines to temper statements encouraging speculation, but no one in authority appreciated the dimensions of the danger.

The slide began erratically. On September 3, the market peaked, sagged, then plummeted. From that point on, the market would sputter for a few days, then drop suddenly. At the end of September people were confused. The market had fallen before. Was this the opportunity to buy low and enter a rebounding market, or was it the beginning of the end?

There was a decline on October 19, followed by a worse one on October 21. October 24 opened with a downward-spiraling vortex. At noon a group of bankers met to create a $240 million pool to stabilize the market. They succeeded only temporarily. October 28 was cataclysmic, October 29 was worse. Not only was the decline rapid; the scale was enormous. On October 30, *Variety* summarized it: "WALL STREET LAYS AN EGG."

In a few weeks the market lost $30 billion, equal to the U.S. expenditure in World War I, almost twice the national debt. Most people, however, expected a temporary decline, then a healthy recovery. Business was top heavy with holding companies, honeycombed with credit, and overexpanded. The conservative Mellon and the liberal John Maynard Keynes predicted the crash would benefit the economy by liquidating unsound businesses. The market bottomed out by November 13, and the economy, unfortunately, continued downward. The Dow Jones average plummeted from $364.90 to $62.70 per share, public utilities from $141.90 to $28.00, railroads from $82.00 to $28.00.

✛ THE GREAT DEPRESSION

There had been earlier panics, but none had been followed by such a severe depression. The chief relationship between the stock market crash and the depression was that the crash destroyed investor confidence. The crash would not have inevitably led to a depression if business had been fundamentally sound, if consumers had been able to continue to purchase the products pouring out of factories. But with overproduction rampant and demand unable to sustain the supply, a depression would have occurred even without the stock market crash, although the timing might have been different. The effect of the crash was to usher in a psychological atmosphere in which industrialists were afraid to invest and consumers were afraid to buy. Unemployment and underemployment were the most conspicuous results. Unemployment rose from about 2 million in 1929 to 13–14 million in 1932. Between 1930 and 1940 only once, in 1937, did the average number of unemployed drop below 8 million.

Labor income declined from $50 billion in 1929 to $29 billion in 1933, a 41 percent drop. Gross farm income fell from $12 billion in 1929 to $5.3 billion in 1932. Corporate income slipped from a profit of $8.7 billion in 1929 to a deficit of $5.6 billion in 1933. The national income plummeted from $81.1 billion to $40 billion, and production fell to 50 percent of capacity by 1933.

Falling production was accompanied by falling prices, but many goods could not be sold at any price. Deflation was problematic for debtors because they had to repay their debts in dollars more valuable than the ones they had borrowed. Like a row of dominoes, banks and businesses collapsed. Backlogs of merchandise accumulated, and as orders slowed factories cut production and laid off workers. Unemployment reduced purchasing power, which lessened demand and led to further cuts and layoffs. Merchants desperately cut prices, exacerbating deflation. The Democrats blamed the Republicans, socialists blamed capitalism, the poor blamed the rich. People lost faith in capitalism, in democracy, in themselves.

People could not consume all that industry and agriculture produced, due partly to an inequitable distribution of wealth. Almost everyone had enjoyed a rising standard of living, yet the rich had grown richer more rapidly than the poor had become less poor. In the 1920s real wages increased 13 percent, but returns to industry rose 72 percent, and in 1926 some 60 percent of the wealth was owned by 1 percent of the people. Two hundred of the largest corporations controlled more than 44 percent of the business assets in 1927, an imbalance that intensified economic inequality. Companies gobbled up others with impunity, creating monopolies, fixing prices, and cowing labor. Trade associations contributed to vast oligopolies, stifling competition and facilitating price fixing. Banks incorporated investment affiliates that made irresponsible investments with depositors' money. Trusts were created to exploit investors; holding companies were formed to eliminate competition, manipulate stocks, and issue securities. The holding company could pyramid values, and the trust could concentrate purchasing, but the pyramid would topple if confidence vanished.

Such concentrated wealth diminished consuming power, made the economy dependent upon the sale of luxuries, and encouraged speculation. Money that might have gone into salaries and wages was invested in stocks and bonds, bloating the market. Because worker productivity exceeded the rate of wage increases, consuming power fell below producing power. Part of the disparity was mitigated by credit purchases. Loans, however, had to be repaid, requiring saving, which necessitated a decline in consumption.

Two additional factors in underconsumption were farmers' inadequate purchasing power, a great influence on the economy, and international trade. Farmers had experienced a depression since the early 1920s and were particularly vulnerable to deflationary prices. When farmers failed, they sought industrial jobs, swelling unemployment and lowering the wage scale. And when the Hawley-Smoot Tariff of 1930 raised rates, American imports fell and other traders were provoked into retaliation.

Many government policies, clearly, had been unwise, and such reforms as stricter regulation of business, higher taxes on the wealthy, and encouragement of labor might have helped to prevent the depression. It would have taken remarkable political will and vision to take necessary actions. Still, no president could have been elected on a platform advocating these changes, and no Congress would have enacted them. Production controls and price supports that might have assisted farmers, for instance, had been advocated but not implemented because farmers opposed the restrictions.

The career of Samuel Insull dramatically illustrates the magnitude of the decline. Insull came to the United States from England at 21 to become private secretary to Thomas Edison and proved an organizational genius. Taking over the small Chicago Edison Company, he absorbed competitors and erected intricate holding companies until he possessed a utility empire worth $3 billion and a personal fortune worth $150 million by 1929, becoming the richest, most influential Chicagoan. President of 11 companies and board chairman of 65, he controlled 6,000 power plants in 39 states. His mansion had gold-plated bathroom fixtures; his estate had the nation's only post office on private property. People swore Insull securities were safer than government bonds. Told he was as powerful as Napoleon, he sneered and said, "Napoleon was only a soldier."

Insull's finances baffled comprehension. He acquired properties for inflated prices, issued overvalued stocks against them, then siphoned profits from operating companies into holding companies. When stock prices fell, his bankers demanded additional collateral, and he could find no profits to sustain his empire, could arrange no more loans. His companies collapsed like a pyramid of sand, the largest business failure in history, and his investors lost $750 million. Pursued by creditors and by the law, Insull fled to Greece, then to Turkey, was extradited in 1934, stood trial in Chicago, and was acquitted. He left the United States and died in Paris in 1938 with 85 cents in his pockets.

From coast to coast, the depression spread misery, at times leaving 25 percent of the work force unemployed. People wandered from one breadline to another, from one soup kitchen to another, from one city to another. Railroads became highways for transients. Blacks moved north, where their suffering was unrelieved. Men lived in sewer pipes in Oakland, in shacks in Central Park; in squalid shantytowns called Hoovervilles; others sat home idly, skills dissipating, self-respect deteriorating. Marriages were postponed, men deserted their families, evictions multiplied. With surpluses on their hands, northwestern farmers gave apples on credit to jobless men, who tried to sell them for a nickel apiece with the slogan, "Buy an apple a day and eat the depression away." On the streets of New York there were 6,000 apple peddlers in 1930, a grim symbol.

While millions hungered in cities or wore ragged clothes, crops rotted in the countryside, and bales of cotton went unsold. Farm income dropped 20 percent in 1930, 30 percent again in 1931. Deepening the despair, in 1930 the worst drought in history struck the Mississippi Valley. With animals dying from the resulting lack of fodder, Hoover provided feed; critics noted that he fed cattle rather than people.

The rich, too, felt the depression—the Rockefeller fortune shrank to one-fifth of its precrash size—but some of the wealthy did not comprehend the anguish of the poor. One of the du Ponts, asked to advertise his products on Sunday afternoon radio, objected, "At three o'clock on Sunday afternoons everybody is playing polo."

✣ HOOVER'S PROGRAM

The activism of Hoover, who marshaled the financial and moral resources of the nation to combat the depression, broke precedent, for in all previous depressions presidents had trusted the economic cycle to bring recovery. Relying initially on consultation and cooperation, Hoover tried to persuade those who could afford it to open their pocketbooks. In addition, he obtained promises from industrialists not to cut wages or dismiss workers and pledges

President Herbert Hoover's reputation as a progressive was ruined by the Great Depression. He was a warm individual who made lasting friends, but the public considered him cold and insensitive to human suffering because he believed direct aid to the poor would undermine personal responsibility.

from union leaders not to strike. Hoover hoped private charity, supplemented by states and cities, could provide effective, decentralized relief, but he resolved that the federal government would intervene if necessary. Curiously, the Red Cross, which Hoover urged to feed the hungry, said it did not want government money, and 47 governors said they did not need federal funds.

At Hoover's request Congress appropriated $800 million and reduced taxes by $160 million to stimulate investment. Hoover also created a pool of funds contributed by bankers to provide loans to business, but the $500 million fund was insufficient. The president then submitted a bill that Congress enacted, creating the Reconstruction Finance Corporation (RFC) to aid exports, stimulate employment, and loan money to agricultural cooperatives, banks, railroads, and manufacturers. Further, Hoover and Congress created a system of Home Loan Discount Banks to enable local banks to borrow funds from the federal government, using mortgages they held as collateral. With federal funds available, banks could avoid foreclosing on homes. By 1937 the system had made more than $1 billion in loans.

Aimed at farmers, the Agricultural Marketing Act of 1929 had created a Federal Farm Board to establish voluntary acreage controls and loan money to cooperatives. Stabilization corporations were established to buy grain, cotton, and other commodities to sustain prices. When the surpluses piled up, the board lost money and finally sold off its produce, permitting prices to fall. An appeal to farmers to limit production was ineffective without compulsion or direct incentives; anyway, Hoover, and most farmers, opposed compulsory planned production. The board, failing to create farm prosperity, preserved price levels until 1931. The prices of 1932 would have been lower without its efforts.

To business morale, the president believed, the gold standard was essential. Gold was fleeing abroad because creditors redeemed securities for gold, considering them safer than paper. It appeared the Treasury might exhaust its gold supply, creating more panic. Dollars were backed by certain kinds of eligible paper as well as gold, however, and by increasing the types of paper that were "eligible," it might have been possible to stem the gold drain and preserve the gold standard. A bill containing such provisions was enacted as the Glass-Steagall Act of 1932. It also liberalized Federal Reserve requirements for collateral, making more member banks eligible for loans, hence more credit available to business.

As an economic stimulus Hoover planned more public works than had any of his predecessors, and by the end of his term 360 public buildings had been completed and 460 were under construction. The Hoover administration began or completed the Supreme Court building, additions to the House and Senate office buildings, a municipal building for the city of Washington, and buildings for the departments of Commerce, Labor, and Justice, the Post Office, the Interstate Commerce Commission, and the National Archives. Highway construction was accelerated, and some 37,000 miles were built with federal money during Hoover's term. Further, he initiated construction of the Golden Gate Bridge.

Hoover's program, although substantial, was limited by his commitment to a balanced budget, which he considered morally responsible and critical to business confidence. Most Democrats shared Hoover's views. Hoover's shy personality handicapped him. He preferred work to bombast when bombast might have been more effective. His speeches, models of rationality, failed to inspire, create confidence, or touch emotions. His bland exterior convinced many that he was insensitive. He had the competence of an engineer, but the heart of a poet and the impossible job of an alchemist.

Hoover's policies were not unreasonable, given his context, and his opponents offered no comprehensive, feasible alternative. Nor was Hoover unimaginative; Raymond Moley and Rexford Tugwell, advisers to FDR, wrote in their memoirs that many of the programs of the New Deal were borrowed from Hoover's ideas. Under Hoover, America weathered the early years of the depression more successfully than much of the Western world, and despite widespread suffering, the nation's institutions remained intact. Hoover's chief failures were political; by putting principle above expediency he made himself unpopular.

The midterm congressional elections of 1930, which brought substantial gains to the Democrats, demonstrated that Hoover was sticking with an inadequate program too long. Relief should have been quickly delivered, centrally administered, and federally financed; the tariff should have been lowered. Hoover should have been more aggressive in leading Congress and should have attempted to be more inspirational. But he could not step out of character or overcome scruples and inhibitions. The Great Depression, a tragedy for millions, was a personal humiliation for Hoover, who came to the presidency with high expectations, assured of a place in history.

✛ THE ELECTION OF 1932

Convinced the depression was licked in 1932, Hoover felt he had to run for reelection to vindicate his record. The Republicans, who had reaped the harvest of prosperity, were trapped in the whirlwind of its disappearance. Nonetheless, Hoover and Curtis were renominated because the Republican party was not prepared to repudiate incumbents.

Democratic aspirants knew Hoover was vulnerable, and competition for their party's nomination was avid. Among the candidates were Al Smith and House Speaker John Nance Garner, yet the leader from start to finish was Roosevelt, the governor of New York. Garner contributed to ending an impasse that gave Roosevelt the nomination and was put on the ticket as vice president. Roosevelt broke tradition by flying to the convention in Chicago and delivering an acceptance speech. "Let it be the policy of our party to break foolish traditions," he said. "I pledge you, I pledge myself, to a new deal for the American people." He added, "This is more than a political campaign; it is a call to arms." A cartoonist highlighted the phrase "new deal" the next day, and it became the label for Roosevelt's program.

Roosevelt and Hoover were similar in some respects. Both were protégés of Wilson, and both were millionaires. Also, Roosevelt basically agreed with Hoover's foreign policy and, like Hoover, advocated a balanced budget. FDR opposed federal relief, as did Hoover, promised to reduce federal expenditures by 25 percent, and condemned Hoover for excessive spending and violation of states' rights. "It is an administration that has piled bureau on bureau, commission on commission, and has failed to anticipate the dire needs and reduced earning power of the people," he said. Because neither candidate had a comprehensive program to end the depression, they talked about less important issues like prohibition. Neither wanted to maintain the status quo, but Roosevelt was considered somewhat stronger for repeal than Hoover. The Democratic platform did not anticipate the social programs of the New Deal.

In personality and temperament, the men were opposites. The gregarious Roosevelt used a battery of speech writers; Hoover wrote his own speeches. Roosevelt's talks were more inspiring, delivered more eloquently than the president's. Hoover had every reason to be glum and appeared so; Roosevelt had every reason to project optimism.

Roosevelt, better at picking other men's minds, had more friendly acquaintances, fewer close friends. He seemed too eager to please, indecisive, superficial. "He is all clay and no granite," Felix Frankfurter said. But Roosevelt had a courage that matched, if not exceeded, Hoover's, and had overcome polio as Hoover had overcome poverty. As men had overestimated Hoover's potential for the presidency, they underestimated Roosevelt's.

A final drama enlivened the campaign, outraged the public, and humiliated Hoover. In the summer of 1932, an army of some 22,000 impoverished World War I veterans descended upon Washington to seek payment of a bonus for their service. They came from all over the country, the largest contingent from Portland, Oregon, led by Walter E. Waters. The press dubbed it the Bonus Expeditionary Force.

Veterans had been paid $1 a day during the war, while shipyard workers received $90 a week, an inequity that Congress redressed by enacting, over Coolidge's veto in 1925, a bill to credit each veteran with an additional $1 a day for domestic and an additional $1.25 a day for foreign service. Veterans were given adjusted credit certificates earning 4 percent interest, cashable in 20 years. Many of them felt they could not wait until 1945 for the money, and in 1931 the government agreed to lend half the face value of the certificates at 4.5 percent interest. The veterans clamored for full, immediate payment, and Representative Wright Patman, a Texas Democrat, introduced a bill to provide it. The veterans came to Washington to lobby for the measure.

Hoover pointed out that all veterans were not poor and that veterans' benefits consumed one-fourth of the national budget. Showing some concern, he supplied the Washington chief of police, Pelham Glassford, with food, tents, and eating utensils for the veterans, many of whom were camping at Anacostia Flats. Glassford sought to conciliate the men. Still, many Washingtonians were alarmed. Hoover refused to meet their leaders, thought it might encourage mob rule, and feared disorder. Waters, warned the bill would fail, was asked what would happen. "Nothing will happen," he said. But no one knew.

On June 15 the bill passed the House and, two days later, failed in the Senate. Waters assembled his men to break the news. A reporter suggested that he ask the men to sing "God Bless America." They did, then returned to their camps.

Glassford was ordered to evict veterans who had occupied abandoned federal buildings scheduled for demolition. He warned there might be violence. There was: two veterans died. Hoover, losing patience, ordered the army to remove the veterans from Washington, leaving their camps intact. He arranged for Congress to appropriate $100,000 to pay for the veterans to return home.

General Douglas MacArthur, in battle dress, directed troops in dispersing the veterans. One of his junior officers, Dwight D. Eisenhower, objected to the procedure; another, George S. Patton, was struck by a brick. Preceded by tanks and tear gas, the troops, bayonets fixed, evicted the Bonus Army from the city. MacArthur then directed his troops to defy Hoover's orders and cross the Anacostia Bridge to destroy the veterans' Camp Anacostia. Some veterans resisted, most fled; the camp was burned. The eviction, on July 28, was a political disaster. "Well, Felix, this will elect me," Roosevelt told Frankfurter. Hoover compounded the error by not disciplining MacArthur, too valuable a soldier to demote, for insubordination.

Only habitual Republicans voted for Hoover, who carried just six eastern states. The voters considered Hoover a failure, yet did not know what to expect of Roosevelt, who polled 22.8 million popular votes and 472 electoral votes to 15.8 million and 59 for Hoover. The Socialist Norman Thomas led the minor parties with 872,840 popular votes, and Communist William Z. Foster polled about 103,000.

Hoover, a transitional figure, was the fulcrum of the age; his administration marked a dividing line between his version of a managed economy and Roosevelt's planned economy. Roosevelt, able to topple the traditional order because it had been undermined by the depression, was the agent of change and its beneficiary.

Elements of transformation and reaction were mixed in Hoover, whose administration was a bridge to modernization. He possessed a defensive mentality in that he wanted to strengthen the system rather than transform it, although he was an enlightened moderate who realized that change was inevitable and accepted some changes.

Hoover made the first break with the past, and Roosevelt, the modernizer, did not entirely abandon traditional institutions; initially he expressed an affinity for rural life and relative isolationism in international affairs. The change from Hoover to Roosevelt appears more a natural progression than a decisive shift; in historical perspective Roosevelt's reforms seem less dramatic than they did at the time, based more on stylistic than on fundamental differences.

Between the election in November and the inauguration in March,

Hoover, lacking credibility, did not act, and Roosevelt was enigmatic about his own plans. The depression reached its nadir as banks closed and business failed. Hoover blamed the decline on fear of Roosevelt, reasoning that the nation had more to fear from an incoming than from an outgoing president.

Roosevelt inspired mixed feelings; already there were those who detested him. On February 15 in Miami, Giuseppe Zangara, who hated the privileged and powerful and tried to assassinate the king of Italy, fired a pistol at FDR. Zangara's aim was deflected, but he killed Chicago Mayor Anton J. Cermak, who accompanied Roosevelt. Some think Zangara intended to shoot Cermak as well as Roosevelt.

Throughout the interregnum the country wondered if Roosevelt could succeed where Hoover had failed. A friend told Roosevelt that if he succeeded he would go down in history as the greatest American president, and that if he failed he would be known as the worst. "If I fail," Roosevelt said grimly, "I shall be the last one."

BIBLIOGRAPHICAL ESSAY

There are many biographies of Herbert Hoover and accounts of the policies of his administration. David Burner, *Herbert Hoover: A Public Life* (1979), considers Hoover's personality flawed but his policies as president constructive. Joan Hoff-Wilson, *Herbert Hoover: Forgotten Progressive* (1975), views Hoover as a progressive out of his element as president. Martin L. Fausold, *The Presidency of Herbert Hoover* (1985), is the most detailed account of Hoover's presidential policies. One should also consult Ray L. Wilbur and Arthur M. Hyde, *The Hoover Policies* (1937), by two members of his cabinet. George N. Nash, *The Life of Herbert Hoover*, 2 vols. (1983, 1988), with a third volume projected, will be the definitive study when complete. Eugene Lyons, *The Herbert Hoover Story* (1959), depicts Hoover as kindly, principled, and loyal, betrayed by a fickle public; and Harris G. Warren, *Herbert Hoover and the Great Depression* (1959), argues Hoover has been unfairly maligned for the depression yet does not deny his flaws. Carol G. Wilson, *Herbert Hoover: A Challenge for Today* (1968), emphasizes Hoover's private life and humanitarian activities more than his presidency. Other studies of Hoover include Robert Sobel, *Herbert Hoover at the Onset of the Great Depression, 1929–1930* (1975); Jordan A. Schwarz, *The Interregnum of Despair: Hoover, Congress, and the Depression* (1970); David E. Hamilton, *From New Day to New Deal: American Farm Policy from Hoover to Roosevelt, 1928–1933* (1991); and Wilton Eckley, *Herbert Hoover* (1980).

The stock market and its decline are the subject of Robert Sobel, *The Great Bull Market: Wall Street in the 1920s* (1968); and John Kenneth Galbraith, *The Great Crash, 1929* (1961). Among the many studies of the Great Depression are John A. Garraty, *The Great Depression* (1986), which provides a worldwide perspective; Bernard Sternsher, *Hitting Home: The Great Depression in Town and Country* (1989), accounts of the effects of the depression in different localities; Edward R. Ellis, *A Nation in Torment: The Great American Depression, 1929–1939* (1971), which describes the human cost of the depression; and David A. Shannon, ed., *The Great Depression* (1960), a selection of readings. Albert U.

Romasco, *The Poverty of Abundance: Hoover, the Nation, the Depression* (1965), is a fine account of the Hoover policies. Other accounts include Gerald D. Nash, *The Great Depression and World War II: Organizing America, 1933–1945* (1979); Robert Bendiner, *Just Around the Corner: A Highly Selective History of the Thirties* (1987); Gilbert Seldes, *The Years of the Locust—America, 1929–1932* (1973); Dixon Wecter, *The Age of the Great Depression* (1948); and Broadus Mitchell, *Depression Decade: From the New Era Through the New Deal, 1929–1941* (1947).

The presidential election of 1928 is described in Edmund A. Moore, *A Catholic Runs for President: The Campaign of 1928* (1956); Allan J. Lichtman, *Prejudice and the Old Politics: The Presidential Election of 1928* (1979); and Oscar Handlin, *Al Smith and His America* (1958). The Bonus Army and the campaign of 1932 are the subjects of Gene Smith, *The Shattered Dream: Herbert Hoover and the Great Depression* (1970); Roger Daniels, *The Bonus March: An Episode of the Great Depression* (1971); and Donald Lisio, *The President and Protest: Hoover, Conspiracy and the Bonus Riot* (1974).

CHAPTER NINE

THE ORIGINS OF THE NEW DEAL

✤ FDR

Franklin Delano Roosevelt came to office facing the greatest challenge to a president since Abraham Lincoln, and there was little in his background to suggest that he would become a great leader. Born to wealth and privilege, descended from the old Dutch aristocracy of New York, he was the only child of James Roosevelt, a railroad executive and businessman, and Sara Delano, also heir to an aristocratic tradition. Roosevelt's childhood was serene; his father spent much time with him, and his overprotective mother, who spoiled him, had him tutored at home. As a child he met some of the most important men in the nation, including President Grover Cleveland, who made a wish for him: that the little man would never become president.

At 14, Roosevelt enrolled at Groton, one of the country's most exclusive prep schools. Roosevelt studied Greek, Latin, and European history at the Connecticut school, excelling neither as a scholar nor as an athlete, maintaining a "C" average and becoming a fourth-string tackle on the football team. "He was a quiet, satisfactory boy of more than ordinary intelligence," headmaster Endicott Peabody said, "taking a good position in his form but not brilliant. Athletically he was rather too slight for success. We all liked him."

In 1900, FDR enrolled at Harvard, where he majored in economics, but his favorite subject was American history. Finding social life more exciting than his studies, he compiled a mediocre academic record. He joined the

Republican Club and cast his first vote for president for his distant cousin, Theodore Roosevelt, in 1904. Sharing the upper-class prejudices of many of his classmates, he was mildly anti-Semitic, opposed to women's suffrage, and believed that Harvard, in seeking "to uplift the Negro, if you like, has sought to make a man out of a semi-beast."

Franklin was attracted to his fifth cousin, Eleanor Roosevelt, whom he met at a Christmas party, and they began courting. In 1903 he proposed, and they were married in 1905, with Eleanor's Uncle Theodore giving away the bride. Eleanor's childhood had been depressing and tumultuous. Her mother, who made her feel unwanted, died when she was 8; her father drank himself to death two years later. The Roosevelts were mismatched; Eleanor was introverted and shy, Franklin was extroverted and demanded attention.

After graduating from Harvard, Franklin enrolled in the Columbia University Law School. He failed two courses and did not graduate, yet learned enough to pass the state bar exam, and he accepted a position with a Wall Street firm. The Roosevelts lived in a house rented by Franklin's mother, then moved into twin townhouses, one for Sara, one for the couple. Sara tried to dominate her son's family and quarreled with Eleanor. Franklin and Eleanor had six children, one of whom died in infancy. Neither was a good parent. Franklin refused to discipline the children and often neglected them. The inexperienced Eleanor, who learned child-rearing from books, tied the hands of her infant daughter Anna to the bedpost so she could not masturbate.

Franklin's father was a Democrat, but the younger Roosevelt's political allegiance wavered until a Democratic delegation, wishing to exploit his name, asked him to run for the state legislature. He ran in 1910 and scored an upset victory in a Republican district. The family moved to Albany, where it became prominent. Franklin earned an undeserved reputation as a reformer, while Eleanor wrote, taught, and filled speaking engagements.

Roosevelt supported Woodrow Wilson for the Democratic presidential nomination in 1912, and after Wilson's election was offered the position of assistant secretary of the navy under Josephus Daniels. Roosevelt planned to use the position as a stepping-stone to higher office. He proved politically astute, although he was inattentive to paperwork and sometimes insubordinate. In 1914 he ran for the Democratic nomination for senator from New York and lost the primary.

In Washington, FDR and his wife's beautiful and charming social secretary, Lucy Page Mercer, who was a dozen years younger than Eleanor, fell in love. Eleanor learned of the affair in 1918 and offered Franklin a divorce, which would have ruined his political career. Moreover, his mother forbade a divorce and Mercer would not marry him. Although she had no scruples about having an affair, she told Franklin that as a devout Catholic she could never marry a divorced man. Eleanor never forgave Franklin and never slept with him again. Their marriage evolved into a partnership of mutual respect without romance, and Eleanor cultivated her interests, developing a network of close friends to compensate for the lack of emotional intimacy with her spouse. She might have had an affair with Earl Miller, her bodyguard, while her husband was governor of New York.

In 1920, Roosevelt was nominated for vice president on the Democratic ticket headed by James M. Cox, and he campaigned energetically. After the ticket's overwhelming loss to Harding and Coolidge, Roosevelt returned to the practice of law, became vice president of a bonding firm, and speculated in business ventures. Despite his recent defeat, a promising political career beckoned.

But in August 1921, Roosevelt was stricken with polio, paralyzed from the waist down, and never walked unaided again. The illness, which might have devastated him, instead made him stronger. Until then he had a reputation as a playboy and an intellectual lightweight. Having never failed seriously, he now failed repeatedly when he tried to walk. His personality did not change overnight, and his political views remained essentially the same, although he learned patience and perseverance. The setback evoked the courageous side of his personality. He read more, talked more, and developed an appreciation for the handicapped. Learning that the mineral waters at Warm Springs, Georgia, contributed to his rehabilitation, he bought a convalescent center there and invested two-thirds of his fortune. Temporarily retired from politics while he tried to regain use of his legs, Roosevelt nominated his mentor, New York Governor Al Smith, for president in 1924 and 1928. In the latter year Smith convinced FDR that he could help the national ticket carry New York if he ran for governor. Roosevelt agreed reluctantly and won narrowly, but Smith lost in New York and the nation.

Governor when the Great Depression began, Roosevelt initially reacted cautiously, rejecting federal aid and calling for retrenchment. As the depression deepened, however, he developed a progressive program, making New York one of the first states to provide public relief. In 1930, Roosevelt was reelected by the massive margin of 725,000 votes, and he and Smith became rivals for the Democratic presidential nomination.

✢ THE BEGINNING OF THE HUNDRED DAYS

Shortly after his election as president in 1932, Roosevelt visited former Supreme Court Justice Oliver Wendell Holmes on Holmes's 92d birthday. After Roosevelt departed, the elder statesman pronounced his judgment: "A second-class intellect. But a first-class temperament." The assessment was accurate.

It was easy to get to know Roosevelt, impossible to get to know him well. Genuine emotional intimacy was beyond him, and he never talked to anyone about his personal philosophy. Nourished by a simple religious faith to which he clung tenaciously, Roosevelt never debated theology and never questioned the tenets of his Episcopalian upbringing. He said to Eleanor, who did not find religion so simple, that "there may be spiritual things which we are simply unable now to fathom." Nor was his personal philosophy complicated.

THE BEGINNING OF THE HUNDRED DAYS ❧ **125**

When a reporter asked if he was a communist, a capitalist, or a socialist, he replied, "I am a Christian and a Democrat—that's all." No analytical thinker, he did not read seriously and disliked paperwork; some considered him imprecise and intellectually lazy. Comfortable with intellectuals, he was no intellectual, borrowing ideas rather than originating them. Preferring action to reflection, he adopted as guiding principles expediency and political pragmatism. Fortunately, the times demanded an experimental temperament.

Disorganized, condescending, superficial, Roosevelt was nonetheless a confident, tough, shrewd, calculating politician—indeed, the best politician of the New Deal—with a streak of deviousness and a tendency to disguise vindictiveness with pleasantries. And he knew how to relax, claiming while president that he fell asleep five minutes after going to bed. Friends marveled at his serenity, which some attributed to his untroubled childhood. Others were awed by his ferocious drive and his refusal to admit defeat. Once, when a friend complimented his resiliency, Roosevelt responded, "If you had spent two years in bed trying to wiggle your big toe, after that anything else would seem easy!" His relentless optimism led Winston Churchill to remark, "Meeting him is like opening a bottle of champagne."

And during the depression Roosevelt was a refreshing toast for the impoverished. He became the first president to use radio periodically, and his warm, simple talks became known as "fireside chats." Sharecroppers and miners sometimes had only two pictures in their cabins: Jesus and Roosevelt. A reporter saw a sentence scrawled in chalk by a hobo in the Denver freight yards: "Roosevelt is my friend." A workingman commented, "FDR is the first President we ever had who would understand that my boss is an S.O.B." But Roosevelt earned the enmity of the upper classes, who came to consider him a dictator. A cartoon from *Esquire* showed a little girl in an upper-class neighborhood telling her mother, "Mommy, Wilfred wrote a bad word." The word, written on the sidewalk, was "Roosevelt."

Roosevelt, no dictator, still enjoyed power, and he assembled a cabinet he could dominate, one in which his will would be virtually unchallenged. The cabinet reflected all political viewpoints and regions, although he excluded businessmen. The average age, 58, made it one of the oldest cabinets, and it was undistinguished.

Roosevelt selected Tennessee Senator Cordell Hull as secretary of state. A former chair of the Democratic National Committee, Hull lacked extensive experience in foreign affairs. His priority was to lower the tariff. The secretary of agriculture, Henry A. Wallace, was well known, son of a Republican secretary of agriculture, a formidable advocate for militant farmers. However, Wallace, a religious mystic, was eccentric and unpredictable. "Henry's the sort that keeps you guessing as to whether he's going to deliver a sermon or wet his pants," one politician said.

Harold L. Ickes, the secretary of the interior, was a Republican reformer, nervous, abrasive, insomniac, a chronic complainer who threatened to resign frequently yet lasted 12 years. A conservationist, a champion of the rights of American Indians, he was scrupulously honest. Roosevelt found it hard to get

President Franklin Delano Roosevelt proved an inspiring communicator. Particularly effective on radio, he used the airwaves to rally the nation during the Great Depression.

along with Ickes, harder to get along without him. FDR's most controversial appointment was Secretary of Labor Frances Perkins, because she was the first woman to sit in the cabinet and the first in the office who did not come from the ranks of organized labor. A social worker, she had served as New York state industrial commissioner and became a member of the inner circle.

Postmaster General James A. Farley, so Irish he signed his letters in green ink, was FDR's principal political tactician, distributing patronage astutely to nourish a party out of power for 12 years. Farley, formerly the New York state boxing commissioner, became chair of the Democratic National Committee and proved the most effective politician in the cabinet.

Roosevelt's more important advisers were outside the cabinet, a group of intellectuals he had assembled while governor, a collection that the press labeled the Brains Trust. It was led by Raymond Moley, a Columbia University professor who, along with Felix Frankfurter of the Harvard Law School, sought out talented minds to advise Roosevelt. Moley recruited Rexford G. Tugwell, an expert on agricultural economics, and Adolf A. Berle, whose expertise involved corporations. A child prodigy who had graduated from Harvard at 17, the temperamental Berle, New Dealers joked, had remained a child after he ceased to be a prodigy.

The Brains Trust also included Benjamin V. Cohen, who excelled at drafting laws; Thomas G. Corcoran, who expedited passage of legislation; and General Hugh S. Johnson, a protégé of financier Bernard Baruch. The advisers, who had contributed position papers during the campaign, seldom met after the election, but many found positions in the bureaucracy.

Roosevelt swore in his entire cabinet at one time shortly after he was inaugurated in an atmosphere of desperation. "It was very, very solemn and a little terrifying," Eleanor wrote. "The crowds were so tremendous, and you felt that they would do anything—if only someone would tell them what to do." In his inaugural address FDR echoed Hoover's belief that the chief problem was a lack of business confidence when he said, "The only thing we have to fear is fear itself." Roosevelt departed from Hoover's cautious approach by declaring that if all else failed, "I shall ask the Congress for the one remaining instrument to meet the crisis—broad Executive power to wage a war against the emergency, as great as the power that would be given to me if we were in fact invaded by a foreign foe." Roosevelt's largest ovation came after he said, "This nation asks for action, and action now."

The new administration, aided by officials from the Hoover cabinet, worked late on inauguration evening to address the banking crisis that was draining the nation of hope. Twenty-two states had closed their banks, and Roosevelt concluded that he must resort to a plan Hoover had advocated, the closure of all banks in the nation. Using authority from a World War I law, Roosevelt issued an executive order that ultimately produced an eight-day bank holiday. Consumers traded with stamps, subway tokens, and IOU's as the nation struggled to get along with the cash on hand. Surprisingly, rather than a panic, there was a sense of relief that action had been taken. "This is the happiest day in three years," Will Rogers wrote. "We have no jobs, we have no money, we have no banks; and if Roosevelt had burned down the Capitol, we would have said, 'Thank God, he started a fire under something.'"

To pass banking legislation, the president summoned a special session of Congress to assemble on March 9. On the first day he submitted the Emergency Banking Act that passed the House in 38 minutes and the Senate in three hours. The bill, not printed in time for most representatives to read it, provided for a federal audit of banks, which were classified according to their stability and permitted to reopen on a staggered basis; 75 percent were cleared to open on the first day. The Treasury was also authorized to print sufficient currency to assure that depositors got their money, and gold hoarding and exportation were prohibited. The crisis did not end, however, because no one knew whether there would be a run on the banks when they reopened. Before reopening the banks, Roosevelt delivered his first fireside chat to convince depositors that the banks were safe. When they reopened, $10 million more were deposited than was withdrawn. The crisis had been met.

Unfortunately for the president, Roosevelt dissipated some of the goodwill earned by surmounting the banking crisis with his next piece of legislation, the Economy Bill, intended to balance the federal budget by reducing government salaries by $100 million and veterans' pensions by $400 million. Roosevelt was influenced by his director of the budget, Lewis Douglas, who felt that only a balanced budget could restore business confidence and that the president had to redeem his campaign pledge to reduce spending. FDR later was pushed, reluctantly, into deficit spending. He considered deficit spending an expediency that should be used only during emergencies. Throughout his presidency he retrenched as the economy improved and spent as it declined. During his first term Roosevelt sought to save money: for example, he cut the defense budget from $752 million in fiscal year 1932 to $531 million in fiscal year 1934.

Many Democrats opposed the Economy Bill as deflationary. It passed only because 69 House Republicans voted for it and because, while it was being considered, Roosevelt introduced a popular bill to permit the sale of beer and wine. The Eighteenth Amendment was on its way to repeal with passage of the Twenty-first Amendment by the last Congress of the Hoover administration. The Beer Bill, an interim measure to permit sale of some alcohol while the states were ratifying the Twenty-first Amendment, passed easily.

Roosevelt, who had planned to let Congress adjourn after a few days, decided to use the momentum gained from his early successes and keep legislators in Washington to deal with other facets of the depression. Congress remained in session for more than three months, a period that became known as the Hundred Days. It was the most productive session of the New Deal era. Roosevelt, with no program ready, had to improvise. When a reporter asked him to define his plans, Roosevelt likened himself to the quarterback in a football game. The quarterback knows what the next play will be, he explained, but beyond that he cannot plan too rigidly because future plays will depend on how the next one works.

✧ GROWTH OF THE NEW DEAL

The New Deal evolved without a grand design, driven more by political necessity than by economic theory. Eclectic, inconsistent, certain programs were crosscut by others. The ideological jumble did not disturb Roosevelt, who learned by trial and error, compromising, preempting rivals, and responding to pressure from interest groups. His objective was to retain the initiative and exert control. Congress let the administration lead, granting unprecedented authority to the chief executive and shifting the balance of power in the federal system from the states to the central government. "I suppose prudence dictates that one should not attempt to swim against the tide," one Republican senator wrote, and another remarked, "We would pass Mother Goose through the Congress if Mr. Roosevelt asks us to."

Democratic majorities of 60–35 in the Senate and 311–116 in the House facilitated passage of the president's program. The opposition seldom mustered more than 35 votes in the Senate or more than 100 in the House, and the Republicans, badly divided, offered no alternatives. Congress, to the left of Roosevelt on spending, labor, and public works, did, however, shape his program. Most bills did not emerge precisely as the administration drafted them, and some ideas originated in Congress. Roosevelt accommodated the initiatives, adding them to his program.

The most pressing problem was unemployment, and one of the first bills the Congress enacted created the Civilian Conservation Corps (CCC) to employ young men, aged 18–25, in semimilitary camps in national forests and parks. Some 250,000 were put to work planting trees, building ponds, digging irrigation ditches, controlling erosion, and improving recreational facilities. Paid subsistence wages, they were required to send money to their parents. By 1936 some 1.6 million young men had been employed by the CCC, which planted more trees than had been planted in the entire prior history of the United States. A poll taken in 1936 showed that 82 percent of the public wanted to continue the CCC, and it lasted until World War II.

Almost simultaneously, the president submitted and the Congress enacted legislation creating the Federal Emergency Relief Administration (FERA) to provide relief to the unemployed. The FERA did not pay the unemployed directly but distributed money to cities and states for unemployment relief. Roosevelt chose Harry Hopkins, a New York social worker, to head the FERA, and by 1935, Hopkins had become the president's most important adviser on domestic affairs. Hopkins had empathy for the poor and a capacity to help them by cutting through red tape. He spent $5 million within two hours of his appointment and became a leading advocate of spending to aid the indigent. No respecter of authority, he took a sarcastic attitude toward members of Congress. When one advised him to focus on long-range solutions to unemployment, he dismissed the idea with the comment that people "don't eat in the long run—they eat every day."

Hopkins helped to convince FDR to create a more ambitious program to help the destitute through the winter of 1933–34, the coldest in fifty years. As part of the effort, the New Deal created the Civil Works Administration (CWA), the first all-federal program concentrating on work relief. Hopkins spent almost $1 billion to employ some 4 million workers before the program was terminated because of its cost and conservative criticism that spring. About one-third of the jobs consisted of building and repairing roads; others involved developing parks, digging sewers, clearing waterways, preventing erosion, and refurbishing neighborhoods. The program was labor-intensive; most funds were spent on wages. Given Hopkins's priority to put people to work quickly and pump spending power into the economy, some of the jobs, inevitably, were no more useful than raking leaves.

Whereas the CWA emphasized help for blue-collar workers, the Reconstruction Finance Corporation, revitalized under the leadership of banker Jesse Jones, distributed as much money as all of Roosevelt's work relief programs to save thousands of banks and businesses. In addition to making loans, the government invested money in banks to insure their solvency.

To address the meager income of farmers, which FDR believed was a primary cause of the depression, the Agricultural Adjustment Act was passed. The word "adjustment" was used because the bill attempted to adjust production to consumption. The Agricultural Adjustment Administration (AAA) paid farmers to limit production in the hope that the surplus would be eliminated and prices would rise. Money to pay the farmers was obtained from a tax on food processing. Because the agency was not organized until May 1933, after spring planting, about one-fourth of the cotton crop was plowed under and some 6 million pigs were slaughtered before maturity. When these moves proved insufficient, a Commodity Credit Corporation was organized to loan money to farmers against sale of their crops.

A limited success, the AAA helped prevent farm conditions from declining further, yet did not solve the farmers' problems. Gross farm income rose from $4 billion in 1932 to $6 billion in 1934, but not until 1941 did income reach 1929 levels. Ironically, more cotton was produced in 1933 than in 1932, despite the destruction of part of the crop, and higher domestic prices for cotton and wheat hurt the export market. Surpluses would have been greater except for a severe drought in the Southwest that dried up fields, created a dust bowl, and sent thousands of desperate farmers on migrations to cities and to California seeking work. The AAA, which lasted until 1935 when the Supreme Court declared it unconstitutional, might have hurt sharecroppers and tenants, for their planting was reduced but they saw nothing of the government checks that went to landowners. Moreover, although higher prices helped farmers, higher food prices hurt consumers, particularly those on fixed incomes. Farmers likewise complained that much of their income was spent on higher-priced industrial goods.

Because most farmers were in debt and had to borrow money to live on until harvest time, many believed cheaper, more plentiful dollars would help them. Senator Elmer Thomas of Oklahoma introduced an amendment to the act that would give the president discretion to create limited inflation by coining silver, issuing paper currency, and devaluing the dollar. Initially opposed to the amendment, FDR decided to support it so he could avert more radical inflationary schemes. After passage of the act with the amendment, he used his authority to take the government off the gold standard.

The administration also helped rural people through creation of the Tennessee Valley Authority, (TVA), an experiment in regional planning to develop the area along the Tennessee River in Tennessee, Alabama, Kentucky, and other states. The intent was to have federal agencies, including the Army Corps of Engineers, implement a program of flood control, soil conservation, tree planting, production of fertilizers and explosives, development of recreational facilities, and generation of electric power. Long advocated by Senator George W. Norris of Nebraska, the plan was bitterly opposed by businessmen because the TVA competed with private utilities and used its cost of generating electricity as a yardstick to determine whether such companies charged fair rates.

Equally important, the government acted to save home owners from foreclosures through the Home Owners Loan Act. Commercial banks could use home mortgages as collateral for government loans, making the government, in effect, the holder of the mortgages. Because the government had more resources than individual banks, it would be less likely to foreclose.

The plan to revitalize industry under the National Industrial Recovery Act (NIRA), the most complex piece of legislation ever presented to Congress, mandated a government-business partnership unprecedented in peacetime. Roosevelt was pressed to develop the scheme to preempt a more radical measure by Senator Hugo Black of Alabama, who wanted to revive industry by limiting the work week to 30 hours without decreasing wages. The president, believing Black's bill unconstitutional, ordered his advisers to weave together competing proposals into a plan to rejuvenate industry.

The NIRA was based on the assumption that ruthless competition and cost cutting were destructive. Creation of the National Recovery Administration under the act was designed to replace competition with cooperation. It involved national planning and industrial rationalization of the business sector with centralized control. Under the auspices of the National Recovery Administration (NRA), each industry would draft and follow codes of competition, including maximum hours and minimum wages, elimination of duplication and, in some cases, industries fixed prices and divided markets. (Because price fixing violated antitrust laws, the president was authorized to exempt industries from antitrust prosecution.) Section 7 (a) guaranteed the right of collective bargaining to unions but made no distinction between company unions and independent ones.

General Hugh S. Johnson, who had worked under Bernard Baruch to coordinate industry during World War I, was responsible for drafting the legislation and was named director of the NRA. Because the law provided no means of enforcing codes, Johnson resorted to social pressure, designed a Blue Eagle as the symbol of the NRA, and added the motto, "We do our part." Only businesses adhering to the codes could display the Blue Eagle, and consumers were expected to patronize only such businesses. Johnson also used devices such as parades and mass rallies.

All of Johnson's work, though, could not redeem the NRA, for its scope was too large to be feasible in a complex society. Small-businessmen had little say in drafting the codes, consumers had virtually no influence in determining prices, and there was little elasticity in the system to compensate for expansion or retraction with demand. Worse, effective enforcement of the codes would have required a monstrous bureaucracy, and soon the cumbrous code-making process bogged down. The results were disappointing: production and employment increased initially, then declined, and national income for 1934 was down $10 billion from the year before.

Roosevelt appointed a review board to investigate the codes, and in 1934 the panel, headed by Clarence Darrow, issued a biased and flawed report criticizing many aspects of the agency. The findings still irritated Johnson, who grew increasingly dictatorial and erratic, indulged in drinking binges, and resigned, with FDR's prodding, in September. The NRA lasted until 1935, when the Supreme Court declared the NIRA unconstitutional. A grandiose flop in producing recovery, the agency did make contributions to industrial reform, particularly in outlawing child labor, requiring collective bargaining, and mandating maximum hours and minimum wages.

The NIRA was responsible for one success, the Public Works Administration (PWA), created under the act with an initial appropriation of $3.3 billion. The president placed it under the direction of Ickes, a cautious administrator concerned with preventing waste. Ickes was ineffective in producing recovery through a rapid infusion of money, but his capital-intensive program, employing skilled workers hired by private contractors, constructed monumental projects, including the Triborough Bridge and the Grand Coulee Dam. From 1933 to 1939 the PWA built 70 percent of the public schools constructed, 65 percent of the courthouses and city halls, 35 percent of the hospitals, and two aircraft carriers. Ickes's prudence was vindicated by the absence of fraud in his projects, which helped convince Congress that additional public works programs were politically feasible.

At the same time that New Dealers were attempting to end the deflationary spiral by limiting production, injecting money into the economy, and reorganizing agriculture and industry, Roosevelt experimented with devices to inflate the currency. Some of his advisers, believing public works would not get money into the economy quickly enough, felt that manipulating the currency might achieve immediate results. By deliberately inflating the currency to produce cheaper dollars he might raise domestic prices and ease credit, and a weaker dollar would make American goods more competitive in foreign markets. One way to put more dollars into circulation was to pay more for gold than the market price. Beginning in October 1933, the government increased the price it paid for gold daily, raising the price by random amounts each day to confuse speculators. An economist remarked that the policy resembled "a gold standard on booze." Businessmen, who disliked uncertainty, were appalled and Lewis Douglas, the director of the Budget Bureau, predicted catastrophe. The gold buying produced neither catastrophe nor recovery, and in January 1934 the president ended the experiment.

Some New Dealers advocated the remonetization of silver with the purchase of gold to stimulate inflation. Farmers, miners, and other inflationists rallied behind silver, and the administration agreed to experiment. In December 1933, Roosevelt announced that the government would purchase the entire domestic production of silver at 21 cents per ounce above the market value. Over the next 15 years the government spent $1.5 billion on silver, more than it spent to support farm prices over that period. The program was remunerative for the silver industry, which employed fewer than 5,000 persons, but failed to revive the economy.

Some economists and most businessmen believed that the depression was an international affair that could be alleviated only by worldwide cooperation. They placed hopes in the World Economic Conference that met in London during June and July 1933. FDR sent a delegation divided between advocates of international and nationalistic solutions; the chief rivalry was between Hull and the nationalist Moley, whom Roosevelt dispatched when the conference reached an impasse. Moley arranged a compromise, yet Roosevelt wrecked the conference by rejecting the accord that his delegates negotiated. Having wavered for months between the advice of nationalists and that of internationalists, Roosevelt finally sided with the nationalists because he believed international currency stabilization would jeopardize his efforts to raise domestic prices.

The search for solutions to the depression also involved a search for scapegoats. From January 1933 to the spring of 1934 the Senate Banking and Currency Committee investigated abuses in banking and business that led to the stock market crash. The hearings facilitated reforms in banking and in the sale of stocks and securities.

The most important reform was passage of a second Glass-Steagall Banking Act in 1933. Separating investment from commercial banking to prevent bankers from speculating with depositors' money, the act also created the Federal Deposit Insurance Corporation, to provide federal guarantees of deposits of less than $5,000. Under this effective law, fewer banks failed for the rest of the decade than in any single year of the prosperous 1920s.

Securities were the focus of another 1933 law, the Securities Act, which required publication of all data relevant to the sale of stocks and securities, and two 1934 laws, the Truth-in-Securities Act and the Securities Exchange Act. The former ordered that new securities issues be accompanied by a statement about the financial condition of the company, as determined by the Federal Trade Commission. The latter created the Securities and Exchange Commission to enforce the 1933 act and to license stock exchanges and brokers.

Pressure for inflation accelerated in 1934 as some early New Deal experiments appeared to falter. In March, Congress restored the salary and pension cuts made in the Economy Act of 1933, overriding the president's veto. In June, Congress enacted the Silver Purchase Act, which required the Treasury to increase the supply of silver until it reached one-third of the value of the gold it held and to issue certificates redeemable in silver. The fiscally conservative Douglas resigned in exasperation in August, predicting that the inflationary experiments would thwart recovery.

❖ NEW POSSIBILITIES

The November 1934 congressional elections furnished the first test of the New Deal's popularity, a test it passed. For only the second time in American history, the president's party increased its congressional majority, gaining nine seats in the House and nine in the Senate. Conservative Republicans were further demoralized to see that Republicans who supported the New Deal fared better at the polls than Republicans who opposed it.

The popularity of the early New Deal owed more to Roosevelt's aggressive leadership than to its success in ending the depression. Despite tangible accomplishments to its credit, particularly its provision of jobs and relief, the New Deal's most significant short-term accomplishment was to inject vitality into politics and to lift the morale of the nation. More important, however inconsistent, wasteful, and disorderly it might have been, however great the gulf between its promise and performance, the New Deal established the principle that the government had a responsibility for the welfare of its people. Its experiments suggested new possibilities that touched every citizen. It overcame the provincialism and decentralization of the American government by concentrating power in the federal government, changing permanently the power balance in the system, and dramatically increasing the power of the president.

Some believed Roosevelt had gone too far in increasing his power. The New Deal, they protested, was a patronage machine designed to spend and spend and elect and elect. Others considered the New Deal flawed by inconsistency, and political scientists complained they could make no sense of a government that gave with one hand and took away with the other. Roosevelt himself chuckled at a widely circulated joke that mocked the hodgepodge nature of the New Deal. A caller asked Democratic headquarters to settle an argument by telling him the principles of the New Deal. "Hold the line," a party official responded. After a long interval he returned and said, "Sorry, but we're having an argument too."

BIBLIOGRAPHICAL ESSAY

The literature on Franklin D. Roosevelt and the New Deal is nearly inexhaustible.
   Geoffrey C. Ward explores Roosevelt's prepresidential years in *Before the Trumpet: Young Franklin Roosevelt, 1882–1905* (1985), and *A First-Class Temperament: The Emergence of Franklin Roosevelt* (1989) as does Frank Freidel, in his study *Franklin D. Roosevelt,* vol. 1, *The Apprenticeship* (1952), vol. 2, *The Ordeal* (1954), and vol. 3, *The Triumph* (1956). Freidel continues his study in vol. 4, *Launching the New Deal* (1973), and he has written a single-volume study, *Franklin D. Roosevelt: A Rendezvous with Destiny* (1990). Kenneth S. Davis has also written a major multivolume study, vol. 1, *FDR: The Beckoning of Destiny, 1882–1928* (1971), vol. 2, *FDR: The New York Years, 1928–1933* (1985), and vol. 3, *FDR: The New Deal Years, 1933–1937* (1986). The best synthesis of the New Deal era remains James MacGregor Burns, *Roosevelt: The Lion and the Fox* (1956). Some of the other excellent studies are two by Rexford Tugwell, *The Democratic Roosevelt* (1957), and *In Search of Roosevelt* (1972), as well as single-volume studies by Ted Morgan, *FDR: A Biography* (1985); and by Nathan Miller, *F.D.R.: An Intimate History* (1983).
Among the many studies of Eleanor Roosevelt are Blanche W. Cook, *Eleanor Roosevelt,* vol. 1, *1884–1933* (1992); Joseph P. Lash, *Eleanor and Franklin: The Story of Their Relationship* (1971); two by William J. Youngs, *Eleanor Roosevelt* (1984), and *Eleanor Roosevelt: A Personal and Public Life* (1985); and Dorothy Dow, *Eleanor Roosevelt: An Eager Spirit* (1984).

Among the plethora of studies of the New Deal are William E. Leuchtenburg, *Franklin D. Roosevelt and the New Deal, 1932–1940* (1963); Paul K. Conkin, *The New Deal* (1992); Arthur M. Schlesinger, Jr., *The Age of Roosevelt*, vol. 2, *The Coming of the New Deal, 1933–1935* (1958); and Dexter Perkins, *The New Age of Franklin Roosevelt, 1932–45* (1967). Basil Rauch, *The History of the New Deal, 1933–1938* (1963), is an excellent summary; Anthony J. Badger, *The New Deal: The Depression Years, 1933–1940* (1988), is a more recent summary. The politics of the New Deal is the subject of Albert U. Romasco, *The Politics of Recovery: Roosevelt's New Deal* (1983); Sean J. Savage, *Roosevelt the Party Leader, 1932–1945* (1991); James T. Patterson, *Congressional Conservatism and the New Deal* (1967); John M. Allswang, *The New Deal and American Politics: A Study in Political Change* (1978); and Frank Freidel, *F.D.R. and the South* (1965). Aspects of the New Deal are covered in Bernard Bellush, *The Failure of the NRA* (1975); Rexford Tugwell, *The Brains Trust* (1968); Bonnie F. Schwartz, *The Civil Works Administration, 1933–1934* (1984); Robert E. Sherwood, *Roosevelt and Hopkins: An Intimate History* (1948); Joseph P. Lash, *Dealers and Dreamers: A New Look at the New Deal* (1988); Raymond Moley, *The First New Deal* (1966); Theodore Saloutos, *The American Farmer and the New Deal* (1982); Van L. Perkins, *Crisis in Agriculture: The Agricultural Adjustment Act and the New Deal* (1969); John A. Salmond, *The Civilian Conservation Corps, 1933–1942: A New Deal Case Study* (1967); and James T. Patterson, *The New Deal and the States* (1969). Studies of New Dealers include T. H. Watkins, *Righteous Pilgrim: The Life and Times of Harold L. Ickes, 1874–1952* (1990); George Martin, *Madam Secretary, Frances Perkins* (1977); John M. Blum, *From the Morgenthau Diaries: Years of Urgency* (1964); Otis L. Graham, Jr., *An Encore for Reform: The Old Progressives and the New Deal* (1967); Peter H. Irons, *New Deal Lawyers* (1982); Frederick H. Schapsmeier and Edward L. Schapsmeier, *Henry A. Wallace of Iowa: The Agrarian Years, 1910–1940* (1968); Michael P. Beschloss, *Kennedy and Roosevelt: The Uneasy Alliance* (1980); Susan Ware, *Partner and I: Molly Dewson, Feminism, and New Deal Politics* (1987); and George McJimsey, *Harry Hopkins* (1987).

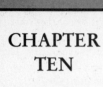

CHAPTER
TEN

A NEW DEAL FOR WHOM?

✤ THE SECOND NEW DEAL

By late 1934 it was clear that neither the NRA nor the AAA had produced recovery, that FDR's coalition of interest groups had broken down, and that the New Deal had lost its momentum and popularity. Unemployment and production had improved only marginally, and the president found it necessary to reevaluate his approach to dealing with the depression. His response was a turn to the left that preempted his critics such as Huey P. Long, Father Charles E. Coughlin, and Dr. Francis E. Townsend (see Chapter 11). Roosevelt engineered the enaction of a series of landmark laws that changed the nation for generations. The importance of the legislation passed in the spring and summer of 1935 prompted some historians to label the period the Second New Deal.

Based more on expediency than on ideology, just as the First New Deal had been, the Second New Deal did not mark a conversion of Roosevelt either to Keynesian deficit spending or to radical ideas. The Second New Deal, also like the first, seemed radical to traditionalists and was a force for modernization, although certain elements of the second departed from the administration's earlier ideas. Roosevelt no longer placed faith in cooperative planning by government and business but in regulated competition. This viewpoint was a retreat, from the liberal idea that planning on a national scale was feasible and desirable, to the conservative conviction that capitalism would function best if all interests were allowed to compete, protected from monopoly. It was also a turn from the centralizing aspects of modernization to a more fragmented economy dominated by local businesses. In the Second New Deal, Roosevelt declared war on big business and devoted special attention to small farmers and organized labor.

New Dealers became convinced that unemployment was a long-range rather than a short-range problem, that the government should replace the dole with jobs, and that putting money into the hands of potential consumers was the most effective means of stimulating the economy. Workers, they argued, must be protected from the ragged edges of capitalist competition by unemployment insurance and retirement benefits, and the government should support organized labor in its struggle to win recognition and higher wages. Further, the life-style of farmers should be improved through electrification, and slum dwellers should be given the opportunity to live in open spaces with clean air.

In his annual address to Congress in January 1935, FDR requested $4 billion for work relief, the largest peacetime appropriation in history. Using part of the appropriation, he created the Works Progress Administration (WPA, later called the Work Projects Administration) as the centerpiece of the administration's work relief program. Employment became a federal responsibility, and care for those considered unemployable, such as the ill, the handicapped, and the elderly, was returned to the states. The WPA, headed by Hopkins, became the longest-running New Deal agency, lasting more than 8 years and employing some 8.5 million workers over 8 years, about 3.5 million in its peak year, one-fifth of the total work force. The labor-intensive program spent 75 percent of its appropriation on wages, and 25 percent on materials, paying wages higher than relief checks but less than the prevailing wage. The workers, three-fourths of them unskilled or semiskilled, built 650,000 miles of highways, 125,000 public buildings, and 8,000 parks, dug irrigation ditches, planted trees, controlled floods and erosion, and strung electric lines to farm homes. The WPA also had programs for writers, artists, and performers (see Chapter 12). The WPA was a limited success, and it fell far short of Roosevelt's goal of providing every able-bodied unemployed person with a job. Yet the economy revived, and the public mood brightened.

Because the WPA did not employ men and women under 24, Eleanor Roosevelt advocated a special program for young people to keep them in school and to teach them skills. Congress thus created the National Youth Administration (NYA), and over seven years the agency hired 600,000 college students, 1.5 million high school students, and 2.6 million out-of-school youths for part-time work. Students received jobs on the basis of need and academic grades, and the program was so successful that college enrollment increased. It also kept students and other young people from competing with adults for full-time jobs. Future President Lyndon Johnson, at 26, became director of the NYA in Texas, and the man who succeeded him in the White House, Richard Nixon, worked his way through the Duke University Law School with the help of the agency.

Yet the most enduring legacy of the New Deal was the Social Security Act, which won the allegiance of the middle class. Drafted largely by Frances Perkins, it furnished unemployment compensation and retirement benefits. Under the act, unemployment compensation was a joint federal-state program financed by a payroll tax, and retirement benefits were a federal program financed by employee and employer contributions. The measure passed despite opposition. Conservatives argued that it would destroy individual responsibility because, with unemployment payments, no one would work and, with retirement benefits, no one would save. Liberals claimed that the program was too conservative, taxing the workers and excluding farm and domestic workers and those employed by educational, charitable, and religious institutions.

The most utopian experiment of the Second New Deal was the Resettlement Administration (RA), headed by Rexford Tugwell, which sought to transplant unemployed city dwellers and farmers working marginal land to planned suburban communities that combined the best of rural and urban lifestyles. Settlers were given tools, equipment, and advice in subsistence agriculture. The government planned to resettle 400,000 families in planned, self-governing communities. The program did not meet expectations, ultimately resettling only 4,441 families. Three "greenbelt" communities were built near Washington, Milwaukee, and Cincinnati, but additional communities proved prohibitively expensive and the plan was flawed by its encouragement of agriculture when farmers were producing a surplus. In 1937 the Bankhead-Jones Farm Tenancy Act created the Farm Security Administration (FSA), the replacement for the RA. The FSA provided low-interest loans that enabled tenants to purchase farmland.

Farmers also benefited from the Rural Electrification Administration, which extended power lines to farm homes where private industry found it unprofitable. It gave loans to farmers for hooking up and provided WPA workers to extend the lines, changing forever the life-style of farm families. When the program began in 1935, 90 percent of farm families lacked electricity; by 1950, 90 percent were electrified.

To rectify some of the abuses through which financiers such as Samuel Insull had gouged consumers and ruined investors, Roosevelt introduced the Public Utility Holding Company Bill. In 1932 the 13 largest holding companies controlled 75 percent of the utility industry, a virtual monopoly that the bill aimed to prevent. It included a "death sentence" clause providing that any company that could not prove its usefulness to the public within five years would be compelled to dissolve. The measure aroused more business antipathy than any previous New Deal measure, and one company spent $700,000 to defeat it, although the bill, including an amended version of the "death sentence," was signed into law.

Business was angered by the Wealth Tax Act of 1935, which raised income, inheritance, and gift taxes. Roosevelt complained that the tax structure was insufficiently graduated; under it, someone who made $5 million annually was taxed at the same rate as someone who made $1 million. The law raised rates on personal incomes above $50,000, peaking at 75 percent on incomes of more than $5 million, and increased the corporate income tax. Opponents called the bill a "soak-the-rich" measure designed to punish the wealthy and win votes. In fact, the measure raised little additional revenue, and it was unwise to enact a deflationary measure during economic contraction. The chief impact of the bill was symbolic. It enabled FDR to portray himself as the champion of the poor and the enemy of the wealthy. Roosevelt's image as a partisan of the needy was nonetheless dimmed when he vetoed the Patman Bonus Bill, which would have made immediate payments to veterans holding certificates due to mature in 1945. (A similar measure had failed during the Hoover administration.) The Senate could not override Roosevelt's veto.

At the same time FDR attacked big business, the effect of his Banking Act of 1935 was to centralize the banking system and provide more federal control. The bill increased the authority of the Federal Reserve System to regulate banking by permitting it to set discount rates and to determine the size of bank loans from federal sources.

The Wagner Act, introduced in 1934 and withdrawn at Roosevelt's request, did not receive the president's endorsement until it was virtually assured of passage in 1935. Throwing the weight of the federal government behind the attempts of organized labor to unionize industry, the law defined some management practices as illegal: it outlawed company unions; provided that a union winning a majority in a plant election would be the exclusive bargaining agent of the workers; created a strong National Labor Relations Board; and required that employers bargain in good faith. It was the most prolabor bill ever enacted.

✦ ORGANIZED LABOR

In the 1930s labor rebuilt its structure, massively increased its membership, and organized new industries in a surge of activity unleashed by the Wagner Act and Section 7 (a) of the NIRA, which made Roosevelt a hero of working people. Section 7 (a) offered a wedge to union activists to force their way into unorganized plants, yet it left a loophole by not outlawing company unions. Many employers responded by organizing company unions subservient to them, touching off in 1934 a wave of strikes by labor leaders seeking to win recognition as the exclusive bargaining agent of workers in key industries. During the spring and summer strikes occurred among auto-parts workers in Toledo, truck drivers in Minnesota, maritime workers in San Francisco (escalating into a general strike), and textile workers in the South and in New England. All but the textile strike resulted in labor victories.

In 1933 labor attempted to organize the Electric Auto Lite factory in Toledo; management refused to negotiate, and the next year the union called a strike. The company hired strikebreakers, and communists supported the workers. After sheriff's deputies clashed with strikers, Ohio Governor George

White deployed the National Guard. The strikers persisted, though, and won a settlement that included union recognition, the rehiring of strikers, and wage increases. The Minneapolis truckers' strike appeared a prelude to class war because the local teamsters' union was led by a Trotskyite faction of communists. The entire state was polarized; the Minneapolis Citizens' Alliance, a business organization, fought unionism, and Governor Floyd B. Olson sympathized with the strikers. After the truckers shut down the city and clashed with police, Olson reluctantly called out the National Guard, but that did not end the violence. The employers refused to fire strikebreakers, and the union continued to strike for 36 days until it broke the power of the alliance and won recognition, a pay increase, and an end to the open shop.

The chief complaint of West Coast longshoremen was the daily shape-up, in which workers report to the wharves to be hired. The system gave employers total control of hiring by enabling them to exclude union sympathizers. In May, longshoremen, soon joined by sailors, struck the entire coast. In July, after violent confrontations with police, maritime leaders called for a general strike, and other unions joined in sympathy. Both sides appealed to FDR, yet he remained neutral. The issues were finally submitted to arbitration, and the settlement in October was a victory for the strikers, who received wage increases and an end to the shape-up.

Less successful was a strike by textile workers that began in Alabama and spread up the East Coast until 376,000 workers were idled. The major issue was the right of the United Textile Workers' Union to represent the laborers. Southern law enforcement officials were unsympathetic to strikers, and National Guardsmen kept southern mills open while sheriff's deputies ejected families from company housing. Employer resistance and military force wore down the strikers, who returned to work in September, a crushing defeat for the union. Employers refused to rehire 15,000 strikers.

The biggest transformation in organized labor involved the American Federation of Labor (AFL), which had dominated the movement since its formation in the 1880s. The AFL was a federation of craft unions that organized workers by their skills or the types of labor they performed. Medieval in origin, based on hand labor, the organization seemed outdated after the assembly line increased the demand for unskilled labor. The failure to organize the unskilled into unions that included all workers in an industry sparked a rebellion against the AFL, led by John L. Lewis of the United Mine Workers (UMW), Sidney Hillman of the Amalgamated Clothing Workers, and David Dubinsky of the International Ladies Garment Workers Union.

The AFL council opposed industrial unions because organizing across work lines would create jurisdictional disputes and dual unions. If workers in automobile plants, for example, were given the choice of joining a craft union or a union that included all automobile workers, the competition could split the labor movement. Lewis argued that industrial unions were the only type possible in industries that made products such as automobiles, steel, and rubber. He promised that industrial unions organized under the Committee for Industrial Organizations (CIO), created by him and his allies, would affiliate with the AFL. The council, claiming that the CIO violated the AFL's constitution, ordered it to disband. When it refused, the council expelled the ten CIO unions affiliated with the AFL in 1935. Three years later the CIO made the break final by transforming itself from a temporary committee into the Congress of Industrial Organizations.

Lewis, who became the preeminent labor leader of the 1930s, began his organizing by creating the Steel Workers Organizing Committee (SWOC) headed by Philip Murray, the vice president of the UMW, and by providing the SWOC with funds from the UMW. The committee won a contract from the United States Steel Corporation in 1937 that recognized it as the exclusive bargaining agent and provided a wage increase of 10 percent. That victory, over Big Steel, had come easily, but Little Steel, led by Tom Girdler of Republic Steel, resisted. In 1937 the union struck, and months of industrial warfare ensued. Roosevelt, who had encouraged Lewis, split with him over tactics used in that strike and professed exasperation with labor and management, calling for "a plague on both your houses." Eventually Little Steel capitulated after the National Labor Relations Board ruled in favor of the union. The warfare left a legacy of bitterness between Roosevelt and the ambitious, aggressive, autocratic Lewis that became hatred.

The automobile industry was the largest remaining unorganized industry, and the CIO used large-scale sitdown strikes for the first time in its efforts to unionize General Motors. In sitdown strikes the workers, instead of walking off the job, sat down at machines and refused to move, a tactic that prevented management from hiring strikebreakers and provoked violent confrontations. Government officials, even those who sympathized with labor, questioned the legality of the tactic, because it appeared to violate the right of private property, or at least amounted to trespassing, yet there was no denying its effectiveness; by seizing a key plant in an integrated industry, strikers could halt production nationwide.

The United Automobile Workers (UAW), which changed its affiliation from the AFL to the CIO in 1936, struck the Fisher Body plant in Flint, Michigan, with a sitdown, paralyzing the entire industry. Provided with food by their wives, the men lived in the plant for six weeks, and the violence escalated. Police used tear gas and attempted to prevent the delivery of supplies, although the men were steadfast. Governor Frank Murphy, who sympathized with the union but believed he must maintain order, encouraged General Motors to negotiate. The chief issue was that the UAW demanded exclusive representation, and General Motors wanted its workers free to affiliate with any union. In February 1937, a compromise gave an organizing monopoly to the UAW for six months, after which an election would be held, and provided a 5 percent pay increase. In the election, the UAW won.

The UAW next focused on Chrysler, which it organized after a sitdown strike. The Ford Motor Company, however, was more recalcitrant. Henry Ford opposed unions and authorized Harry Bennett, a former boxer who headed the Ford Service Department, to assemble an antilabor army. Bennett hired spies, beat union organizers, and encouraged agitators such as Gerald L. K. Smith to deliver antiunion speeches at Ford plants. After the UAW struck in April 1941, Ford's wife threatened to leave him if he did not sign a union contract; otherwise, he would destroy his company. Ford signed a contract and provided the most generous terms in his industry.

By Pearl Harbor the automobile industry was unionized. The industrial unions were coveted by competing unions, and a struggle raged within labor for control of the industry. Eventually the UAW split, one faction affiliating with the AFL and another with the CIO.

Rubber was another industry that the CIO organized. The United Rubber Workers of America was founded in Akron in 1935 and affiliated with the CIO the next year. In 1936 it staged a sitdown strike against the major companies in Akron, and in 1937 signed contracts making it the exclusive bargaining agent for Firestone, Goodyear, Goodrich, and U.S. Rubber. In addition to rubber workers, the CIO organized seamen, radio and electrical workers, longshoremen, journalists, furniture makers, and lumbermen.

The 1930s was one of the most tumultuous decades in the history of American labor: massive strikes for union recognition, then a civil war between the AFL and CIO, and, finally, fragmented, competing unions in almost every major industry by 1941. Government policies and Lewis's aggressive leadership made possible a renaissance. In 1935 there had been 2,104 strikes involving 1,120,000 workers, exceeded by 4,740 strikes involving 1,860,000 workers in 1937. Membership of organized labor almost tripled, from 2,805,000 members in 1933 to 8,410,000 in 1941, when it encompassed 23 percent of all nonagricultural workers.

Appearances, though, were deceiving. The South still lagged in organizing, and labor was deprived of a potent weapon when the Supreme Court ruled sitdown strikes illegal in 1939. The CIO, which appeared to dominate the movement by the end of the 1930s, had most of its membership (71 percent) in just six unions, and the greatest pool of unorganized workers was among white-collar professionals, a condition that favored the AFL. Among some, the CIO had acquired a questionable reputation because of its militance and because of the influential positions of communists in the organization. Moreover, Lewis's hunger for power was unsated. In 1940 he vowed to destroy Roosevelt by endorsing his Republican foe, Wendell Willkie, promising to resign as CIO president if the Democrat were reelected. When Roosevelt won convincingly, Lewis was forced out, and Philip Murray succeeded him.

✣ DISCRIMINATION AND THE NEW DEAL

The New Deal produced a revolution in the voting habits of blacks. Until 1936, most voted Republican, then began to vote Democratic and have continued to do so. Minorities became a key element in the New Deal coalition that included organized labor and the South.

Blacks became Democrats for economic reasons. The New Deal, chiefly through the FERA, CWA, WPA, NYA, and RA, provided desperately needed jobs. Some blacks received better housing through the efforts of the PWA,

WPA, RA, and FSA. Black interests had a representative in the New Deal, Clark Foreman, a white southerner, whom FDR appointed. Ickes advocated the appointment of a person to represent blacks in each cabinet department, and such appointments were made in the Interior, Agriculture, Commerce, and Labor departments.

A network of blacks in government organized themselves into a Black Cabinet and met at their initiative, presided over by Mary McLeod Bethune, the head of the Division of Negro Affairs at the NYA. They sought to end discrimination in relief. Bethune's efforts were largely successful in the NYA, and Ickes rooted out discrimination in the Interior Department, but prejudice persisted at the local level.

Eleanor Roosevelt made black concerns a priority, and black lobbyists used her to influence her husband. She served as an ambassador to black America, addressed interracial audiences, and invited black entertainers to the White House; she and Ickes arranged for black singer Marian Anderson to hold a concert at the Lincoln Memorial after Anderson was denied other facilities in Washington.

Unlike Eleanor, Franklin had no black friends and was uninterested in black culture. A cautious politician, he never made black problems a priority because he feared alienating southern members of Congress whose support he needed for his economic programs and because he rarely thought of blacks as a distinct interest group. He avoided talking about racial issues and appointed some advisers who were segregationists. He refused to work to amend the Wagner Act and Social Security Act to prohibit discrimination in the implementation of the laws, and although he prohibited discrimination in New Deal agencies it was practiced anyway. Blacks, often the last hired for work relief, received lower wages than whites; NRA codes permitted wage discrimination against blacks; and the CCC hired few blacks, especially in the South. In the South, an NAACP leader remarked, "The white gets the apple and the Negro gets the core."

FDR's position on antilynching legislation was indicative of his expediency on racial issues. A bill to make lynching a federal crime was introduced in 1922 in the House and in the Senate in 1934, but it always was killed in committee or thwarted by a southern filibuster. Resisting Eleanor's pleas to endorse the bill, Franklin feared it would jeopardize more important legislation and the bill was never enacted. Nonetheless, working-class blacks, placing a higher priority on jobs and relief than on civil rights, did not punish FDR for his lack of aggressive leadership on racial issues. For the first time the government was touching the lives of ordinary blacks, and they felt encouraged to participate in politics, which suddenly seemed relevant to them.

In the South racism included not only segregation and lack of opportunity, but lynching and discrimination in the legal system. A poignant miscarriage of justice occurred after nine young blacks were arrested in 1931 near Scottsboro, Georgia, and accused of raping two white women who had been riding a freight train. Although the women were prostitutes and there was no physical evidence of rape, a jury convicted the "Scottsboro boys," and all save one were sentenced to death. An appeals court set aside the verdict and a series of further legal proceedings ensued, extending over 11 years and involving three additional trials. The obvious prejudice against the boys aroused national indignation, and their incarceration became a cause célèbre. Communist attorneys led the defense of the boys, and the party exploited the injustice to promote anticapitalist propaganda. Langston Hughes wrote a poem about the affair, and prominent Americans called for the release of the defendants. In the fourth trial, four defendants were acquitted and the other five convicted and sentenced to long prison terms. Paroled in the early 1940s on the condition that they not leave Georgia, they were reincarcerated for violating parole and later paroled again. The last was freed in 1950, completing one of the more obviously biased proceedings in the history of American jurisprudence.

During the 1930s, Communists worked diligently to convert southern blacks, promising to carve out a black republic in the southern states after a revolution in America. Their efforts were unsuccessful; only 1,300 of the 6,000 members of the Communist party in the South were blacks.

A young black, Angelo Herndon, who became a recruiter for black labor unions in Birmingham, Alabama, was arrested in Atlanta for his Communist activities and, while imprisoned, was further charged with inciting an insurrection. Tried for advocating the overthrow of the government in January 1933, he was convicted and sentenced to 20 years at hard labor. Released on appeal, he became a popular speaker at Communist rallies. Several state and federal courts upheld his conviction, but the Supreme Court overturned it in 1937 on the grounds that his recruiting for the Communists was protected by the constitutional guarantee of free speech. Like the "Scottsboro boys," Herndon became a martyr to the communist cause.

W. E. B. Du Bois, who continued to be among the most influential black intellectuals, was attracted to Russian communism yet condemned American communists for putting class ahead of race. Also, he denounced their cynical exploitation of the Scottsboro tragedy. "American Negroes do not propose to be the shock troops of the Communist Revolution, driven out in front to death, cruelty and humiliation in order to win victories for white workers," Du Bois wrote.

Du Bois became alienated and controversial in the 1930s, resigning his position as editor of the *Crisis* in 1934 after quarreling with NAACP Executive Secretary Walter White. White advocated racial equality through integration, whereas Du Bois argued for cultural and economic separatism, including black schools and black unions. Du Bois returned to Atlanta University, where he wrote three books dealing with black history and founded *Phylon,* a journal that explored black culture. He supported the domestic programs of the New Deal but opposed its foreign policies and, in the late 1930s, became an apologist for Soviet and Japanese aggression, even approving of the Hitler-Stalin Pact of 1939.

Perhaps the most charismatic mass leader of blacks in this period was George Baker, a minister who called himself Father Divine and claimed to be

W. E. B. Du Bois was the most prominent black intellectual of the interwar era, a prolific writer and editor of the *Crisis*, organ of the National Association for the Advancement of Colored People. He became increasingly militant in the 1930s.

God. Born in Rockville, Maryland, he preached in the South, was convicted of lunacy in Georgia, then headed north, attracting a wide following. A self-taught preacher with no formal training, a brilliant speaker, he championed New Thought, which held that channeling thought could help one heal disease, overcome adversity, and ensure prosperity.

In 1917 Divine moved to Brooklyn and married his most fervent disciple, Peninniah, who became Mother Divine. In 1919 he bought a house and organized a commune at Sayville, Long Island, where his services attracted such crowds that he was convicted of creating a public nuisance. When the judge died suddenly a few days after the sentencing, the story spread that Divine had put a curse on him. "I hated to do it," Divine said.

Divine's influence peaked in the mid-1930s after he moved to Harlem,

George Baker, a charismatic black minister who called himself Father Divine, attracted a mass following in the 1930s. His followers gave all their possessions to his movement and refused to accept government aid.

established Peace Missions, fed the hungry, and rehabilitated alcoholics and addicts. One letter arrived at his door addressed to "God, Harlem, U.S.A." and politicians, including FDR, sought Divine's support; in 1932 he endorsed Hoover. Divine's followers, who gave all their possessions to his movement, refused to accept government relief. Divine opposed separatism, and after Peninniah died in 1943, he married a white woman who carried on the movement after his death in 1965.

American Indians suffered during the depression as much as any minority, but the Roosevelt administration produced an Indian New Deal, and Indian affairs were debated as an integral facet of policy. FDR appointed John Collier, a humanitarian who had worked for improvement of conditions for Indians, as commissioner of Indian affairs. In addition, the program included the Indian Reorganization Act of 1934, intended to return to Indians some control over their lives. Seventy-five percent of tribes voted to organize self-governing councils under the act, which slowed the pace of forced assimilation into white society. The act made the secretary of the interior the final authority over Indian affairs, a provision that harmed Indian interests after the sympathetic Ickes retired.

The prominence of Jews among New Dealers exacerbated the rise of anti-Semitism, which peaked in the 1930s. Bigots such as Gerald Smith, Elizabeth Dilling, and Father Charles E. Coughlin blamed Jews for the depression and the rise of communism; labeled Roosevelt a Jew; denounced the "Jew Deal"; and spoke of Jewish plots to control the world economy and eradicate Christianity through manipulation of money and control of the gold supply. Organizations such as the Ku Klux Klan and pro-German groups proposed a solution to the "Jewish problem" in America comparable to Hitler's solution in Germany, and Representative Louis V. McFadden of Pennsylvania denounced Jewish "money power" on the floor of Congress. Despite such adversity, Jews worked for philanthropic efforts, for racial justice, and for a foreign policy that would rein in dictators.

Hispanic immigration declined markedly, a result of the depression. In fact, during the 1930s more Mexican Americans returned to Mexico than entered the United States. With jobs in high demand, Hispanics found their language a significant disadvantage in finding work. Many were confined to menial labor in city barrios or migrant labor. In some states there was discrimination against Hispanics at restaurants, bars, movies, hotels, swimming pools, churches, public buildings, and toilets. Worse, because Hispanics rarely voted, politicians ignored their interests. The economic boom of the World War II period brought a surge in immigration from Latin America but also increased tensions.

The condition of Japanese in the United States deteriorated in the 1930s. Japanese born in Japan clung to traditional ways, while their offspring born in America, the Nisei, rebelled and were strongly influenced by American culture. Unfamiliar with Japan as their parents knew it, they were anxious to conform to American ways; their parents blamed the adolescent revolt on America. Many highly educated Japanese Americans faced job discrimination, which increased as tensions in the Far East escalated. Japanese Americans trained as teachers and engineers had to take jobs as houseboys, dishwashers, migratory laborers, and cannery workers.

The experience of Chinese Americans differed, although they, too, suffered economic privation. White Americans began to view the Chinese in America as hardworking, frugal, and intelligent and admired their ability to survive despite destitution, to struggle, to save, and to refuse to seek government relief. They also came to view the Chinese as victims of Japanese aggression and potential allies in hostilities with Japan.

⸭ LIMITED CHANGES FOR WOMEN

In the work force, the percentage of women increased marginally, from 24.3 percent in 1930 to 25.4 percent in 1940. From 13 percent to 19 percent of WPA employees were women, most engaged in sewing, and some 8,000 women worked in CCC camps, compared to 2.5 million men. Some 20 percent of white women and 40 percent of black women worked outside the home, almost all of them because of economic need; black women worked in larger numbers as domestics and agricultural laborers. Many men resented the competition of women for scarce jobs, and in a 1936 Gallup poll, 82 percent of men and women believed wives should not work if their husbands had a job.

Among professional women, three-quarters were teachers or nurses. Jobs for female teachers, musicians, and doctors declined, and women who wished to attend medical or law schools faced quotas. The percentage of women college professors, most of whom taught at women's colleges, declined slightly. But more women worked as journalists, and in 1937, Anne O'Hare McCormick of the *New York Times* became the first woman to win a Pulitzer Prize for journalism.

In the cause of racial equality, southern women were prominent, notably Jessie Daniel Ames, creator of the Association of Southern Women to Prevent Lynching. Her organization investigated and exposed lynchers and denounced lynching, which had been justified as necessary to protect white women, as misguided chivalry. Lillian Smith and Paula Snelling, editors of literary journals, urged fellow southerners to cease using derogatory terms for blacks. Whites, the editors wrote, would benefit by sitting next to blacks on buses, talking to them, and learning from them.

Following the lead of Eleanor Roosevelt, women took an active role in New Deal politics. Molly Dewson, chair of the Women's Division of the Democratic National Committee, was one of the most effective political leaders in the country. More women were appointed to political positions in the New Deal than under any previous administration—including the first cabinet member, ambassador, and appeals judge—a prominence that was not reflected among governors or members of Congress.

Some women were active in radical causes, including the Communist party, which required women to sacrifice their personal lives and seldom permitted them a voice in policy making. Membership was fashionable among intellectuals and the wealthy, who were ashamed to see so many poor. On the other end of the ideological spectrum, Elizabeth Dilling led a growing number of women in opposition to the New Deal. A zealous anticommunist, Dilling claimed FDR wanted to communize America.

❖ THE PERSISTENCE OF CHANGE

Dictating massive changes in the economy, in government, and in politics, the Great Depression overpowered the reluctance to change that had characterized the politics of the 1920s. Most changes, abetted by an administration eager to experiment, were made out of expediency rather than ideology, but there is no question that the political mainstream shifted to the left. America was moving from a single-interest, single-race, single-gender politics to a system that was more fluid, more diverse, more dynamic.

BIBLIOGRAPHICAL ESSAY

The second New Deal is covered by Arthur M. Schlesinger, Jr., *The Age of Roosevelt*, vol. 3, *The Politics of Upheaval* (1960); and William R. Brock, *Welfare, Democracy, and the New Deal* (1988). Roger Biles, *A New Deal for the American People* (1991), discusses how the New Deal affected various groups. Roy Lubove, *The Struggle for Social Security, 1900–1935* (1986), discusses enactment of Social Security; W. Andrew Achenbaum, *Social Security: Visions and Revisions* (1986), discusses its implementation as well. Specific agencies are discussed in Donald S. Howard, *The WPA and Federal Relief Policy* (1943); Sidney Baldwin, *Poverty and Politics: The Rise and Decline of the Farm Security Administration* (1938); and Betty Lindley and Ernest K. Lindley, *A New Deal for Youth: The Story of the National Youth Administration* (1938).

The best studies of labor under the New Deal are three by Irving Bernstein, *Turbulent Years: A History of the American Worker, 1933–1941* (1971), *A Caring Society: The New Deal, the Worker, and the Great Depression* (1985), and *The New Deal Collective Bargaining Policy* (1950). See also Stanley Vittoz, *New Deal Labor Policy and the American Industrial Economy* (1987); and Walter Galenson, *The C.I.O. Challenge to the A.F. of L.* (1960).

Biographies of labor leaders include Melvyn Dubofsky and Warren Van Tine, *John L. Lewis: A Biography* (1977); Matthew Josephson, *Sidney Hillman* (1952); and John Barnard, *Walter Reuther and the Rise of the Auto Workers* (1982). The most important strike is described in Sidney Fine, *Sit-Down: The General Motors Strike of 1936–37* (1969).

There are many accounts of minorities under the New Deal. Kathleen Wright, *The Other Americans: Minorities in American History* (1969), is a useful survey. Blacks are covered in numerous studies, including Nancy J. Weiss, *Farewell to the Party of Lincoln: Black Politics in the Age of FDR* (1983); John B. Kirby, *Black Americans in the Roosevelt Era: Liberalism and Race* (1980); Harvard Sitkoff, *A New Deal for Blacks: The Emergence of Civil Rights as a National*

Issue (1978); Raymond Wolters, *Negroes and the Great Depression* (1970); Bernard Sternsher, ed., *The Negro in Depression and War* (1969); John Hope Franklin and August Meier, eds., *Black Leaders of the Twentieth Century* (1982); and Ralph J. Bunche, *The Political Status of the Negro in the Age of FDR* (1973). Biographies of Father Divine include Jill Watts, *God, Harlem, U.S.A.: The Father Divine Story* (1992); and Robert Weisbrot, *Father Divine* (1983).

Studies of American Indians and their advocate, John Collier, include Don L. Parman, *The Navajos and the New Deal* (1975); Graham D. Taylor, *The New Deal and American Indian Tribalism: The Administration of the Indian Reorganization Act, 1934–1945* (1980); Kenneth R. Philip, *John Collier's Crusade for Indian Reform* (1977); and Lawrence C. Kelly, *The Assault on Assimilation: John Collier and the Origins of Indian Policy Reform* (1983). On Mexican Americans, see Mark Reisler, *By the Sweat of Their Brow: Mexican Immigrant Labor in the United States, 1900–1940* (1976).

The best studies of women and the New Deal are by Susan Ware, *Holding Their Own: American Women in the 1930s* (1982), and *Beyond Suffrage: Women in the New Deal* (1981). For other aspects of the history of women in the 1930s, see Lois Scharf, *To Work and to Wed: Female Employment, Feminism, and the Great Depression* (1980); Susan Strasser, *Never Done: A History of American Housework* (1982); Winifred D. Wandersee, *Women's Work and Family Values, 1920–1940* (1981); Jacqueline Jones, *Labor of Love, Labor of Sorrow: Black Women, Work, and the Family from Slavery to the Present* (1985); and Jacquelyn Dowd Hall, *Revolt Against Chivalry: Jessie Daniel Ames and the Women's Campaign Against Lynching* (1987).

CHAPTER
ELEVEN

DISSENT

✢ OPPOSITION FROM THE RIGHT AND THE LEFT

A s an advocate of gradual transformation, albeit somewhat limited transformation, Roosevelt sought change as a means of saving important values. "Reform if you would preserve," counseled the president, who, in implementing a welfare state, provided a middle ground between Marxism and unfettered capitalism. Those who wanted radical change and those who wanted no change condemned him. Most of his critics were on the right, but the most charismatic critics were on the left, and some, such as Huey Long, evinced characteristics of transformers and of reactionaries. Alone, none of these dissenters was formidable; in a stable coalition, they might have been a threat. Because they opposed the New Deal for different reasons, however, a coalition was difficult.

Foes on the far right believed that Roosevelt was part of a conspiracy of Jews, blacks, communists, and organized labor, whose aim was to make him world dictator, eradicate Christianity, and establish communism. (Gerald Smith and other anti-Semites distributed copies of a bogus genealogy "proving" that Roosevelt was descended from Dutch Jews.) On the other hand, some on the left, including the socialist Norman Thomas, accused Roosevelt of being a fascist no better than Hitler. And the wealthy considered him a traitor to his class.

Nor was the opposition entirely on a political level. Much of it, in fact, was personal. Roosevelt was accused of being insane, of being an alcoholic, of having contracted syphilis. Rumors circulated that Senator William E. Borah had found him cutting out paper dolls in the White House study, that maniacal laughter could be heard in the house, that his friends kept him in a straitjacket and put bars on his bedroom window to prevent him from hurting himself. Some argued that because his legs were crippled, his mind must also be crippled; Gerald Smith remarked that God would not have crippled Roosevelt if the president had been a decent man. FDR was even blamed for kidnapping the Lindbergh baby.

Roosevelt's critics on the far right included women such as Elizabeth Dilling and Agnes Waters. Dilling, who had traveled in the Soviet Union, became an anticommunist lecturer, writing books asserting that a conspiracy of Jews and communists were planning to take over America with FDR's help. "In my opinion, Benedict Arnold's treasonable acts against the U.S., by comparison with Roosevelt's aid to Communism, should rank as a petty misdemeanor," she wrote. Waters, once a Democrat, broke with Roosevelt because she believed him a communist. She had lived in the Soviet Union and served as secretary to Alice Paul, founder of the National Woman's Party, but after the death of her husband she dedicated her life to political crusading. Waters claimed FDR was an honorary member of the Third International and that the Soviets had praised him "as the first Communist President of the United States." As proof, she said that every key member of his staff was a communist. Among the first women to lead large movements on the far right, Dilling and Waters claimed to have entered the fight because men had failed to halt the tide of communism.

Other foes of Roosevelt joined organizations such as the Sentinels of the Republic, which was founded to stop the spread of communism, arrest the centralization of government power at the federal level, and eradicate Jewish influence in the New Deal. The American Taxpayer's League protested high taxes in a series of radio broadcasts. The Southern Committee to Uphold the Constitution opposed the New Deal for destroying states' rights and claimed that Roosevelt had created a bloated bureaucracy to keep himself in office.

Perhaps the best-known anti–New Deal group was the American Liberty League, organized in 1934. Most members were conservative businessmen, many of them Republicans, but the leadership included prominent Democrats Al Smith and John W. Davis. The Liberty League desired a smaller government and condemned the New Deal for destroying private enterprise by overtaxation, overregulation, and currency inflation. Amply financed by wealthy business interests, the League peaked at 125,000 members in 1936, when it campaigned against Roosevelt's reelection.

At first the far right had little impact on Congress. In 1933–1934 only 25 Republicans and 5 Democrats in the Senate and about 100 House Republicans consistently opposed the New Deal. Gradually opposition mounted: some members of Congress resisted Roosevelt's leadership because they did not want to become rubber stamps; conservatives disliked deficit spending and bureaucracy and believed the dole destroyed individual responsibility; southerners feared that the erosion of states' rights threatened racial segregation. By 1936 a coalition of Republicans and conservative Democrats could muster 40 percent of the congressional vote on some issues.

Communism should presumably have grown in the United States during the depression, which was seemingly the fulfillment of Karl Marx's prophecy of the collapse of capitalism. Membership in the Communist party, however, grew only slowly; in 1919, the year the Communist International was created, some 60,000 Americans had belonged to the party, a figure not exceeded until 1938. Moreover, the party failed to attract certain groups. Despite organizing efforts, only 1,200 of the 6 million farmers in the country had joined by 1936, and party membership was almost exclusively urban: three-quarters resided in four major cities, one-half in New York and in Chicago. The Communists also sought black recruits, won the sympathy of such intellectuals as Paul Robeson and Langston Hughes, and nominated a black, James Ford, as vice president in 1932 and 1936. Still, they never won over the black masses, who remained loyal New Dealers.

Communists had condemned New Dealers as social fascists whose policies of limited reform would only postpone a communist revolution. They proposed to nationalize industry, collectivize agriculture, eliminate churches, and move the national capital to an industrial center such as Chicago or Detroit. But in 1935, at the direction of the party in the Soviet Union, American communists suspended their opposition to Roosevelt's program. Deciding that fascism posed a greater danger than liberalism, the chief party ordered its satellites to cooperate with liberal reformers in a popular front. American communists worked for Roosevelt's reelection in 1936, abandoned efforts to organize independent unions, and began cooperating with the CIO, contributing field organizers and working strenuously to take over the UAW.

Under the moderation of the popular front, party membership, a meager 30,000 in 1935, grew to 82,000 in 1938 and to almost 100,000 in 1939. Then, the Soviet Union twice ordered its parties in other countries to reverse direction: in 1939, when it signed a treaty with Hitler, and in 1941, when the Führer invaded. The revelation that the Communist party of the United States was a puppet of the Soviet Union destroyed its capacity for growth, and after 1939 it was never a mass movement.

❖ COMPETING ECONOMIC PROGRAMS

The most serious challenge to the New Deal came from American demagogues who offered competing programs. The depression created an audience for anyone who pretended to have a solution to the economic decline, and the biggest challenger was Senator Huey P. Long of Louisiana, the only major dissenter who was a professional politician with demonstrated appeal.

Few men have packed so much into a short, explosive career. Married at 19, Long was a lawyer at 21, a public official at 25, governor at 35, a senator at 37. He combined a superb mind with animalistic vitality, a charismatic personality, and an intuitive understanding of popular psychology. Possessing only a rudimentary formal education but a prodigious memory, an unquenchable thirst for power, and a compulsion that drove all his actions, he became the most unconventional governor in Louisiana's history, erecting buildings and highways, dominating the legislature, and thwarting an attempt to impeach him in 1929.

After taking his seat in the Senate in 1932, Long used it to win a national following. Claiming the depression occurred because of an inequitable distribution of wealth, he said, "There is no rule so sure as the one that the same mill that grinds out fortunes above a certain size at the top grinds out paupers at the bottom." Long's solution was to confiscate the property of millionaires and redistribute it. The government would take all annual income above $1 million, and all wealth in excess of $5 million, and use it to give every family a home, car, and radio worth at least $5,000 and guarantee an annual income of at least $2,500. He would also provide old age pensions, a bonus for veterans, massive public works, and free college educations. Some aspects of his program appealed to conservatives—no one but millionaires would pay any taxes—and wealthy Republicans helped bankroll his attempts to embarrass Roosevelt.

In 1934, Long organized a Share Our Wealth Society to publicize his plan and hired Reverend Gerald L. K. Smith to promote it nationwide. The minister, an even better orator than Long, was so successful that the society had 200,000 members within a month, 3 million by the end of 1934, and 7.5 million by February 1935. Long planned to launch a third-party candidacy for president in 1936, and a secret poll taken by Roosevelt showed he might receive 11 percent of the vote. Long, who could not win, might draw enough liberal votes from Roosevelt to elect a Republican, setting the stage for Long to run again and win in 1940.

Roosevelt cut off all patronage to Long, used federal money to support his enemies in Louisiana, and ordered the Internal Revenue Service (IRS) to investigate the senator. The IRS found gross corruption in Louisiana, including bribes, kickbacks, and tax evasion and was planning to indict Long in the summer of 1935, but an assassin struck first. Long, wounded by a lone gunman, and possibly by a ricocheting bullet from a bodyguard, on September 8, 1935, died the next day after bungled surgery. Long probably could not have been elected president, although victims of his dictatorship in Louisiana had learned not to underestimate him. He was the only prominent dissenter who was an actual dictator, not merely a potential one.

Before Long's assassination, some journalists predicted that the Louisianan might forge an alliance with Father Charles E. Coughlin, a Catholic priest who was another major critic of the New Deal. Born in Canada, Coughlin was asked to found a church in Royal Oak, a suburb of Detroit, in 1923. In 1926 he began broadcasting sermons, and by 1932 he was addressing the largest radio audience in the world and receiving a half million dollars annually through the mail for support of his program. Coughlin's appeal was based on his warm, resonant, mellow voice rather than on the content of his talks. He was one of the first Americans to push radio to its potential as a medium for political speeches.

Initially Coughlin addressed theological issues, yet as he turned to politics his audiences increased dramatically, and he began to seek political power. Coughlin backed Roosevelt in 1932, became increasingly critical of the New Deal, then broke with the president by late 1934. He organized a pressure group, the National Union for Social Justice, and later a weekly newspaper, *Social Justice,* as an outlet for his views. Believing that FDR's reforms were cosmetic at a time when the depression required economic restructuring, Coughlin proposed to back paper dollars solely with silver, establish a system of national banks, and nationalize industry.

Coughlin was less effective in proposing solutions to the depression than he was in blaming scapegoats for it. He claimed that an international conspiracy of Jews, bankers, and communists had created the depression so it could control the world. Gold, he said, was "Jewish currency," silver was "Gentile currency." Coughlin used some of his donations to speculate in silver futures, and the administration's revelation of his secret speculation turned him into an implacable foe of Roosevelt. "So help me, God, I will be instrumental in taking a communist from the chair once occupied by Washington," he vowed. If he could have allied his movement with Long's, Coughlin might have posed a significant threat to the New Deal, but both men had colossal egos and were competitors as well as potential allies.

The unlikeliest demagogue of the depression era was Francis E. Townsend, a California physician who advocated generous pensions to the elderly as a panacea. In 1933 he wrote a letter to a newspaper proposing that the government pay a pension of $200 per month to every person over 60 who retired from work and spent each check before receiving the next. The response to the proposal was overwhelmingly favorable, and letters of support, some containing money, poured in. In partnership with his friend Robert E. Clements, a real estate agent, Townsend launched a national movement in 1934. Within six months they had organized 3,000 Townsend Clubs and required a staff of 95 to answer mail. By the end of 1935 the movement had 10 million members, and Townsend was publishing a newspaper with a circulation of 300,000. After the Townsend Plan was introduced in Congress, a special committee was created to investigate the Townsend organization so it could be discredited. Summoned to testify, Townsend walked out on the arm of Gerald Smith, who had left Louisiana after Long's assassination in search of a new movement. Smith, hoping to merge the Long and Townsend followings, injected vigor into the Townsend movement. He also viewed himself as a potential bridge between Townsend and Coughlin.

Townsend unleashed the elderly as a new force in American politics. He attracted sincere old people, many of them destitute and many religious fundamentalists. Townsendites sang "The Battle Hymn of the Republic" and "Onward, Christian Soldiers" at their meetings and condemned city vices such as cigarettes, lipstick, and premarital sex. Such an audience was highly susceptible to Smith's demagogic oratory.

California proved a mecca not only for Townsendites but for followers of novelist Upton Sinclair, who created a movement called End Poverty in California (EPIC) in 1933. Sinclair proposed that the government seize all unused land and colonize it with the unemployed, who would grow their food and manufacture clothing and furniture, living in colonies with dormitories, a common dining hall, and recreational facilities. Sinclair said he would finance these colonies with a 10 percent tax on unimproved land, a state income tax, and a tax on stock sales. Some 8 million people signed petitions supporting EPIC, and Sinclair won the Democratic nomination for governor in 1934. Although FDR supported him, Sinclair was trounced in the general election by the Republican incumbent, Frank Merriam, and his movement faded.

Another movement that mushroomed and vanished in the early 1930s was technocracy, advocated by Howard Scott, an amateur theorist who was given a laboratory at Columbia University on the basis of forged academic credentials. Scott claimed that engineers could increase productivity by 1,000 percent, so with rational use of machines people would need to work only four hours a day, two days a week, to make an average annual family income of $20,000. He advocated replacing dollars with a currency based not on precious metals but on energy, using units called ergs and joules. The fad of technocracy faded after Scott was revealed to be a charlatan with little scientific knowledge.

✢ THE ELECTION OF 1936

As the presidential election of 1936 approached, the New Deal became the scapegoat of dissenters on the left and the right. Some journalists predicted that Roosevelt would become a one-term president if the Republicans could produce an attractive alternative.

Within the Democratic party Roosevelt faced no major opposition. In January 1936, Governor Eugene Talmadge of Georgia, a champion of farmers, free enterprise, racial segregation, and states' rights, explored the possibility of running in the primaries by staging a grass-roots convention in his state. The principal speaker was Gerald Smith, who vowed, "We're going to drive that cripple out of the White House and we're going to do it in 1936." Other speakers condemned Eleanor Roosevelt for inviting blacks to dine and sleep at the White House. The convention received financial support from the American Liberty League and the Southern Committee to Uphold the Constitution, but Talmadge, too reactionary to pose much of a challenge to FDR, decided not to enter any primaries.

FDR's strategy was to represent the interests of the poor in his campaign, and he declared war on big business in the spring and summer. In June, Congress passed a windfall profits tax and an act to protect small businesses from chain store competition by requiring wholesalers to sell at the same price to all retailers regardless of volume. Roosevelt also launched the first antitrust prosecution of his administration.

Roosevelt and Garner were renominated by acclamation at the convention in Philadelphia. The president's acceptance speech was the most eloquent of his career. One passage summed up his crusade and contrasted his humane experimentation with the alleged callousness of the Hoover administration:

> Governments can err. Presidents do make mistakes, but the immortal Dante tells us that divine justice weighs the sins of the cold-blooded and the sins of the warm-hearted in different scales. Better the occasional faults of a government that lives in a spirit of charity than the consistent omissions of a government frozen in the ice of its own indifference.

The president called upon the nation to meet the challenges it faced. "There is a mysterious cycle in human events," he said. "To some generations much is given. Of other generations much is expected. This generation has a rendezvous with destiny."

Governor Alfred M. Landon of Kansas received the Republican nomination for president on the first ballot at Cleveland, and Frank Knox, publisher of the *Chicago Daily News,* was nominated for vice president. Because the Republicans could think of nothing to rhyme with Landon, they coined the slogan, "Off the rocks with Landon and Knox." A simple, homespun man who personified middle-class respectability, Landon was a moderate associated with neither the Hoover wing of his party nor with eastern financial interests. In 1932 he had been the only Republican elected governor of a state west of the Mississippi and had defied the Democratic tidal wave by winning reelection in 1934. Because he had balanced the Kansas budget and was a reticent speaker, he was called Frugal Alf, and the Kansas Coolidge. He supported the New Deal's relief and public works but denounced the bloated bureaucracy, deficit spending, and politicization of work relief. Roosevelt, he complained, had usurped the power of Congress, antagonized business, and destroyed morale by raising taxes. Landon promised that as president he would furnish jobs and still balance the budget.

Landon received many newspaper endorsements, including that of the Hearst chain and the *Chicago Tribune,* and had the backing of eminent Americans such as Henry Ford, Al Smith, and H. L. Mencken. Mencken claimed Roosevelt would do anything to get votes. "If he became convinced tomorrow that coming out for cannibalism would get him votes he so sorely needs, he would being fattening a missionary in the White House back yard come Wednesday," Mencken quipped.

But Landon had serious liabilities. He was unknown outside the Midwest, faced a popular incumbent with extensive patronage, and was an ineffective campaigner in person and on radio. He had no broad program to offer as an alternative. His speeches were filled with trivialities; in one he said, "Everywhere I have gone in this country I have found Americans."

Roosevelt fought the campaign along class lines, blaming big business and the Republican party for the depression. Since New Deal reforms in 1935, he pointed out, not a single bank had failed, the best record in 50 years. FDR also noted that he had spent $4 billion on relief and $5 billion on public works, and that unemployment had declined by 4 million since 1932. His best argument was that the New Deal had mitigated the effects of the depression. The Republicans countered by arguing that the New Deal had not solved the depression; that although 1936 compared favorably with 1933, it did not compare favorably with 1929; and that there were still 9 million unemployed.

Both parties made vigorous efforts to woo blacks. The Democrats accredited ten black delegates to their convention, the first ever; the party also admitted black reporters to the press box and published testimonials by blacks whom relief had helped. Landon endorsed an antilynching bill, advertised in black newspapers, and sponsored a national tour by black Olympic track star Jesse Owens, who endorsed him.

John L. Lewis campaigned for Roosevelt, and the CIO contributed $770,000 to the Democratic campaign. John A. Ryan, a priest and prominent Catholic spokesman, refuted Coughlin's charges that Roosevelt was a communist and recruited Catholics to the Democratic cause. Coughlin appealed to uneducated Catholics while Ryan appealed to educated ones.

The Communists nominated Earl Browder, who realized he had no chance of winning, wanted FDR to be reelected, and made Landon's defeat his highest priority. Denouncing other minority candidates as stooges for Landon, Browder instructed Communists to vote for Roosevelt in states where the Communist ticket was not on the ballot. The Socialists nominated party stalwart Norman Thomas, who bitterly assailed the Communists and Roosevelt and charged that the president had offered mere palliatives; the depression would not end, he said, until the capitalist system was abolished.

Coughlin, Townsend, and Gerald Smith created the Union party and chose North Dakota Congressman William Lemke as its presidential candidate. His running mate was Thomas O'Brien, a Boston attorney and Coughlin organizer. Lemke, a bland speaker who had built a career fighting for lost causes, advocated inflation, aid to farmers, and mortgage relief. Coughlin promised to cease broadcasting if he could not deliver 10 million votes for Lemke. Smith blamed Roosevelt for the assassination of Long and, two weeks before the election, announced that he was forming a front to seize the government.

Underfunded, on the ballot in only 35 states, Lemke was virtually unknown outside North Dakota and was overshadowed by his trio of demagogic supporters, who were more interested in their own programs than in electing him. Coughlin seldom mentioned Lemke in his speeches, and Townsend instructed his followers to vote for Landon in states where Lemke was not on the ballot. Then Smith provoked a rivalry with Coughlin, who refused to campaign with him, and shortly before the election Townsend and Lemke denounced Smith as a fascist. Smith, for his part, considered his candidate unappealing. Years later he said of Lemke, "He was a complete composite of unattractiveness. He looked like a hayseed. He wore a cap. He was not eloquent, and all he could talk about was money and agriculture." Lemke, Smith complained, was a "colorless zombie."

The *Literary Digest*, which had predicted the outcome in 1932, mailed out

10 million ballots and reported the results in August: Landon would win 32 states and 57 percent of the vote. But the magazine, taking its mailing list from telephone directories and automobile registration lists, did not count the millions of Roosevelt supporters who owned neither telephones nor cars. The Democratic ticket won 523 electoral votes to 8 for the Republicans, who carried only Maine and Vermont in the most one-sided election since 1820. Roosevelt won 60.7 percent of the popular vote, a percentage not exceeded until 1964. Lemke polled 882,000 votes, Browder 80,000, and Thomas 190,000. All the extremist parties together won only 2.9 percent of the vote, less than the 3.1 percent they had polled in 1932. The Democrats won a greater percentage of the black vote than of the white vote, 81 percent of the Catholic vote, and 94 percent of the southern vote. Annihilating the Republicans in the congressional elections, the party wound up with three-fourths of the Senate seats and almost four-fifths of the House seats.

The election transformed the political landscape. From the Civil War to the Great Depression there had been only two Democratic presidents; from 1932 to 1968 there was only one Republican president. The Democrats became the majority party, embracing a coalition of minorities, labor, intellectuals, immigrants, Catholics, Jews, and the city masses. The election was a watershed in the tense struggle between change and reaction, the point at which modernization triumphed in politics. Economic issues became more critical than any others, and the campaign set the agenda for presidential campaigns for the next half century. Every Democrat would follow Roosevelt's example; every Republican would denounce the legacy of the New Deal.

✥ THE ATTEMPT TO PACK THE SUPREME COURT

Only one formidable obstacle to consolidation of the New Deal remained: the Supreme Court. The Court was divided along ideological lines, with four conservatives, three liberals, and two moderates. No important New Deal legislation reached the Court until 1935. Then, in quick succession, the Court nullified the NIRA, the AAA, and a New York state minimum wage law, knocking the props from under the New Deal. The Court ruled that New Deal legislation had granted excessive power to the president, had preempted states' rights through extension of the interstate commerce clause, and had entered areas it was constitutionally unauthorized to regulate, such as agriculture. Roosevelt feared that such reforms as the Wagner Act and the Social Security Act would be nullified for similar reasons. He denounced the Court for ruling on the wisdom rather than on the constitutionality of reform legislation and complained that it had rendered the federal government impotent by a "horse-and-buggy" interpretation of interstate commerce.

Without consulting Congress or the cabinet, Roosevelt, who did not have the chance to appoint a justice in his first term, framed legislation that would enable him to appoint enough justices to ensure a liberal majority. Introduced on February 5, 1937, his bill authorized the president to appoint an additional justice whenever any justice with at least ten years of service did not retire within six months of his seventieth birthday, limiting appointments to a maximum of six to the Supreme Court and 44 to the district and appeals courts. The objective, the president said, was to inject youthful vigor into the legal system and enable it to meet its obligations promptly. His real objective, as everyone knew, was to transform the Court into a rubber stamp for the administration. Six of the nine justices were over 70.

An avalanche of opposition developed in Congress, in the states, in public opinion, and on the Court. Liberals and conservatives feared the president would endanger the balance of power among the three branches of government established in the Constitution, although the document did not specify the size of the high court. Even those who agreed with his goals disagreed with his methods and ridiculed his hypocrisy in pretending that his only objective was to increase the efficiency of the judiciary. Mencken quipped that if the bill passed "the Court will become as ductile as a gob of chewing gum." Senator Burton K. Wheeler, who led the Democratic opposition, said, "It merely places upon the Supreme Court six political hacks."

The Court counterattacked. Chief Justice Charles Evans Hughes subjected Roosevelt's rationale for the bill to withering ridicule in a letter Wheeler read to the Senate Judiciary Committee. Hughes pointed out that the Court had ruled on a case it had received only four weeks earlier and predicted that more justices would require more conferences and discussions that would only prolong hearings. Then the Court, in a series of decisions, upheld a Washington state minimum wage law and ruled that the Social Security Act and the Wagner Act were constitutional. During the same period the conservative Justice Willis Van Devanter announced his retirement. These events convinced wavering members of Congress that the bill was unnecessary.

In April, Senate Majority Leader Joseph Robinson urged Roosevelt to agree to a compromise that would permit him to appoint one justice per year when a sitting justice reached 75. Refusing the offer at first, Roosevelt agreed to accept it in July, when it was too late. The compromise was recommitted to the committee, where it died. Roosevelt lost Robinson, who had labored vainly for the president's plans, when the majority leader collapsed and died of a heart attack on July 14. Vice President Garner, at the president's request, arranged a second compromise that streamlined judicial procedure but provided no appointments. It passed easily, and FDR signed it in August.

Roosevelt appointed liberal Alabama Senator Hugo Black to succeed Van Devanter, a choice that angered southerners, but senatorial courtesy mandated that the Senate not reject one of its members, and Black was confirmed. A few weeks later a journalist revealed that Black had once been a member of the Ku Klux Klan. Black admitted it, yet said the membership had been brief and perfunctory, and did not resign from the Court.

Roosevelt liked to claim that he had won the battle of wills with the Court, if not with Congress, by frightening the justices into approving the constitutionality of the Second New Deal. If so, it was at the price of appearing to be the village bully. It is more likely that it was Roosevelt's electoral victory, rather than the Court-packing bill, that convinced the Court to change direction; the case involving the Washington state minimum wage law, for example, had been decided before the judicial bill was introduced. The defeat of the Court bill was the sharpest congressional rebuke FDR suffered, and, from that point onward, a coalition of Republicans and conservative Democrats would frustrate his program. In the end, Roosevelt got his liberal Court. Vacancies permitted him to appoint five justices within three years and seven within six years, more than any president since George Washington.

✧ THE ROOSEVELT RECESSION OF 1937–1938

An economic decline followed the setback over the Court bill. Concerned about the deficit, particularly about the cost of the WPA and the PWA, Roosevelt slashed spending in the summer of 1937, cutting WPA employment by 50 percent and ordering Ickes to phase out the PWA. By August the economy had ceased to grow. Between September and December unemployment increased by nearly 2 million, and another million lost their jobs after Christmas. The national income began to fall at the rate of nearly $800 million per month, steel production declined by three-fourths, and factory production sank to 1933 levels. By the New Year there were nearly as many unemployed as there had been under Hoover.

Roosevelt summoned a special session of Congress in November, but it adjourned without enacting any of his recommendations, among them a new farm bill and an executive reorganization bill. Ickes, Hopkins, and Perkins recommended that the administration resume spending, and Roosevelt consulted with the British economist John Maynard Keynes, who remarked afterward, "I don't think your president knows anything about economics." Roosevelt, who knew a lot about politics, proposed a $3 billion spending package in April, which Congress approved. Unwilling to spend at the levels recommended by Keynes, he nonetheless considered the deficit a lesser evil than unemployment. The economy recovered by the summer of 1939.

✧ ROOSEVELT'S ATTEMPT TO PURGE CONGRESS

Despite Roosevelt's genial personality, he never sustained a defeat without retaliating. Bitter over the desertion by certain senators during the Court-packing debate, he cut off patronage to several conservatives. Convinced that only liberals would be faithful allies, he decided to try to transform the Democrats into the party of liberalism. To assure ideological purity, it would be necessary to purge his party of conservatives. This decision necessitated campaigning against incumbents in the 1938 primaries. Although it is common for a president to campaign in general elections, it is almost unprecedented for him to intervene in primaries. Roosevelt targeted about 9 of the 29

Democratic senators standing for reelection, delivering radio speeches against them and sending cabinet members to campaign for their opponents. Roosevelt's principal foes were three conservative southerners: Ellison D. ("Cotton Ed") Smith of South Carolina, Walter George of Georgia, and Millard Tydings of Maryland. He also campaigned for some liberals threatened by conservative challengers.

But the attempted purge was almost a total failure, as all of the senators FDR wanted to defeat were reelected. His sole significant victory was the defeat of John O'Connor of New York, chair of the House Rules Committee, who had blocked administration legislation. In the November elections the Republicans made their first gains of the New Deal era, winning 81 seats in the House, 8 in the Senate, and 13 governorships.

Roosevelt was not invincible, and for the rest of his presidency conservatives would frustrate his domestic policy. Yet the Democrats retained comfortable majorities in both houses, and even though the conservatives might be effective in opposition, they could not put over a program of their own. The result was stalemate.

The New Deal had run its course, and its history included successes and failures. It had not lifted the nation out of depression, but it had implemented long-overdue reforms in the economy and impressive, long-term changes in politics. In both spheres, transformation had vanquished reaction. Meanwhile, the battle raged on the cultural front.

BILIOGRAPHICAL ESSAY

For opposition to FDR from the right, see Leo P. Ribuffo, *The Old Christian Right: The Protestant Far Right from the Great Depression to the Cold War* (1983); Glen Jeansonne, *Gerald L. K. Smith: Minister of Hate* (1988); Seymour Martin Lipset and Earl Raab, *The Politics of Unreason: Right-Wing Extremism in America, 1790–1970* (1970); and two books by George Wolfskill, *The Revolt of the Conservatives: A History of the American Liberty League, 1934–1940* (1962), and *All But the People: Franklin D. Roosevelt and His Critics, 1933–1939* (1969). Also see William Anderson, *The Wild Man from Sugar Creek: The Political Career of Eugene Talmadge* (1975); William E. Akin, *Technocracy and the American Dream: The Technocrat Movement, 1900–1941* (1977); the contemporaneous work, Raymond Gram Swing, *Forerunners of American Fascism* (1935); and the novel, Sinclair Lewis, *It Can't Happen Here* (1935).

For opposition from the left, see Harvey Klehr, *The Heyday of American Communism: The Depression Decade* (1984); David A. Shannon, *The American Socialist Party* (1955); Mark Naison, *Communists in Harlem During the Depression* (1983); Donald R. McCoy, *Angry Voices: Left of Center Politics in the New Deal Era* (1958); and two books by Frank Warren, *Liberals and Communism: The "Red Decade" Revisited* (1966), and *An Alternative Vision: The Socialist Party in the 1930s* (1974). Biographies of Norman Thomas include William Swanberg, *Norman Thomas, The Last Idealist* (1976); James C. Duram, *Norman Thomas* (1974); and Harry Fleischman, *Norman Thomas* (1964).

Among demagogues with competing programs, Huey Long has attracted the most biographers. Glen Jeansonne, *Messiah of the Masses: Huey P. Long and the Great Depression* (1993); William Ivy Hair, *The Kingfish and His Realm: The Life and Times of Huey P. Long* (1991); and Harnett T. Kane, *Louisiana Hayride: The American Rehearsal for Dictatorship, 1928–1940* (1971), are critical of Long, although T. Harry Williams, *Huey Long* (1969), considers him a great man. Ed Reed, *Requiem for a Kingfish* (1986), is the most recent account of the Long assassination. Robert Penn Warren, *All the King's Men* (1946), is a novel based on Long's career.

Alan Brinkley, *Voices of Protest: Huey Long, Father Coughlin, and the Great Depression* (1982), is a joint biography of Long and Coughlin. Other Coughlin biographies include Sheldon Marcus, *Father Coughlin: The Tumultuous Life of the Priest of the Little Flower* (1973); and Charles J. Tull, *Father Coughlin and the New Deal* (1965). General accounts of unrest include Reinhard H. Luthin, *American Demagogues* (1954); and Ralph Lord Roy, *Apostles of Discord: A Study of Organized Bigotry on the Fringes of Protestantism* (1953).

For the election of 1936, see David R. McCoy, *Landon of Kansas* (1967). Excellent accounts of the Union party campaign are found in David H. Bennett, *Demagogues in the Depression: American Radicals and the Union Party, 1932–1936* (1969). On FDR's attempt to pack the Supreme Court, see C. Herman Pritchett, *The Roosevelt Court: A Study in Judicial Politics and Values, 1937–1947* (1948); Joseph Alsop and Turner Catledge, *The 168 Days* (1938); and two books by Merlo J. Pusey, *The Supreme Court Crisis* (1937), and *Charles Evans Hughes,* 2 vols. (1951).

CHAPTER
TWELVE

A SOCIETY
TRANSFORMED

✣ THE ARTISTIC AGENDA

With many joining the ranks of the unemployed in the 1930s, writers, artists, musicians, and actors found themselves in humble lives and in the struggle to exist in the face of adversity. Having waged cultural fights to defend individualism in the 1920s, they now focused on collectivism. Disillusionment with capitalism and sympathy with Marxism permeated their community, and some became partisans in the class war, defending the poor against the predatory rich and calling upon the government for help. Common people, their lives full of cruelties and crudities, were portrayed as heroes and victims, in triumph and, more frequently, in defeat. The popularity of Marxism faded as the economy recovered, but the artists of the 1930s contributed ideas that have endured: ordinary people can furnish the raw material of a rich art; there is honor in failure; and most lives are mixtures of happiness and despair.

✣ THE FEDERAL ARTS PROJECT

The WPA broke with precedent by offering work relief to white-collar workers, including artists and humanists. Making government a patron of the arts, Congress appropriated $27 million in 1935 to fund projects in writing, music, the theater, and the visual arts. The Federal Writers Project employed some 6,500 at its peak in 1936 and permitted such promising novelists as Conrad Aiken, Richard Wright, John Cheever, and Ralph Ellison to practice their vocation. Considering fiction too subjective and too controversial to underwrite, the project employed writers at practical tasks such as preparing guidebooks, taping oral histories, indexing newspapers, making inventories of historical records, and interviewing former slaves, thus furnishing material useful to travelers and to future writers and historians. The American Guide Series included a tour guide for each state, for 30 major cities, and for highways, rivers, national monuments, historic sites, and parks. This work bored many creative writers, yet it enabled them to support themselves while they wrote novels, poems, and plays during their time off.

More than 50,000 musicians were out of work, the result of the depression, the decline of vaudeville, and the popularity of radio and sound movies. The Federal Music Project employed about 15,000 of them to perform and teach. They played in orchestras and bands and sang in choral groups, performing free of charge in parks and schools. By the time the project expired in 1939, some 150 million Americans had heard 225,000 public performances, and about 500,000 children had received free music lessons. Forty-five cities established WPA symphony orchestras.

The most controversial art project was the Federal Theater Project (FTP), headed by Hallie Flanagan, a Marxist playwright who viewed the stage as a weapon in the class struggle. Some of the performances were experimental: the Living Newspaper dramatized news stories, and Orson Welles produced *Macbeth* with a black cast. The project's most ambitious production was a dramatization of Sinclair Lewis's *It Can't Happen Here,* a chilling depiction of fascism coming to America. Not all plays were ideological; the project staged *Cinderella,* Mark Twain stories, puppet shows for children, and Gilbert and Sullivan light operas for adults. The FTP, which spent 90 percent of its money for salaries, employed such future stars as Welles, Burt Lancaster, and Arlene Francis. Aiming primarily at blue-collar audiences, performers put on plays in schools and public buildings and at CCC camps. By 1938 12.5 million Americans had seen 924 plays, free or for a nominal charge.

Painters and sculptors who could not earn a living due to the decline in the market for art found employment under the Federal Arts Project (FAP). Among the 5,300 employed were easel painters and muralists who painted on walls inside public buildings. FAP artists painted 4,500 murals, more than 450,000 paintings, and made some 19,000 sculptures, some of which were featured in traveling exhibits. In addition, community art centers received federal aid, and some artists taught children. Like the government-sponsored dramas, some of the art had ideological content that was critical of capitalism and sympathetic to socialism.

Some of the most provocative photography of the 1930s was done by photographers hired by Roy Stryker for the Farm Security Administration to document the depression. Eminent photographers, Margaret Bourke-White, Dorothea Lange, Walker Evans, and Ben Shahn among them, photographed breadlines and Hoovervilles, finding dignity where the squeamish saw squalor.

The quality of the WPA-financed artistic productions was often mediocre, as could be expected from any endeavor making employment rather than the product the chief priority. However, the effort set a precedent for government aid to the arts, recognized the artistic community as a national resource, and helped millions of Americans develop an appreciation for art.

✣ A NEW GENRE OF THE NOVEL

A new genre in writing developed in the 1930s, the proletarian novel, which focused on the struggles of the laborer. Tough-minded realism characterized these novels, with profanity, violence, and sex spicing the plots. Most proletarian novels were ephemeral because they were often morals with stories instead of stories with morals, although some were great, lasting works.

Many of the best writers of the 1920s remained active and popular during the depression era, including the nation's most erudite novelist, John Dos Passos. Bridging the gulf between the decades, Dos Passos turned his rage at materialism into passionate proletarian novels and captured the revolutionary fervor of the times before his faith in Marxism faded and he turned to conservative themes. Dos Passos's *U.S.A.*, a trilogy collected in 1937 after being published as the separate novels *The 42nd Parallel* (1930), *1919* (1932), and *The Big Money* (1936), was intended to be an autobiography of the United States in the twentieth century. It was the most ambitious literary task of his generation.

Like Dos Passos, James T. Farrell wrote a trilogy concentrating on proletarian themes centered around his protagonist, Studs Lonigan, a young Irish American raised in the ghettos of Chicago. The raw story of a tough boy whose life revolved around violence, sex, crime, and hardship, Farrell's trilogy depicted the difficult lives of the young in depression America.

The most influential writer who established his reputation as a proletarian novelist in the 1930s was John Steinbeck. Born and raised in California, he set his most memorable novels in the West, depicting migrant workers, ranch hands, and union organizers. His first critical success, *Tortilla Flat* (1935) described the Mexican community of Monterey. *In Dubious Battle* (1936) was the story of a young man who joined the Communist party and organized apple pickers after his family was ruined by capitalism. *Of Mice and Men* (1937) portrayed two itinerant workers, one of them feebleminded. Steinbeck's greatest work, *The Grapes of Wrath* (1939), described the migration of an Oklahoma farm family from the dust bowl to the fields of California. A gripping human interest story, it proved a catalyst to social reform, provoking Americans to realize that the economic crisis was also a spiritual crisis. *The Grapes of Wrath* won a Pulitzer Prize.

Ernest Hemingway, who was not influenced by proletarian themes, remained popular but was less productive in the 1930s. His *To Have and*

Severe drought and windstorms created a dust bowl in the Southwest in the 1930s. John Steinbeck depicted the plight of an Oklahoma farm family fleeing the dust bowl in his 1939 novel *The Grapes of Wrath*.

Have Not (1937) sold well, but a bigger artistic success, *For Whom the Bell Tolls* (1940), was set amid the Spanish Civil War, which Hemingway covered as a journalist.

William Faulkner, still chronicling the dark passions of families in his fictitious Mississippi county, finally received popular as well as critical acclaim. *Sanctuary* (1931), shocking for its sex and violence, was a best-seller, as was *Absalom, Absalom!* (1936). From 1933 to 1940 Faulkner published almost a novel a year and wrote dozens of short stories. Two of his best stories, "Spotted Horses" and "The Bear," were written in the early years of the decade.

Thomas Wolfe, like other writers of his generation, lived so passionately and captured his experiences so intensely that he literally sacrificed his life to his art. Wolfe virtually wrote himself to death in the 1930s, dying in 1938 at 38 after getting most of the experiences of his life into print. His novels, including *Of Time and the River* (1934), *The Web and the Rock* (1939), and *You Can't Go Home Again* (1940), read like the scribbling of a brilliant, compulsive diarist determined to put his soul on paper. He described the anguish of growing up better than any writer in America.

The greatest humorist of the 1930s, James Thurber, published seven books in the decade after beginning his career as a satirist for the *New Yorker*. Thurber caricatured his autobiography, combining comic sketches with humorous drawings. Among his most famous short stories is "The Secret Life of Walter Mitty," the tale of a timid man who lived a daring life in his imagination. T. S. Eliot termed Thurber's humor a profound critique of the human condition, and Thurber described it as "a kind of emotional chaos told about calmly and quietly in retrospect."

Some writers who produced only a handful of works nonetheless proved popular and enduring. Among them were Katherine Anne Porter, best known for her exquisitely crafted short stories, and Nobel Prize–winner Pearl Buck, whose *The Good Earth* (1931), set in China, was a best-seller made into a movie. Then there was Margaret Mitchell, an Atlanta housewife who published *Gone With the Wind* in 1936 after ten years of writing. The epic novel of the Civil War and Reconstruction in Georgia sold 1 million copies within six months and became the most successful motion picture of all time. But Mitchell, whose only writing experience came during a brief period as a reporter for the *Atlanta Journal,* never wrote another book.

✤ CONTINUITIES IN POETRY

The 1930s did not break many paths in poetry: T. S. Eliot and Ezra Pound remained the two most influential poets in the artistic community, and Robert Frost was still the most read. Eliot, after converting to Catholicism, professed the need for belief in absolutes and ideals. He completed two verse dramas, *Murder in the Cathedral* (1935) and *Family Reunion* (1939). Pound continued to write his *Cantos,* and Frost continued with his austere celebrations of rural New England. Frost's work, enjoyed by thousands who found most modern poetry arcane, earned him a reputation as the national poet. Frost, who said he had "never been radical when young for fear of being conservative when old," proved a better prophet than his Marxist contemporaries. In "Build Soil" he wrote:

> You see the beauty of my proposal is
> It needn't wait on general revolution.
> I bid you to a one-man revolution—
> The only revolution that is coming.

✤ JOURNALISM AND POLITICS

Magazines were more widely read than books by a generation in a hurry, and family journals, featuring fiction that reinforced traditional values, were especially popular. Demand for short magazine stories was keen, and some leading writers made more money from them than from novels. Mass audience magazines included *Time, Newsweek, Esquire, Fortune, Harper's, Atlantic, Ladies' Home Journal, Cosmopolitan, Saturday Review, Reader's Digest, New*

Yorker, and *Collier's.* The *Literary Digest* ceased publication in 1938, the victim of spicier competition and its prediction that Roosevelt would lose to Landon in 1936.

Newspapers and magazines reflected the growing importance of political stories; the Washington press corps doubled, and foreign correspondents reported the rise of Hitler, Mussolini, and Stalin. Political columnists were popular, among them Walter Lippmann, Arthur Krock, and Mark Sullivan. But also popular were gossip columnist Walter Winchell, etiquette columnist Emily Post, and humor columnist Will Rogers. Mencken, who resigned as *American Mercury* editor to return to newspapers in 1933, continued to be the most influential journalist, although his appeal had declined since the 1920s. He lost much of his following as he became increasingly critical of the New Deal.

✛ HISTORY AND BIOGRAPHY

Historians began to utilize more original source materials, such as letters, memoirs, diaries, and newspapers. Biographies tended to be long and generally sympathetic, more narrative than analytical. Some of the most successful historians of the 1930s were journalists, including Douglas Southall Freeman and Allan Nevins. Freeman and Nevins, skilled writers who aimed at a broad audience, were also meticulous researchers.

Freeman, a Virginian, wrote multivolumed biographies of George Washington and Robert E. Lee. Carefully organized, brilliantly written, his biographies seek to depict what happened accurately without a deep analysis of the motives of his subjects. Nevins, a Pulitzer Prize winner, was one of the most prolific American historians and one of the finest craftsmen. His early publications were so successful that he left journalism to become a professional historian and taught at Columbia University. One of the first historians to use taped interviews, he founded the Columbia Oral History Project.

Charles A. Beard, who still published prolifically, still was controversial. In the 1930s he became interested in historical relativism and concluded that the scientific ideal was an illusion. Skeptical of the ability of a historian to remain completely objective, he believed that one must begin research with a particular point of view. An isolationist and an increasingly bitter critic of FDR's foreign policies, Beard devoted almost all of his writing in the decade to keeping the United States out of war. He argued that the nation usually went to war not because of foreign threats but because of domestic conspiracies.

Beard aside, the social vision of historians in the 1930s was not unanimously liberal. For example, William A. Dunning, Ulrich B. Phillips, William Dodd, and Frank Owsley focused on slavery, the Civil War, and Reconstruction from a prosouthern perspective, viewing Reconstruction as a harsh period of northern domination of the South.

✣ THE VISUAL ARTS

Painting, like literature, was critical of capitalism. A furor was created when Diego Rivera, whom Nelson Rockefeller had paid $14,000 to paint a mural in Rockefeller Center, depicted Lenin scowling as American police beat strikers; Rockefeller fired Rivera and had the scene painted over. Other muralists depicted proletarian themes, and abstract art was enlisted in the battle against capitalism. Among representational painters, Grant Wood, Thomas Hart Benton, and Andrew Wyeth were popular. Anna Mary Robertson, known as Grandma Moses, who had not painted until her late 70s, was acclaimed as a primitive regionalist after her work appeared at an exhibition of unknown artists in 1939. She had her first one-artist show in 1940.

Photography continued to progress as a new art form, and markets opened with the publication of mass circulation magazines that featured photojournalism. *Life* pioneered the photo essay in 1936, a sequence in which the individual photo was secondary in importance to the group.

✣ RELIGION

During the Great Depression millions of Americans turned to religion for solace, and some ministers believed the depression might help bring the United States back to God. The attendance at fundamentalist churches with an otherworldly orientation rose 50 percent, although attendance at mainline Protestant churches that offered less emotional support declined by 11 percent. Urban Protestant churches tended to less emotionalism, but emotionalism and revivals still flourished among southern Protestants.

Catholics were enthusiastic about the New Deal, and about 80 percent of them consistently supported the Roosevelt administration. Some Catholics believed the New Deal was implementing the program that Pope Pius XI outlined in *Quadragesimo Anno* (1931), an encyclical that condemned laissez-faire capitalism, rejected unregulated competition, and called for a living wage for labor and a new partnership between capital and labor. FDR encouraged the belief that he was inspired by Catholic doctrines and appointed more Catholics to the bureaucracy than any previous president. Catholics considered themselves a part of the New Deal coalition and approved of national planning.

John A. Ryan, a priest, was passionately committed to the New Deal and to social reform. Ryan taught theology at the Catholic University of America from 1915 to 1939 and, from 1919 to his death in 1945, served as director of the social action department of the National Catholic Welfare Conference. A widely read author, he argued that social and labor legislation was the obligation of the government, and he campaigned for minimum wages, government health insurance, and retirement benefits. He was an official in the American Civil Liberties Union and was active in the National Council for the

Prevention of War. Defending FDR's foreign policies, he moved from near-pacifism to advocating that the United States contain the spread of fascism. On theological issues, Ryan was conservative, opposing birth control and believing that Catholicism should be the state religion in any nation with a majority of Catholics.

The Catholic clergy were more radical than the masses in calling for social justice. However, Dorothy Day, a prominent lay Catholic, had a radical vision of social reform. Living in Greenwich Village, Day led a bohemian life as a radical journalist, had an abortion, married and divorced, and wrote a success-ful novel. After selling the movie rights to her novel, she purchased a house on Staten Island, which she shared with a lover. When her daughter was born, she converted to Catholicism to baptize the infant and broke with her lover, an atheist. Day began writing for Catholic magazines and in 1933 founded the *Catholic Worker,* a newspaper that sold for a penny. She also created hospital-ity houses to feed the homeless and farms where the poor could work. There was no attempt to convert those who sought shelter, but she hoped her exam-ple would help them find religion. Her movement, known as the Catholic Worker movement, was passionately committed to social improvement and world peace. One writer noted that Day might have been the most important lay Catholic in the history of the church in America.

Many Protestant ministers were also advocates of social reform: a poll of 20,000 in 1932 found that 34 percent supported socialism, but in the large cities the proportion rose to 50 percent. Yet the congregations rarely reflected the radicalism of church leaders, and Protestants who found the liberal churches spiritually sterile turned increasingly to fundamentalism. There were fewer nervous breakdowns and suicides among fundamentalists than among mainline congregants.

Reinhold Niebuhr, the foremost Protestant theologian of the 1930s, helped revive interest in Protestant theology by making it relevant to contem-porary society. Advocating a theological position he termed neo-orthodoxy, he argued that utopia would not come in this world because all solutions to earthly problems were temporal. Critical of capitalism and Marxism, a social reformer despite his pessimism, he argued that humankind should strive for social justice. He emphasized the ambiguity of the human condition: human beings were imperfect, tainted by sin, yet made in God's image. "Neo-ortho-doxy was what was left after faith in social science, in liberalism, in Marxism . . . was excluded," a philosopher wrote.

Norman Vincent Peale became the leading Protestant popularizer. A mainstream Methodist, he rebuilt his Marble Collegiate Church in Manhattan and launched a career as a lecturer who preached positive thinking. With a simple, personal preaching style, he told his congregants that "you can if you think you can." In 1933 Peale started a radio program called "The Art of Living" that continued for 40 years and, in 1952, published *The Power of Positive Thinking,* which became a best-seller.

American Jews increasingly drew away from their European roots and became assimilated into American society during the 1930s. Some 82 percent supported the New Deal, which was filled with brilliant young Jews such as Benjamin Cohen, a member of Roosevelt's inner circle. Also prominent were speechwriter Sam Rosenman, Treasury Secretary Henry Morgenthau, and Supreme Court Justice Felix Frankfurter. Frankfurter recruited dozens of Jewish intellectuals to serve in the administration before his appointment to the Court.

✛ EDUCATION

The depression had both debilitating and salutary effects on education. Public schools and colleges suffered a decline in funding and were burdened by overcrowding because enrollment increased more rapidly than the population. Public spending per pupil in elementary and secondary schools dropped from $108.49 in 1920 to $76.22 in 1934. On the other hand, the depression encouraged students to stay in school longer, and a higher percentage graduated from high school and attended college, although many found it necessary to work part time. Greater numbers of women attended high school and college in the 1930s, but their percentage among college students declined from 43.7 percent in 1930 to 40.2 percent in 1940. Women still went to college to attract a husband and tended to concentrate in the humanities rather than in the sciences.

Because many could attend only by virtue of family sacrifices, collegians were more serious and more vocationally oriented than their counterparts in the 1920s. Most students in the 1930s were relatively conservative but some were radicalized by the depression. The American Student Union, a communist front, enlisted thousands. Many students were pacifists and signed the Oxford pledge stating that they would not fight for their country under any condition.

Sex, alcohol, fraternities, sororities, and football kept their hold on students. Social competition on campus remained keen, particularly in dating. Few women wished to go steady; their objective was to have as many dates as possible to demonstrate their popularity. "Going steady is like buying the first car you see—only a car has trade-in value later on," one woman said. Another commented, "One is a bore—I want more." An advice columnist in *Women's Home Companion* told college women not to be rude to an unattractive man because "he may come in handy for an off-night." At dances, women hoped to dance with as many men as possible and considered themselves social failures if they danced with one man all night. Men, expected to "cut in" on dances with popular women, also considered good-looking dates evidence of their social standing. Concerned about the high cost of dating, they nevertheless vied to outspend one another to secure the company of beautiful women. "You don't win prom princesses, you buy them—like show horses," a book for men said.

Petting and premarital sex were more common than in the 1920s but received less publicity. Most students learned about birth control from their peers, and condoms were the most often-used method.

✧ MARRIAGE AND THE FAMILY

The depression sometimes made it too expensive to get married, to have children, or to get divorced, as all declined. Weddings were postponed, and the average age at marriage was the highest since before the turn of the century (26.7 for men, 23.3 for women). Getting married and raising a family, however, were still goals of most people. The percentage of women who did not marry, 20 percent in 1890, plunged to 5 percent by 1950, and in the 1930s almost 90 percent of wives had children. Birth control was increasingly practiced: contraceptives were sold through such sources as the Sears catalog and rest rooms in gasoline stations, and by 1940 information on the subject could be disseminated legally in all except two states. Chronic fatigue caused by the difficulty of earning a living somewhat lessened interest in sex and contributed to the declining birth rate.

Women who married and had children compensated for shrinking family income by canning, baking, laundering, and sewing at home. Fewer women had servants, yet household burdens were eased by the greater availability of electric appliances. Wives usually did the shopping, and deflation enabled them to stretch their budgets; those who shopped wisely could feed a family of six on just $5 per week.

✧ THE MOVIES OF THE 1930s

Overall movie attendance declined between 1929 and 1933, and in 1931 theaters began cutting prices. The tactic was successful, and by 1933 attendance revived and remained high for the rest of the decade. Furnishing escape from the mental and economic depression, movies, which were the most frequent dating activity, became so important that families skimped on necessities to attend. Hollywood met demand by turning out a large volume of cheap films.

In the early 1930s, there was a series of gangster films such as *Little Caesar* (1931). Gangsters were viewed as the only credible examples of financial success, but the prevailing morality required that they be killed off at the end, usually by another gangster. Initially, the police were depicted as inept, yet by 1935 movies showed the FBI "G-Men" as heroes who stepped in to rescue local police. Many of the crime movies were set in New York, which was depicted as a sewer of vice.

The greatest comedians of the 1930s were the Marx brothers, who combined slapstick with puns. Groucho, Harpo, Chico, and Zeppo made five films between 1929 and 1933, including *Animal Crackers,* Paramount's most lucrative film of 1930, and two later smash hits, *A Night at the Opera* (1935) and *A Day at the Races* (1937). Another popular comedian, W. C. Fields, who had an unhappy childhood, was depicted as a braggart who drank excessively and hated children.

Sometimes Fields was paired with the funny and seductive Mae West, who launched a new genre, films about the sexually aggressive female. She had two hits in 1933, *She Done Him Wrong* and *I'm No Angel,* both of which depicted the woman as the hunter rather than the hunted. In *She Done Him Wrong,* West asked Cary Grant, "Why don't you come up and see me sometime?" Another of her famous lines was, "When a girl goes wrong, men go right after her." Partly concerned with West, the Catholic Legion of Decency began rating films in 1934, and thereafter overt sexuality declined; passionate embraces became taboo, and married couples slept in separate beds.

Frank Capra directed a series of successful "screwball" comedies from 1931 to 1941, including *It Happened One Night* (1934), a romance starring Claudette Colbert and Clark Gable. Gable, a journalist, aided Colbert, a woman seeking freedom from her rich family. After a series of comic misadventures they fell in love and got married. *It Happened One Night* won Academy Awards for best film, screenplay, director, actor, and actress.

The motion picture industry also featured Walt Disney, who turned the animated cartoon into a new art form; monster movies; child star Shirley Temple, the number one box office attraction from 1935 to 1938 and the inspiration for a line of dolls, clothes, and books; Greta Garbo, a beautiful, talented, and mysterious Swede; and musicals whose quality has never been surpassed, many of them starring Fred Astaire and Ginger Rogers. In addition, the decade had one of the most successful box office extravaganzas of all time, *Gone with the Wind* (1939), an early Technicolor film. The four-hour film, which starred the unknown Vivien Leigh opposite Gable, captivated audiences and helped make Gable the number two box office attraction of the late 1930s. Gable, who came to be known as the world's greatest lover, said, "It's a living."

÷ RADIO

Radio, the most pervasive cultural influence of the time, enjoyed a golden age in the 1930s. In 1929, there were 9 million radios in America; by 1940, there were 29 million, and 85 percent of all Americans had access to a set. The technical aspects of broadcasting improved; radios became smaller and no longer required long outdoor antennas; there were more stations broadcasting; and radios were being installed in cars.

Music remained the principal item on the radio menu, and the medium helped popularize swing, a variation on jazz, and classical music. Politicians increasingly turned to radio to promote their ideas and themselves, not only Roosevelt with his fireside chats but demagogues such as Huey Long and Father Charles E. Coughlin. The Federal Communications Commission

(FCC) developed the policy of requiring stations to offer equal time to each candidate in a political campaign. Between 1932 and 1939, the volume of news broadcast doubled.

Radio occupied a central role in family life. Daytime radio included soap operas, cooking shows, and programs for housewives on raising children. In the early evening there were fantasies such as "Superman," "The Lone Ranger," and "Tarzan"; quiz programs such as "Information Please" and "Quiz Kids"; and comedy shows from performers including Fred Allen and Jack Benny, George Burns and Gracie Allen, and ventriloquist Edgar Bergen with his dummy, Charlie McCarthy.

The most popular show of all time was "Amos 'n' Andy," which remained on the air in some form from 1928 to 1960 and inspired books, a movie, a comic strip, and a television series. It was the creation of white comedians Freeman F. Gosden, who played Amos, and Charles J. Correll, who played Andy. Initially set in Chicago, then in Harlem, the program's humor was derived from the misadventures of the owners of a taxi company with one cab. The protagonists, southern blacks, were complex, human characters, and the show did not employ racial humor; nonetheless, some blacks found it offensive. "Amos 'n' Andy," one of the first successful serials, had the largest regular audience of any show.

The credibility of radio was so great that when Orson Welles broadcast an imaginary invasion by Martians on Halloween night in 1938, thousands fled their homes. A Pittsburgh man found his wife in the bathroom holding a bottle of poison, screaming, "I'd rather die this way than like that!"

✤ THEATER AND PROLETARIAN THEMES

Dramatists shared some of the sociopolitical tendencies of novelists, viewing the masses as victims oppressed by capitalism and workers as heroes. The playwright most in tune with the radical tendencies of the time was Clifford Odets, whose *Waiting for Lefty* (1935) was the biggest hit of the decade and has been performed more frequently than any play in American history. Audiences responded enthusiastically to the play, based on a New York taxi-cab strike. One of the strikers, Lefty, who was absent from a union meeting, was found dead, presumably murdered by company thugs. Odets had two other hits during the decade: *Awake and Sing* (1935), an affectionate portrait of a Jewish family, and *Golden Boy* (1937), the story of a violinist who became a prizefighter.

Lillian Hellman became a successful playwright in the 1930s. Although she was a political leftist like Odets, her plays did not reflect proletarian themes. Her first hit, *The Children's Hour* (1934), concerned false allegations of a lesbian relationship between two teachers at a boarding school, a theme considered shocking. Her next hit, *The Little Foxes* (1939), depicted a turn-of-the-century southern family dissipated by greed, and in 1941 she produced *Watch on the Rhine,* a highly acclaimed anti-Nazi polemic.

Robert E. Sherwood, a speechwriter for Roosevelt as well as a successful playwright, was an exception to the proletarian bias of the period. Anti-Marxist, antitotalitarian, he believed that most Americans were decent people. Sherwood won Pulitzer prizes for *Idiot's Delight* (1936); *Abe Lincoln in Illinois* (1938), his most popular play and a celebration of democracy; *There Shall Be No Night* (1940); and the book *Roosevelt and Hopkins: An Intimate History* (1948).

Other hits included George Gershwin's *Porgy and Bess* (1937), Moss Hart's and George S. Kaufman's *You Can't Take It with You* (1937), and Thornton Wilder's *Our Town* (1938). Drama was more serious than film, focusing upon psychological analysis rather than melodrama. The plays of the 1930s that have endured were not concerned primarily with the economic problems of the period.

✣ MUSIC

Music benefited from improvements in the technology of recording, the dissemination of songs by radio and jukeboxes, and the innovation of sound movies, which made musicals possible. Popular music never had a larger audience.

Some of the leading composers wrote Hollywood scores. Many were already established, including Irving Berlin, George Gershwin, Ira Gershwin, Jerome Kern, Cole Porter, and Hoagy Carmichael. Swing was still popular, and musicians who won reputations in the 1930s included Tommy Dorsey, Artie Shaw, and Glenn Miller. The new singers included Bing Crosby, Frank Sinatra, Ethel Merman, and Billie Holliday. The most popular songs included "I Got Rhythm," "Goodnight Sweetheart," "Smoke Gets in Your Eyes," "Red Sails in the Sunset," "Pennies from Heaven," and "Brother, Can You Spare a Dime?" Among the favorite dances were the fox trot, the samba, and the rumba, the last two imported from Latin America.

✣ SPORTS

Spectator sports provided another form of escape, served as a vehicle of upward mobility for immigrants and minorities, and competed for scarce entertainment dollars. Although attendance at professional events declined, larger audiences followed athletics over radio.

Amateur boxing flourished with the introduction of the Golden Gloves championship tournament, sponsored by the *Chicago Tribune,* and professional boxing was dominated by Joe Louis. Son of an Alabama sharecropper, Louis turned professional in 1934 and won the world heavyweight title in 1937 at the age of 23, becoming an inspiration to black athletes.

Attendance at major league baseball games declined early in the decade, then revived once recovery began. The Yankees remained the dominant team, and Lou Gehrig, the team's first baseman and captain for 16 years, set a record for consecutive games played. Nearly as talented as Ruth, he lacked his teammate's excessive appetites and faced death with courage after contracting a fatal muscular disease. Late in the decade Yankee center fielder Joe DiMaggio became a dominant player, starring at the plate, in the field, and on the bases.

College football remained the most popular amateur sport. There was no single back with the glamor of Red Grange, but players, becoming bigger and faster, increased their overall skills, and the offenses grew more sophisticated. A few blacks starred at northern universities.

Blacks dominated the sprints in Olympic track competition. In the 1932 Olympic Games held in Los Angeles, Americans Eddie Tolan and Ralph Metcalfe finished first and second, respectively, in the 100-meter dash. In the 200-meter dash, won by Tolan, Americans swept all three medals.

By the time of the 1936 Olympics at Berlin, Jesse Owens, who set five world records and equaled a sixth in 45 minutes in 1935, was the leading sprinter. At Berlin, Owens won the 100 meters, the 200 meters, the long jump, and anchored the winning 400-meter relay team. Hitler, frustrated by the defeat of his Aryan heroes, personally presented medals to German medalists but refused to do so to any of the foreign athletes.

Sprinter Jesse Owens won four gold medals in the 1936 Olympics. Blacks were not permitted to participate in most professional sports, but they began to dominate the sprints in track and field.

Millions of Americans took up golf, which began to be played at municipal courses open to the public as well as at exclusive country clubs. Bicycling revived, particularly among women, and there were more bicyclists in 1935 than in any year since the 1890s.

Women increasingly participated in golf, tennis, bicycling, and swimming, and some women athletes achieved fame. Their inspiration was Mildred ("Babe") Didrikson, the greatest female athlete of all time and the most versatile athlete of either sex. Didrikson won five events, tied for first in a sixth, and finished fourth in a seventh at the National Amateur Athletic Union track meet in 1932, single-handedly winning the team championship. At the Los Angeles Olympics she won gold medals in the javelin and the high hurdles and a silver medal in the high jump. Turning professional, she pitched for a women's baseball team; taking up golf, she dominated women's professional play in the 1940s. The range of her activities was astounding: Not only could she run and jump, but she could swim, shoot, ride, and box and excelled at tennis, basketball, polo, and billiards. Asked if there was anything she did not play, she replied, "Yeah, dolls."

✤ CULTURAL TRANSFORMATION AND ECONOMIC CRISIS

Cultural transformation carried over from the 1920s into the 1930s but was subordinated by the crisis of the depression. Because much creativity was channeled into government rather than into art, the art of the 1930s, although still animated by alienation, was less original than the work of the preceding decade. Like economics and politics, culture oscillated between transformation and reaction, as seen in the difference between the taste of the intellectuals and that of the masses, which was substantially less radical. Soon the struggle between transformation and reaction would dominate on an international scale, a development announced by the thunderclap of war that followed the cloud of depression.

BIBLIOGRAPHICAL ESSAY

For federal patronage of the arts in the 1930s, see Jane De Hart Mathews, *The Federal Theatre, 1935–1939: Plays, Relief, and Politics* (1967); Edward C. Banfield, *The Democratic Muse, Visual Arts and the Public Interest* (1984); Jerre Mangione, *The Dream and the Deal: The Federal Writers Project, 1935–1943* (1972); Karal Ann Marling, *Wall-to-Wall America: A Cultural History of Post-Office Murals in the Great Depression* (1982); Frances V. O'Connor, ed., *Art for the Millions, Essays from the 1930s by Artists and Administrators of the WPA Federal Art Project* (1973); Frances V. O'Connor, *Federal Art Patronage, 1933–1943* (1966); Marlene Park and Gerald E. Markowitz, *New Deal for Art: The Government Art Projects of the 1930s, with Examples from New York City and State* (1977); and Richard D. McKinzie, *The New Deal for Artists* (1973).

Two writers who were active in the 1930s have written excellent accounts of the literature of the period: Edmund Wilson, *The Shores of Light: A Literary Chronicle of
the Twenties and Thirties* (1952), and *The Thirties* (1982); and Malcolm Cowley,
The Dream of the Golden Mountains: Remembering the 1930s (1980). Other
accounts include Alfred Kazin, *Starting Out in the Thirties* (1980); Robert
Crunden, *From Self to Society: Transitions in American Thought, 1919–1941*
(1972); Richard H. Pells, *Radical Visions and American Dreams: Culture and
Social Thought in the Depression Years* (1973); John Aldridge, *After the Lost
Generation* (1951); Leo Gurko, *The Angry Decade* (1947); and Maxwell
Geismar, *Writers in Crisis: The American Novel, 1925–1940* (1961).

For popular culture in general, see Frederick Lewis Allen, *Since Yesterday, 1929–1939*
(1940); Alice G. Marquis, *Hopes and Ashes: The Birth of Modern Times,
1929–1939* (1986); and Robert S. Lynd and Helen M. Lynd, *Middletown in
Transition* (1937), a follow-up to their famous case study of a community in the
1920s. For the visual arts, see Milton W. Brown, *American Painting, 1908–1935*
(1977); Henry Geldzahler, *American Painting in the Twentieth Century* (1967);
Barbara Rose, *American Art Since 1900* (1967); Michael F. Braive, *The
Photograph: A Social History* (1966); Nathan Lyons, *Photography in the
Twentieth Century* (1967); and Wayne Andrews, *Architecture in America* (1960).

The contours of religious changes brought by the depression are outlined in Samuel C.
Kincheloe, *Research Memorandum on Religion in the Depression* (1937).
Catholicism is covered in George Q. Flynn, *American Catholics and the
Roosevelt Presidency, 1932–1936* (1968); Robert D. Cross, *The Emergence of
Liberal Catholicism in America* (1958); and Charles E. Curran, *American
Catholic Social Ethics: Twentieth Century Approaches* (1982). Among the many
works about Dorothy Day are Mel Piehl, *Breaking Bread: The Catholic Worker
and the Origin of Catholic Radicalism in America* (1982); Nancy Roberts,
Dorothy Day and the Catholic Worker (1984); and two books by William D.
Miller, *Dorothy Day: A Biography* (1982), and *A Harsh and Dreadful Love:
Dorothy Day and the Catholic Worker Movement* (1973). Leading Protestant
ministers are discussed in Richard W. Fox, *Reinhold Niebuhr* (1986); and Arthur
Gordon, *Norman Vincent Peale: Minister to Millions* (1963).

Andrew Bergman, *We're in the Money: Depression America and Its Films* (1971), is a
monograph concentrating specifically on the 1930s. More general studies include
Leo Rosten, *Hollywood: The Movie Colony and the Movie Makers* (1941);
Gilbert Seldes, *The Movies Come from America* (1937); Edward Wagenknecht,
The Movies in the Age of Innocence (1962); and Arthur Knight, *The Liveliest
Art: A Panoramic History of the Movies* (1957). The memoirs of two participants
are important: Will H. Hays, *The Memoirs of Will H. Hays* (1955); and Donald
Hayne, ed., *The Autobiography of Cecil B. DeMille* (1959). George Eells and
Stanley Musgrove, *Mae West* (1984), is the story of one of the biggest stars of the
era.

Among the studies of popular culture that include radio programs are Norman F.
Cantor and M. S. Worthham, eds., *The History of Popular Culture* (1968); and
Melvin Patrick Ely, *The Adventures of Amos 'n' Andy: A Social History of an
American Phenomenon* (1991). Orson Welles's famous broadcast that incited
panic is described in Hadley Cantril, *The Invasion from Mars: A Study in the
Psychology of Panic* (1940). Books covering music in the 1930s include Paul

Henry Lang, *One Hundred Years of American Music* (1961); Neil Leonard, *Jazz and the White Americans* (1962); Sigmund Spaeth, *A History of Popular Music in America* (1948); Barry Ulanov, *A History of Jazz* (1952); Cecil Smith, *Musical Comedy in America* (1950); Alec Wilder, *American Popular Song: The Great Innovators, 1900–1950* (1972); and Jay Gold, ed., *The Swing Era,* 3 vols. (1970).

CHAPTER THIRTEEN

THE ROAD TO WAR

✣ WORLD TRANSFORMATION

Technology urbanized the community of nations, binding them as neighbors. But the new proximity facilitated tension and was made ominous by the transformation of military technology. Prepared technologically for global war, the world was not conditioned to prevent it, for diplomacy worked traditionally and slowly, the reactionary aspect of the international tension with transformation. Having entered the twentieth century with faith in progress, the world seemed on the precipice of a new dark age by 1939.

✣ ROOSEVELT'S DIPLOMATIC BACKGROUND

Franklin D. Roosevelt was a relatively cosmopolitan president, at least superficially. His family had traveled and lived abroad; he had been tutored in German and French by European governesses and had studied European history at Groton and Harvard; and between 1900 and 1912 he toured Europe three times and the Caribbean twice. Still, he came to the White House with few general principles to guide his foreign policy. He would improvise as the situation dictated, learning through trial and error. He made no speeches on foreign affairs in the 1932 campaign and, upon taking office, reduced appropriations for the small, underequipped army and used the money for domestic

priorities. He paid little attention to international events until they commanded his attention and ultimately dwarfed domestic priorities. A nationalist in
placing American interests first, he was an internationalist in realizing that the
fate of the United States was tied to that of other nations.

✣ THE GOOD NEIGHBOR POLICY AND SOVIET RECOGNITION

In his first inaugural address, devoted primarily to the domestic crisis,
Roosevelt said, "In the field of world policy, I would dedicate this nation to
the policy of the good neighbor." Reporters isolated the phrase "good neighbor" and applied it to Roosevelt's policy of nonintervention in the Western
Hemisphere, although the phrase and the policy of restraint had originated
with Hoover. Roosevelt went further than Hoover, however. Eight months
after his inauguration he specifically renounced intervention, then translated it
into policy.

In 1934 Roosevelt negotiated a treaty abrogating the Platt Amendment,
which had asserted that the United States had the right to intervene militarily
in Cuba, and before the end of the year, the withdrawal of American troops
from Haiti, begun by Hoover, was complete. Two years later the United
States concluded a treaty with Panama, relinquishing the unilateral right to
intervene in that republic and promising to share defense of the Panama Canal
with Panama.

The United States also loosened the reins on its major colony, the
Philippines. In 1934 FDR signed into law the Tydings-McDuffie Act, providing for independence in 1946; in the interim the Philippines would have
dominion status and would be gradually given self-rule. The measure gratified
American sugar and tobacco farmers who competed with duty-free Philippine
agricultural products that would now be subject to tariffs. More important,
Roosevelt was among the first Western leaders to recognize that the period of
colonialism was ending, and the United States was the first Western nation to
relinquish voluntarily a colony. The objective of Roosevelt's policies toward
Latin America and the Philippines was to give America a clear anticolonial
record in contrast to the dictatorships of Europe. Also, the policies welded the
hemisphere into an alliance against external threats. Roosevelt solidified the
alliance with the Declaration of Lima (1938), which bound all nations in the
hemisphere to act together to defend the hemisphere, and the Act of Havana
(1940), which stated that an act of aggression against any of them would be
considered an attack on all. During World War II every hemispheric nation
except Argentina cooperated completely with the Allies.

FDR neither rebuilt the economies nor reformed the politics of the Latin
American republics, yet he proved more tolerant of their independence than
previous presidents. This approach became apparent when Mexico nationalized foreign property, including oil, in 1938, and Roosevelt accepted compensation to owners on terms favorable to Mexico.

In another departure from the policies of his predecessors, Roosevelt, hoping that closer relations with the Soviet Union would stimulate trade, extended diplomatic recognition to that nation in November 1933. In return, the Soviets agreed to cease efforts to overthrow the American government and to permit the free practice of religion to Americans in the Soviet Union. Neither promise was kept, and little trade developed, but recognition facilitated the collaboration of the two nations against Adolf Hitler.

✧ THE RISE OF HITLER AND DESTRUCTION OF THE EUROPEAN ORDER

The Great Depression and the stigma of defeat in World War I facilitated Hitler's rise to power in a Germany starved for economic order and thirsty for revenge. A charismatic speaker with the determination of a zealot, Hitler believed in the power of will as opposed to reason, in the use of force instead of restraint, and he considered war the supreme test of a race. For him, racial struggle was the dominant force in history, and the fate of the race took precedence over the rights of the individual. Hitler defined Germans, or Aryans, as a superior race whose destiny was to rule the world. Germany must fight to expand its Lebensraum, or living space, enslaving the inferior peoples of eastern Europe and the Soviet Union and creating a superior race by eradicating Christianity and communism and by liquidating the old, the ill, and the entire Jewish people. Paranoid about Jewish influence, Hitler said, "The heaviest blow ever struck humanity was the coming of Christianity. Bolshevism is Christianity's illegitimate child. Both are the inventions of the Jews."

Hitler considered Americans a mongrel race incapable of thwarting him, and he detested the Roosevelts. He said, "All half-caste families—even if they have but a minute quantity of Jewish blood in their veins—produce regularly, generation by generation, at least one pure Jew. Roosevelt affords the best possible proof of the truth of this opinion." He added, "The completely negroid appearance of his wife is also a clear indication that she, too, is a half-caste."

Facing no significant opposition from the Americans, British, or French, within six years of coming to power Hitler had overturned the European order. The United States was preoccupied with the depression, Britain struggled to hold its empire, and France put its hopes for defense against a resurgent Germany in the Maginot Line, a series of concrete pillboxes and artillery emplacements near the German border. Designed to fight a war of limited maneuver, the line gave the French a false sense of security.

Hitler led Germany out of the League of Nations in 1933, began rearmament in 1934, and introduced conscription in 1935, in defiance of the Versailles Treaty. In March 1936, the German army marched into the Rhineland, a demilitarized zone, in further defiance of the treaty. Had France resisted, the German generals, who were not prepared to fight, had sealed orders to withdraw. France did not resist. Then in October, Hitler signed an alliance with Italian dictator Benito Mussolini. Mussolini described the future of Europe as centered in a Rome-Berlin axis, giving the name Axis powers to the new allies.

The fascist Mussolini had seized power in 1922, pledging to prevent communist expansion and to restore Italy to the greatness of the Roman Empire. Believing a great power must have colonies, and hoping to restore Italian pride by conquest, he attacked Ethiopia in 1935. Emperor Haile Selassie appealed to the League of Nations to save his country. The League took no military action and implemented economic sanctions but did not embargo coal or oil, the things Italy most needed.

✧ THE AMERICAN RESPONSE

The determination of the American people never again to become involved in a foreign war tempered Washington's response to German and Italian aggression. Many Americans, who pointed to a long history of isolation from European affairs, had concluded that participation in World War I was a mistake that should not be repeated. America was invulnerable to invasion because of two great moats, the Atlantic and the Pacific, and had no stake in the outcome of European quarrels, they argued. The argument made sense in the nineteenth century, although technology had since transformed warfare. The Atlantic and the Pacific were no longer moats; they were highways. If Lindbergh's single-engine plane had flown the Atlantic, it was feasible for enemy bombers to fly it. However, as in domestic policy and culture, every technological advance stimulated a conservative reaction. The reaction to the technology of modern weaponry was a further retreat into the cocoon of isolation.

Isolationists dominated the midwestern and western heartland and were numerous among liberals, conservatives, and reactionaries. Most isolationists in Congress were to the left of Roosevelt, among them the Republicans William E. Borah of Idaho, Gerald P. Nye of North Dakota, and Arthur H. Vandenberg of Michigan; Progressives George W. Norris of Nebraska and Robert M. La Follette of Wisconsin; and the Democrat Burton K. Wheeler of Montana. Outside of Congress, the broad isolationist stream had a channel of far right fringe groups led by such demagogues as Father Charles E. Coughlin, Gerald Smith, and Elizabeth Dilling. They imagined a conspiracy among Jews, who wanted Gentiles to slaughter themselves in a war; the British, who wanted Americans to fight to preserve their empire; and the communists, who wanted to rule the world. To these reactionaries, communism, not fascism, was the chief threat.

In 1934 the isolationist Senator Hiram Johnson introduced a bill to prohibit loans to any foreign government in default to the United States. Enacted as the Johnson Act, it applied to most of Europe. At about the same time a Senate committee chaired by Nye, whose state constituency included no defense industry, launched an investigation into the role of armament makers in involving the United States in World War I. The committee, whose hearings continued until 1936, implied that the country had gone to war because of a domestic conspiracy. Strength was added to the conspiracy argument by books about the armaments industry, including *Merchants of Death* by Helmuth C. Englebrecht and *Iron, Blood and Profits* by George Seldes, and a *Fortune* article, "Arms and the Men." The isolationist impulse crested in January 1935 when Congress, intimidated by a coalition including Huey Long, Father Coughlin, and William Randolph Hearst, defeated American membership on the World Court.

FDR wanted to respond to Mussolini's attack on Ethiopia by placing an embargo on arms shipments to Italy. The president hoped Congress would authorize him to distinguish aggressors from victims in implementing such embargoes. Instead, Congress substituted a blanket embargo against all belligerents. Roosevelt, who feared the defeat of bills essential to the Second New Deal if he put up a fight, reluctantly approved the mandatory embargo, contained in the Neutrality Act of 1935. The isolationist theory was that if the United States sold no arms to belligerents, it would avoid involvement in war, but in practice the law favored the well-armed Italians over the poorly armed Ethiopians. Only weapons were covered by the embargo, and the United States continued to sell oil to Italy.

European events hurtled out of control in 1936, this time in Spain. In July, General Francisco Franco, backed by most of the Spanish army, led a revolt against the republican, or Loyalist, government in Madrid. Many Americans supported the Loyalists, and some 4,000 fought for them in a voluntary brigade. Most Catholics, though, sympathized with Franco because the republic had persecuted Catholics. The Soviet Union supported the republic, but Germany and Italy favored Franco: by 1939 almost 40 percent of Franco's troops and almost all of his arms came from the Axis powers. The war would last three years, cause more than 1 million deaths, and end with Franco's victory.

Roosevelt's priority was to prevent the spread of war, not to preserve Spanish democracy. In keeping with that priority, Congress passed in January 1937 a joint resolution applying the Neutrality Act of 1935 to civil wars such as the one in Spain. And on May 1, the day the 1935 law was set to expire, Roosevelt signed the Neutrality Act of 1937, which would last two years. The new act gave the president the discretion to certify whether a state of war existed; if he did, an arms embargo would be implemented against both sides. Commodities other than arms could be sold to belligerents only on a cash-and-carry basis.

❖ AGGRESSION AND APPEASEMENT

In March 1938, German troops marched into Austria and Hitler proclaimed the Anschluss, the union of Austria and Germany, claiming it was the will of the Austrian people. Britain and France issued mild protests, and the United States did nothing, although the Versailles Treaty specifically prohibited the Anschluss. Hitler next began making demands upon Czechoslovakia, claiming that the Sudetenland, a part of Czechoslovakia with a large German population, should be annexed to Germany. Each time the Czechs yielded to a German demand, Hitler upped the ante.

With war appearing imminent, Hitler, Mussolini, British Prime Minister Neville Chamberlain, and French Premier Edouard Daladier met at Munich to seek a compromise; Czechoslovakia, whose fate was being discussed, was not invited. The British and French decided to appease Hitler by giving him the Sudetenland. Hitler declared, "This is the last territorial demand I have to make in Europe," and Chamberlain returned to England to announce that he had achieved "peace with honor . . . peace in our time." Chamberlain's chief political opponent in Britain, Winston Churchill, dissented. "Do not suppose that this is the end," he warned. "This is only the beginning of the reckoning."

If Hitler's ambition had been limited to rectifying injustices, appeasement might have worked at the expense of Germany's immediate neighbors. But Hitler had an insatiable appetite for territory, and by refusing to commit themselves to containing him at an early date, the other European nations and the United States made his expansionist dreams feasible. Britain, France, the Soviet Union, and the United States each looked for someone else to do the job. Each feared to oppose him alone, yet they were unwilling to work together. Such trepidation increased Hitler's confidence and invited his contempt of his potential adversaries. His strategy of dividing and conquering worked initially because his adversaries distrusted each other as much as they feared him.

Even more sinister were Hitler's plans for the Jewish people. There were only 500,000 Jews among his country's 85 million inhabitants, yet Hitler made them scapegoats for defeat in World War I, the depression, and all other German ills. The repression began with the Nuremberg Laws of 1935, which severely limited their activities. Then in November 1938, after a young Polish Jew assassinated a minor German official in Paris, the Nazi government precipitated the Kristallnacht, or Night of Broken Glass, when German soldiers and civilians beat Jews, arrested them, destroyed their businesses, burned their synagogues, and compelled them to pay not only for the damage to their own property but a huge fine to the state. New regulations barred Jews from engaging in retail trade, attending college, using public libraries, or driving cars. Most ominous, some 25,000 Jews were sent to concentration camps.

Jews attempting to flee Germany, sadly, could find no nation to take them. The United States refused to relax immigration laws, and Congress failed to pass a bill to allow 20,000 Jewish children to be admitted outside quotas. A refugee ship carrying 930 Jews from Hamburg to Cuba, the *St. Louis,* was not permitted to land. The refugees, many of whom were on waiting lists to emigrate to the United States, pleaded with American authorities to admit them. After being refused, they returned to Europe, where many perished.

Hitler's intent to dominate all of Europe became clear when, on March 15, 1939, German troops invaded the remainder of Czechoslovakia. Hitler planned to conquer Poland next, a move that necessitated neutralizing the

Soviet Union. Joseph Stalin, eager for a slice of Poland, distrusting the British and French, and naïvely trusting Hitler, obliged by negotiating a neutrality treaty with Germany that made World War II inevitable. Even as he completed the treaty, Hitler planned to turn on the Soviets once he had defeated his enemies in the West. Announcement of the treaty, signed August 23, shocked the world because the fascists and communists were inveterate enemies; since 1935 the Soviet Union had maintained that all democratic nations should cooperate to contain fascism.

Hitler next began a familiar scenario, making demands on Poland, then escalating them beyond Poland's ability to respond. Britain, finally recognizing the futility of appeasement, declared that it would defend Poland. On September 1, Hitler invaded Poland, and two days later Britain and France declared war on Germany.

Stalin emulated Hitler by seizing the eastern half of Poland, annexing the Baltic republics of Estonia, Latvia, and Lithuania, and insisting on territorial concessions from neighboring Finland. When the Finns refused, he invaded Finland. The huge Red Army, embarrassed by the stiff resistance mounted by the Finn army, suffered heavy casualties before overwhelming Finland, which received only sympathy and token aid from Washington. Albania, attacked by Mussolini in April 1939, was also now under Axis control. At Roosevelt's urging, Congress repealed the arms embargo in November and enacted the Neutrality Act of 1939. The Allies could purchase arms and civilian goods from the United States only on a cash-and-carry basis. In addition, the president was authorized to designate combat zones into which American ships could not sail.

Hitler quickly conquered Poland with the tactics of a Blitzkrieg, or Lightning War, characterized by rapid penetration with tanks, planes, and personnel carriers. Having subdued Poland, he did not pursue conquests in the winter of 1939–1940. Military experts predicted that this war would become a war of stationary fronts and limited maneuver much like World War I. They labeled the inactivity the Sitzkrieg, or Phony War.

In April 1940, Hitler burst out of his defensive positions to conquer Norway and Denmark, and in May he conquered Belgium, the Netherlands, and Luxembourg. Then, outflanking the Maginot Line to the north, he invaded France. The Blitzkrieg pinned the British and French armies against the sea; more than 300,000 troops were saved by a heroic evacuation at Dunkirk, yet they lost all their equipment. Less than ten days after the invasion, German troops entered Paris, and on June 22 the humiliated French signed a surrender in the same railway car in the forest of Compiègne in which Germany had surrendered in 1918. General Henri Petain established a collaborationist government in Vichy for the unoccupied southern part of France.

Only Britain, which no longer had an army on the continent, remained unconquered, and only the English Channel stood between Germany and Britain. The British fleet still controlled the North Sea, deterring a cross-channel invasion. Hitler hoped that an invasion would not be necessary, that perhaps his Luftwaffe could bomb Britain into submission. Just the opposite happened: the much smaller Royal Air Force, with the aid of radar and the incentive of self-preservation, won the Battle of Britain. A frustrated Hitler shifted his attacks from air bases to cities and the bombing of civilian populations; rather than breaking the British, his actions stiffened their will. Britain retaliated by bombing Berlin. Henceforth civilian populations on both sides would be targeted; the conflict became a total war.

✛ THE ELECTION OF 1940

For Americans, Hitler's aggression made the issues more clear-cut than they had been in World War I. A Gallup poll indicated that 82 percent of them wanted the Allies, Britain and France, to win; just 2 percent favored Germany. If Britain fell, Americans asked, would the United States be next? Some isolationists still considered the nation immune from attack; FDR was not so sure. Moreover, what would be the quality of life for Americans in a world dominated by tyrants? Doing business with the Nazis, who viewed trade as a weapon, not merely a method of exchange, seemed unlikely. And even if Germany did not attack America, the United States would have to become an armed camp indefinitely to deter aggression. It was a grim prospect.

While France collapsed and Britain struggled to survive, the United States held a presidential election. The great riddle of 1940 was whether Roosevelt would decide to break the two-term tradition established by George Washington. For months he vacillated, refusing to campaign for the nomination yet not encouraging anyone else to campaign. A few weeks before the Democratic convention in Chicago, though, he decided that the Axis threat justified his seeking another term, a decision that drove away some of his close advisers, including James A. Farley and John Nance Garner. To overcome tradition, FDR felt he must appear to be drafted, so he publicly disavowed ambitions for a third term and secretly planned a demonstration for himself that would appear spontaneous. In addition, he stole the thunder of the GOP by appointing two eminent Republicans to his cabinet shortly before the Republican convention in Philadelphia: Henry L. Stimson as secretary of war and Frank Knox as secretary of the navy.

The leading candidates for the Republican presidential nomination were Minnesota Governor Harold Stassen, Ohio Senator Robert Taft, and Michigan Senator Arthur Vandenberg. The front-runner, New York County District Attorney Thomas E. Dewey, made a strong showing in the primaries. But the Republicans rejected their established leaders and turned to an eleventh-hour entrant, Wendell Willkie, a business executive who had never run for office. Willkie won the nomination on the sixth ballot, and the delegates selected isolationist Oregon Senator Charles McNary, best known as cosponsor of the McNary-Haugen farm bill, as his running mate. Despite Willkie's political inexperience, he was the strongest candidate the

Republicans could have nominated. President of a major utilities company, he was a husky, handsome man, an eloquent debater with a winsome personality. He was an internationalist and a supporter of many New Deal reforms, although he became an articulate opponent of the New Deal when his company was overwhelmed by the TVA.

Roosevelt—easily eclipsing the other Democrats put into nomination, Farley, Garner, and Millard Tydings of Maryland—was nominated on the first ballot. A bitter dispute erupted over Roosevelt's running mate, Henry Wallace, a faithful liberal who appealed to farmers. Wallace was anathema to conservatives, and many considered him unstable, but he was the president's choice and FDR prevailed. Wallace remained controversial throughout the campaign. When the Republicans obtained a letter revealing that Wallace had set corn prices upon advice from a spiritualist, even Roosevelt considered dumping him. However, the Democrats received information about Willkie's affair with Irita Van Doren, book editor of the *New York Herald Tribune.* A deal was cut, and the letter and the affair remained secret.

Willkie initially concentrated on attacking the New Deal for inefficiency and on charging that Roosevelt had an insatiable appetite for power. FDR, doing little campaigning, focused on the foreign crisis, which prompted him to take two controversial steps in September. First, he responded to a request from Churchill, Chamberlain's successor as prime minister, for 50 World War I destroyers for use against Hitler's submarines in the battle of the Atlantic. Roosevelt signed an executive agreement sending the destroyers in exchange for 99-year leases on naval and air bases on British territory in the Western Hemisphere. Second, FDR signed a conscription bill that had been introduced in the Senate without administration backing. The Burke-Wadsworth Selective Service Act, the first peacetime conscription act in American history, provided for the creation of an army of no more than 900,000 to be trained for a year.

Willkie supported the destroyer deal and the draft. Yet late in the campaign, finding himself far behind in the polls, he began to charge that FDR was a warmonger. Defensively, Roosevelt said, "I have said this before, but I shall say it again and again and again. Your boys are not going to be sent into any foreign wars." Willkie, who rose in the polls with the accusations, responded that if Roosevelt's promise "to keep our boys out of foreign wars is no better than his promise to balance the budget, they're almost on the transports!"

But every time a new danger appeared in Europe or Asia, the incumbent rose in the polls. Indeed, without the threat of Hitler, it is doubtful that Roosevelt would have won a third term. Roosevelt garnered 27 million popular votes and 449 electoral votes to 22 million and 82 for Willkie—the smallest plurality of any successful presidential candidate since 1916. No third party candidate made a significant impact; the Socialist Norman Thomas polled just more than 100,000 votes and the Communist Earl Browder about 40,000. Temporarily allied with Hitler, the Communists, who had supported FDR in 1936, condemned Roosevelt as an imperialist.

✣ THE ISOLATIONIST OPPOSITION TO ROOSEVELT

Isolationists mounted substantial, if unsuccessful, opposition to FDR's reelection. In May, with administration encouragement, internationalists had created the Committee to Defend America by Aiding the Allies, and a smaller, more militant group, Fight for Freedom, Incorporated, was organized a few months later. The isolationist organizations were more formidable and better financed, however. In July midwestern businessmen created the America First Committee, supported by prominent Americans such as Charles A. Lindbergh, Henry Ford, William Randolph Hearst, and Robert McCormick. Boasting 850,000 members at its peak—about two-thirds of them living within 300 miles of Chicago—America First was not pacifist, although it occasionally cooperated with pacifists. Rather, it argued that America weakened its defenses by shipping weapons to Britain that were needed by the United States armed forces.

Lindbergh was the most effective critic of Roosevelt's foreign policies. The famous aviator had left America disillusioned with his homeland, then returned in 1939 to became the most influential isolationist. Lindbergh had traveled to Germany five times, mostly to inspect the Luftwaffe, and was impressed by German might. Foolishly, he accepted the Service Cross of the German Eagle, a high civilian medal, given by the government for his service to aviation. He kept it so he would not offend the Germans.

Lindbergh condemned aid to Britain, arguing that America was wasting resources because the British faced certain defeat by Germany. Also, he denounced three groups for leading the United States into war. These groups, "responsible for changing our national policy from one of neutrality and independence to one of entanglement in European affairs . . . are the British, the Jewish and the Roosevelt administration." In particular, Jews posed a threat to the United States, Lindbergh claimed, because they dominated the radio, the press, and the motion picture industry.

America First was embarrassed by the anti-Semitic overtones of Lindbergh and its extremist allies, including some German Americans and groups that implicitly sympathized with Hitler. The numbers of such extremists were larger than the transparent perfidy of their views might suggest. Strategically allying themselves with respectable isolationists and pacifists, they roiled the atmosphere, limiting the president's ability to thwart aggression.

✣ THE AMERICAN RESPONSE TO BRITAIN'S PERIL

The British, who were rapidly depleting their financial resources by purchasing weapons and food abroad, faced a crisis. To avert it, Roosevelt introduced the Lend-Lease Bill in January 1941, which would allow Britain to purchase arms on credit or to borrow them for the duration of the war. Roosevelt used a homely analogy to illustrate his objective. If the home of one's neighbor caught fire, he said, one would not try to sell his neighbor a hose, but one would loan it to him and get it back after the fire was out.

Lend-Lease outraged isolationists. Dilling brought 600 mothers to Washington to picket and was arrested twice for trespassing. Robert Taft quipped: "Lending war equipment is a good deal like lending chewing gum. You don't want it back." More viciously, Wheeler denounced Lend-Lease as the "New Deal's triple-A foreign policy," which would "plow under every fourth American boy." FDR replied angrily, "That is really the rottenest thing that has ever been said in public life in my generation." To isolationist charges that the bill would inspire Germany to attack the United States, Roosevelt responded: "Such aid is not an act of war. When the dictators are ready to make war on us, they will not wait for an act of war on our part. They did not wait for Norway or Belgium or the Netherlands to commit an act of war." After strenuous debate, the bill passed, and the president signed it in March.

What the British needed more desperately than supplies was an ally. In the summer of 1941 they got one—from an unexpected quarter. On June 22, Hitler sent a wave of troops into the Soviet Union, forcing Stalin into alliance with the Allies. Some Americans on the far right, such as Dilling, Smith, and Coughlin, preferred a German to a Soviet victory. Others hoped the two great armies would grind down one another. Senator Harry Truman said, "If we see that Germany is winning, we ought to help Russia, and if Russia is winning, we ought to help Germany." Churchill, however, considered the Soviets valuable allies. "If Hitler invaded Hell," he said, "I would at least make a favorable reference to the Devil in the House of Commons." American Communists, once Hitler's opponents, then his allies, became his foes again.

With the war expanding, the army feared that it would have to release one-year draftees just as the world crisis peaked. The administration wanted to extend the term of enlistment for the duration, although the Senate substituted a bill providing for an 18-month extension, which passed easily. The House approved the extension by the vote of 203–202, testimony to the continued strength of isolationism.

On August 9, Roosevelt met secretly with Churchill off the coast of Argentia, Newfoundland. Their chief objective, the formulation of war aims, was manifested in the Atlantic Charter, calling for the right of people to live under a government of their choice and access to raw materials by all the world's peoples. The meeting was the beginning of a warm friendship between Roosevelt and Churchill. "It is fun to be in the same decade with you," the president cabled the prime minister.

By fall, the United States, which had begun convoys to Britain, was fighting an undeclared war in the Atlantic. On September 4, the destroyer *Greer* exchanged shots with a German submarine it had been stalking. Roosevelt branded the incident as an unprovoked German attack. On October 16, eleven crewmen perished when a German torpedo struck the destroyer *Kearny,* and two weeks later 115 sailors went down with the destroyer *Reuben James,* the first American warship sunk by a German submarine. Congress responded by passing legislation authorizing the arming of merchantmen.

⊹ THE COMING OF THE WAR IN ASIA

War did not come in the Atlantic, where everyone expected it, but in the Pacific, from Japan, which seized a Far East empire while Americans were preoccupied with Hitler. Positively packed, with one of the highest population densities in the world, Japan lacked resources and sought to expand to become a great power. There were no strong neighbors in the Pacific and only one potential competitor, the United States. Japanese prosperity, however, depended on America for 90 percent of its scrap iron, steel, copper, and aviation gasoline.

In 1937 the war in China expanded beyond Manchuria. Japan seized the major cities of China, Chiang Kai-shek retreated to the interior, and communists waged a guerrilla war against the invaders. Roosevelt did not proclaim a state of war, using the pretense that Japan had not declared war, and American arms flowed to China. With his mind on the conflict there, the president delivered his first major speech on foreign policy on October 5. "War must be quarantined like an epidemic disease," he said, yet he offered no specific proposals, and public opinion did not demand any.

On December 12, Japanese planes sank the American gunboat *Panay* on the Yangtze River, killing 3 people and wounding 74. Isolationists questioned the stationing of a warship in such dangerous waters, and there were few demands for punitive measures against Japan. After Japan apologized and paid an indemnity, the incident was dropped. Within 24 hours of the sinking, a constitutional amendment requiring a national referendum before the United States could go to war (unless attacked) was brought to the House floor, where it was defeated 209–188.

Encouraged by the dazzling German victories in 1940, the Japanese discussed plans for an empire that included China, French Indochina, Thailand, British Malaya, British Borneo, the Dutch East Indies, Burma, Australia, New Zealand, and possibly India and the Philippines. In September, the same month the Japanese cabinet considered these schemes, Japan occupied northern Indochina and signed the Tripartite Pact, an alliance with Germany and Italy. The United States responded by placing embargoes on aviation gasoline, lubricating oil, and scrap metal. The next spring Japan signed a nonaggression treaty with the Soviet Union; Stalin freed Japan to attack the United States just as he had freed Germany to attack Poland. Then in July, Japan moved into southern Indochina despite warnings from Washington, which froze Japanese assets in the United States. Further, Roosevelt closed the Panama Canal to Japanese shipping and called General Douglas MacArthur from retirement to command American forces in the Far East, and the State Department placed an embargo on oil, Japan's most important need.

The embargo created a crisis in Japan, and in August, Premier Fumimaro Konoye proposed a summit in the Pacific to settle differences. Roosevelt, stalling for time while he dealt with more pressing matters in the Atlantic, thought a conference would bring a showdown too quickly. He also believed that without prior agreements, the Japanese would blame a failed conference on him and use it as a pretext to charge that the United States was unreason-able and as a means for unifying their people for war. Therefore, he refused to meet Konoye, whose cabinet fell October 18. Konoye was succeeded by the militarist war minister, General Hideki Tojo.

Throughout the fall Japanese Ambassador Kichisaburo Nomura conduct-ed intensive negotiations with Secretary of State Cordell Hull. China was the ultimate stumbling block. The United States demanded that Japan withdraw, and Japan demanded that the United States cease sending arms to China. Neither would budge.

Japan had a brief window of opportunity for an attack upon the United States: it had no more than a six-month supply of oil and, by 1942, would lose its naval superiority to the American construction program. Weather condi-tions led the supreme command to favor an attack by December at the latest. After that, the weather would not be favorable until spring, and the oil short-age would be critical. The Japanese objective was an American base 3,900 miles from their home islands: Pearl Harbor.

Japanese contemplation of an attack on a nation so much larger, with more natural resources, seems mad. But realizing that they would lose a pro-tracted war, the Japanese planned a knockout blow against the American Pacific Fleet, believing that the United States would need to concentrate its remaining resources against Hitler and thus concede the Pacific to Tokyo. So on November 25, 1941, a task force including six aircraft carriers, two battle-ships, and nine destroyers started for Hawaii. To minimize the chance of meeting foreign vessels on the way, the Japanese selected a route far to the north of the usual shipping channels.

Since late in 1940 American cryptanalysts had been able to read the most secure Japanese diplomatic codes, called Magic. On November 22, they decoded a message to Nomura and his associate, Saburo Kurusu, ordering them to seek a compromise by November 29, because afterward "things are automatically going to happen." And on November 26, navy experts decoded a long message that seemed to indicate that an attack was being planned. Among the mass of secret messages intercepted were some that pointed toward Pearl Harbor, yet many others seemed to indicate an attack on the Philippines or Singapore. Rumors abounded, including one that a dog on an Oahu beach was "barking in Morse code to [a] Japanese sub offshore."

On December 6, Roosevelt wrote a personal message to Emperor Hirohito, urging him to withdraw from Indochina, but the message, intercept-ed by the Japanese war cabinet, never reached the emperor. That evening, Roosevelt read the final message from the Japanese cabinet to its negotiators in Washington and commented, "This means war." Although Roosevelt expect-ed war, he did not instigate it, as conspiracy theorists argued later. The last thing he wanted to do was to begin a war with a massive American defeat. He did not tempt the Japanese to attack Pearl Harbor; in fact, he did not believe that they were capable of attacking, and he was not prone to jeopardize the navy and its ships, which he loved. If there was no conspiracy in Washington to provoke war, there was nevertheless plenty of incompetence. The Pearl

Harbor commander responded to a warning from the War Department by alerting his troops for sabotage, not for attack. Planes were parked wingtip-to-wingtip so they could be guarded from saboteurs; it would have taken four hours to scramble them. Antiaircraft ammunition was stowed and locked. No patrols were operating to the north of Oahu. Radar was in use only on an experimental basis. An operator of a portable station reported a mass of blips on his screen—airplanes coming in from the north; headquarters dismissed it as an aberration. A civilian aviator reported hundreds of planes; the report was considered a joke.

At daybreak the first wave of dive bombers and torpedo planes roared in, followed by the second an hour later. By ten o'clock battleship row was a smoldering ruin, the Japanese having sunk or damaged 8 battleships, 3 light cruisers, and 188 planes. The United States suffered 3,345 casualties, the Japanese less than 100.

The defeat was not so massive as it seemed at the time. The battleship, the ultimate weapon in World War I, had been made obsolete by air power, and America's three carriers were safely in port or at sea. In the long run, it would have been more effective for Japan to attack the harbor facilities, which would

The Japanese attack on Pearl Harbor, which destroyed the USS *Arizona* and much of the Pacific fleet, brought the United States into World War II. No other event could have so united the American people.

have required the recall of the fleet to California, instead of the ships. The Japanese had actually committed a kamikaze attack on a national scale by starting a war they could not win. They had done the one thing that could quiet the isolationists and unite Americans for war. Admiral Isoruku Yamamoto, the planner of the attack, said soberly, "I fear we have awakened a slumbering giant."

The next day Roosevelt appeared before Congress and requested a declaration of war. The Senate vote was unanimous; in the House, only one vote was cast against war, that of Montana Representative Jeannette Rankin, who had also voted against the declaration of war in 1917.

On December 11, Germany and Italy declared war on the United States, and the next day the United States reciprocated, with no dissent in Congress. Hitler, who was not obligated to fight America because he was not consulted about the attack on Pearl Harbor, thought victory was certain. Had he been a wise man, he would have declared war on Japan rather than on the United States, placing Americans in a ticklish position.

Twenty-three years and 26 days after the armistice of 1918, America was at war again, this time in a war that would transform the United States and the world more than any previous human experience. America's rendezvous with destiny had arrived.

BIBLIOGRAPHICAL ESSAY

On Roosevelt's role in diplomacy, see Robert A. Divine, *Roosevelt and World War War II* (1971); Robert Dallek, *Franklin D. Roosevelt and American Foreign Policy, 1932–1945* (1979); Basil Rauch, *Roosevelt: From Munich to Pearl Harbor* (1975); and Warren F. Kimball, *Franklin D. Roosevelt and the World Crisis, 1937–1945* (1974). See also Lloyd C. Gardner, *Economic Aspects of New Deal Diplomacy* (1964); and Julius Pratt, *Cordell Hull* (1964).

On relations with the Soviet Union, see Raymond H. Dawson, *The Decision to Aid Russia, 1941: Foreign Policy and Domestic Politics* (1959); and two books by Edward M. Bennett, *Franklin D. Roosevelt and the Search for Security: American-Soviet Relations, 1933–1939* (1985), and *Franklin D. Roosevelt and the Search for Security: American-Soviet Relations, 1939–1945* (1984).

Roosevelt's Latin American policy is covered in Bryce Wood, *The Making of the Good Neighbor Policy* (1961). The coming of the war in Europe is described in James A. Leutze, *Bargaining for Supremacy: Anglo-American Naval Collaboration, 1937–1941* (1977); Arnold Offner, *American Appeasement: United States Foreign Policy and Germany, 1933–1938* (1969); two books by Robert A. Divine, *The Illusion of Neutrality* (1962), and *The Reluctant Belligerent* (1965); T. R. Fehrenbach, *F.D.R.'s Undeclared War* (1967); and Samuel Eliot Morison, *The Battle of the Atlantic, September 1939–May 1943* (1947).

The two best books on isolationism and the coming of the war are by Wayne S. Cole, *Roosevelt and the Isolationists, 1932–1945* (1983), and *America First: The Battle Against Intervention, 1940–1941* (1953). Highly detailed accounts of all aspects of the coming of the war are available in two books by William L. Langer and S.

Everett Gleason, *The Challenge to Isolation, 1937–1940* (1952), and *The Undeclared War, 1940–1941* (1953). On isolationism, see Manfred Jonas, *Isolationism in America, 1935–1941* (1966); John E. Wiltz, *From Isolation to War, 1931–1941* (1968); Selig Adler, *The Isolationist Impulse* (1959); and Walter Johnson, *The Battle Against Isolationism* (1973). On other efforts to maintain peace, see John K. Nelson, *The Peace Prophets: American Pacifist Thought, 1919–1941* (1967); and Ernest C. Bolt, Jr., *Ballots Before Bullets: The War Referendum Approach to Peace in America, 1914–1941* (1977).

For American attempts to aid the Allies, see Warren F. Kimball, *The Most Unsordid Act: Lend-Lease, 1939–1941* (1969); David Reynolds, *The Creation of the Anglo-American Alliance, 1937–1941: A Study in Competitive Cooperation* (1981); and Waldo Heinrichs, *Threshold of War: Franklin D. Roosevelt and American Entry into World War II* (1988).

On the coming of the war in Asia, see Akira Iriye, *The Origins of the Second World War in Asia and the Pacific* (1987); David J. Lu, *From Marco Polo Bridge to Pearl Harbor: Japan's Entry into World War II* (1961); Samuel Eliot Morison, *The Rising Sun in the Pacific: 1931–April 1942* (1948); Herbert Feis, *The Road to Pearl Harbor* (1964); John Toland, *The Rising Sun: The Decline and Fall of the Japanese Empire, 1936–1945* (1970); Robert J. Butow, *Tojo and the Coming of the War* (1961); Richard Dean Burns and Edward M. Bennett, eds., *Diplomats in Crisis: United States–Chinese–Japanese Relations, 1919–1941* (1974).

The attack on Pearl Harbor is the subject of many books. The best is Gordon W. Prange, *At Dawn We Slept: The Untold Story of Pearl Harbor* (1981). John Toland, *Infamy* (1972), blames Roosevelt for complicity in the attack, as do earlier works such as Charles A. Beard, *President Roosevelt and the Coming of the War, 1941* (1948); and Charles C. Tansill, *Back Door to War: The Roosevelt Foreign Policy, 1933–1941* (1952). Walter Lord, *Day of Infamy* (1957), is a popular account. Books offering varying views of the attack include George M. Waller, ed., *Pearl Harbor: Roosevelt and the Coming of the War* (1976); and Dorothy Borg and Shumpei Okamoto, eds., *Pearl Harbor as History* (1973). Roberta Wohlstetter, *Pearl Harbor: Warning and Decision* (1962), describes American analysis of the Japanese code.

**CHAPTER
FOURTEEN**

A NATION AT WAR

✜ TRANSFORMATIONS

World War II is the story of a nation that stumbled into 1941 confused and divided and was in a sense remade. Facing the greatest challenge they would ever confront, Americans were caught up in the greatest collective experience of their lives. Sharing a sense of purpose, they were more united than at any time in their history.

Those who remained on the home front desperately wanted to contribute to the war effort. They donated blood, bought bonds, planted victory gardens, and collected newspapers and tin cans for reuse. When the War Production Board asked for 4 million tons of scrap metal in two months, Americans responded with 5 million tons in three weeks. One town with 207 citizens collected 225 tons. Women volunteered to work at hospitals, day care centers, and schools. Cities organized civil defense programs, volunteer fire brigades, amateur aircraft spotters, and first aid classes; in 1942 the *Red Cross Handbook on First Aid* sold more than 8 million copies, making it the best-selling book in the nation.

The war involved large and small sacrifices. Some 300,000 workers were killed in industrial accidents, and 1 million were permanently disabled. More people relocated than at any time in American history. Consumers were deprived of new cars, tires, electrical appliances, and nylon hose. Ten major items were rationed, including meat, shoes, and sugar. Beaches became grimy from oil slicks from sunken tankers. More pollution of the seas occurred almost every day during the war than during the entire decade of the environmentally conscious 1980s.

Army and navy bases and war industries transformed communities and entire regions. In Florida resort hotels were used to house troops, beaches were converted into firing ranges, and military parades were staged on golf courses. The West Coast, which had been isolated, became the most dynamic region of the nation, producing 20 percent of the war goods with 10 percent of the population. Industrial growth anticipated to take 50 years occurred in 4.

People traveled less for pleasure, got to know their neighbors better, and dressed more informally. Women wore slacks, overalls, or pants, and skirts rose several inches above the knee. Men's suits were made without cuffs and with narrow lapels to conserve cloth. People entertained in their homes, and most parties broke up before midnight. Circulation of library books increased 15 percent in 1942. Parlor games, especially checkers, gained in popularity; in 1943 *How to Play Winning Checkers* became a best-seller. Some types of leisure activity were circumscribed: hunting and fishing were banned, and the government forbade the manufacture of tennis and golf balls to conserve raw materials.

On the unsavory side, teenage crime, delinquency, illegitimacy, prostitution, and venereal disease soared. Teenagers called "victory girls" crowded bus depots in large cities so, they said, they could pick up soldiers for sex and thus sustain military morale. Gangs fought with handguns and switchblade knives, and youthful vandalism became a major problem. In New York City, a high school teacher was tortured to death in her classroom. Still, overall crime declined, and some of the nation's most dangerous prisons, such as San Quentin, Sing Sing, and Folsom, were only half full.

The 4 years of war brought more social reform than the preceding 12 years of the New Deal. Medical and dental care improved, and the army provided some men and women with the best diets they ever had. The American Medical Association dropped its opposition to prepaid insurance, and Blue Cross and Blue Shield enrolled tens of millions. People earning more spent more on health care. Even with the nation at war, the death rate was lower than ever. Between 1939 and 1945, life expectancy increased three years, and for blacks it increased five years. Many cities built recreational facilities that would have been considered social reforms but were now thought of as part of the war effort.

Because classrooms were depleted by teachers going to war, parents became involved as volunteer teachers. The federal government offered scholarships and loans to college students in fields that could augment the national defense, and more students took science courses. In 1944, Congress passed the Rankin-Barden Bill, called the "GI bill of rights," to provide veterans with unemployment compensation, loans to buy homes or start businesses, and funds to attend college. The college program marked the greatest entry of the federal government into education since the Morrill Land Grant Act of 1862.

The United States became more of a middle-class nation than ever.

Personal income more than doubled during the war, and it was more fairly distributed than liberals had ever envisaged. For example, the share of the national income earned by the wealthiest 5 percent declined from 23.7 percent in 1939 to 16.8 percent in 1944. The proportion of the national income going to interest and rent, having dropped 20 percent in the 50 years preceding the war, dropped another 20 percent during the war and has not dropped appreciably since. In fact, it took more than 20 years of postwar prosperity for income to increase comparably. "The more cheerful side of this tale is that the underprivileged third of America's population undoubtedly lived better during the war and for some time afterward than they had ever lived before," an economist wrote. The prosperity of the 1920s was eclipsed in gross national product, national income, retail sales, and new investment. The war also brought full employment; by 1945, in addition to the 12 million in the armed services, there were 55 million employed, up from 45 million in 1939.

✥ ECONOMIC MOBILIZATION

The war was won as much on the assembly lines as on the front lines. The United States not only possessed far more natural and human resources than the Axis powers; it utilized them more skillfully. American labor proved more productive and more flexible than German or Japanese labor, more adaptable to the demands of war. American workers proved more willing to sacrifice than their German counterparts and mobilized the greatest labor reserve—women—far more willingly and effectively than the Germans, with their reputation for efficiency. Within six months after Pearl Harbor American factories were producing more than all the Axis nations combined, and before the end of the war the United States was producing twice as much as the enemy. During the course of the war Americans built 86,000 tanks, 296,000 airplanes, 15 million rifles, 5,400 merchant ships, and 6,500 navy ships. Even prisoners at San Quentin staged a riot to demand that they be permitted to bid on war contracts. They were allowed to make war goods and worked 12-hour shifts.

Further, the war brought a reconciliation of government and big business and revived the prestige of businessmen. Some business executives took leaves from their jobs and ran government agencies for the nominal wage of $1 a year. The government provided low-interest loans and tax deductions to enlarge plants and to retool for war production; relaxed enforcement of antitrust laws; and offered contracts that guaranteed a profit. Because it was faster and more efficient than small enterprises, big business received most military contracts and small companies concentrated on consumer goods.

Crucial to production was the auto industry, which ceased making cars after January 31, 1942, and built planes and tanks. The most dramatic increase in productivity was in shipbuilding under the leadership of Henry J. Kaiser. Sacrificing quality for quantity, Kaiser turned out merchant vessels more rapidly than anyone had thought possible.

The United States was faced with a crisis when its supply of raw rubber from the Dutch East Indies was cut off. Roosevelt appointed industrialist

Bernard Baruch to head a committee to solve the problem. Baruch's program included conservation and synthetic rubber production. Gasoline and tires were rationed, private cars were not permitted to carry spare tires, recreational driving was banned, and a national speed limit of 35 miles per hour was established. Scrap rubber was collected, and the government spent $700 million to build 51 synthetic rubber plants and leased them to rubber companies. Synthetic rubber production in 1944 was 100 times greater than it had been in 1941.

To coordinate war production, Roosevelt created the Office of Production Management under William S. Knudsen in 1940. The War Production Board headed by Donald M. Nelson superseded it in 1942. That year Roosevelt created the Office of Economic Stabilization, which was replaced by the Office of War Mobilization in 1943. Both were headed by James F. Byrnes, who resigned from the Supreme Court. His task was to coordinate the policies of all the war agencies.

Coordination was also the aim of the Office of Defense Transportation, created in 1941, and of the War Manpower Commission formed in 1942. The former got truck lines, buses, and railroads to operate as an integrated system. Railroads, remaining in private hands, doubled the amount of freight carried. The Big Inch pipeline was built to transport oil from Texas to Pennsylvania, reducing the incidence of oil tankers sinking in coastal waters. The commission, charged with moving people into jobs vital to the war effort, used the threat of the military draft.

For American agriculture, the war was a bonanza. The income of farmers rose by 250 percent between 1939 and 1945. Civilian food consumption was the highest in history, and one-quarter of agricultural goods went to feed the armed forces and America's Allies. Although the farm population declined by 20 percent and the number of tenant farmers and sharecroppers fell by one-third, farm productivity increased by 28 percent. This greater efficiency was made possible by mechanization, longer hours, fertilizers, hybrid crops, and pesticides. The government encouraged agriculture by exempting farm workers from the draft and by guaranteeing 110 percent of parity for most farm products.

During the war the United States killed some 500,000 enemy troops at a cost of more than $360 billion—amounting to almost $800,000 for every enemy soldier killed. The nation also paid a high price for the property its armed forces destroyed; in fact, it would have cost less to buy the property. From 1940 to 1945 the United States spent nearly twice as much as it had spent in the preceding 150 years. The annual budget was more than ten times what it had been in prewar years, $100 billion in 1945 alone, and the national debt soared from $43 billion in 1940 to $269 billion in 1946. About 46 percent of the expenditures were paid by taxes, the remainder by borrowing.

Individual and corporate income taxes, which had provided 30 percent of government revenue in 1933, provided 76 percent by 1944. The Revenue Act of 1942 raised income taxes to their highest rates in history: 81 percent in the highest bracket. In addition, the act reduced exemptions and taxes fell on lower-income groups for the first time. Only 4 million people paid income taxes in 1939, but some 17 million paid in 1942, and 42 million paid in 1944. In 1943, a new Revenue Act introduced payroll deductions for income taxes, and in 1944 Congress passed a tax increase, though less than the president had requested. In addition, increased corporate and excise levies taxed away much of the profits of industry, and few industrialists and investors got rich off the war.

The government sold bonds for a threefold purpose: to borrow money, to soak up money available for consumer goods and thus control inflation, and to give people a sense of patriotic participation in the war effort. Some $156.9 billion of war bonds were sold to about 85 million investors in seven war loan drives and one victory loan drive. Schoolchildren bought about $1 billion worth of bonds and war stamps, equivalent to $21 per child per year.

In labor unions, membership rose from 9 million in 1942 to 15 million in 1945, and for the first time in history more Americans belonged to labor unions than worked on farms. In 1941, FDR created the National Defense Mediation Board to handle labor disputes, and in 1942 it was succeeded by the National War Labor Board (NWLB), which had equal representation for labor, business, and the public. The NWLB applied the "Little Steel formula" to wages, so called because it was first worked out in a dispute involving the smaller steel mills. Because the cost of living had risen 15 percent from 1941 to 1942, the NWLB permitted wage increases of up to 15 percent, exclusive of overtime, a move that helped to control inflation. The NWLB handled 17,650 disputes involving 12 million workers, and in 40 cases Roosevelt seized plants to ensure continued production. When a national railroad strike threatened in 1944, for instance, the government took over the railroads, then returned them within three weeks after the president had arbitrated the dispute. Work stoppages involved the equivalent of only one day per worker for the duration of the war. John L. Lewis became a national villain for leading his United Mine Workers on strikes in 1941 and 1943, but he won wage increases for his miners.

The United States also won the war in scientific laboratories. Scientists developed the bazooka, which enabled infantrymen to pierce a tank; the radio proximity fuse, which exploded according to nearness to the target; and napalm flamethrowers. They also improved navigational aids, perfected radar and sonar, and created amphibious vehicles for landing on beaches. They developed medical techniques to aid the wounded, including new drugs, and invented insect repellents.

Revolutionary advances in physics made the atomic bomb possible. In 1939, several scientists aware of German progress in nuclear physics persuaded Albert Einstein to sign a letter to FDR calling attention to the possibility of producing bombs from uranium. The president responded by establishing a scientific panel, but little progress was made until the summer of 1941 when Vannevar Bush, Roosevelt's top scientific adviser, told him that a bomb appeared feasible. In 1942, the first controlled nuclear reaction took place beneath Stagg Field at the University of Chicago. The next year a new administrative unit of the Army Corps of Engineers, the Manhattan District, under Brigadier General Leslie R. Groves, took over research. British and Canadian scientists joined the team. Three important centers developed: Oak Ridge, Tennessee; Hanford, Washington; and Los Alamos, New Mexico. Scientists under J. Robert Oppenheimer at Los Alamos brought together fissionable material to produce an explosion in July 1945. The entire project, costing about $2 billion, was unknown to most members of Congress and to Vice President Harry S Truman.

Winning the war required the work of journalists and advertising executives as well as workers and scientists. In 1941, Roosevelt created the Office of Facts and Figures (OFF) to disseminate information about the war to the press and the public. Its head, poet and Librarian of Congress Archibald MacLeish, disliked emotionalism and tried not to slant the truth. The OFF was succeeded in 1942 by the Office of War Information (OWI) under journalist Elmer Davis. An editor, Byron Price, was appointed to head the Office of Censorship (OC), created in 1941. The OC prohibited the publication or broadcast of weather forecasts that might aid enemy bombers and excised sensitive information from letters written home by GIs.

Hollywood produced movies to increase patriotism, some depicting handfuls of GIs defeating swarms of Germans and Japanese. Comic books, which reached millions who read nothing else, were sent abroad, showing superheroes winning battles single-handedly. The OWI produced some propaganda comic books and hired advertising executives to put the American war effort in the best light.

Most wartime movies and novels depicted Americans as reluctant soldiers doing their best at a job they disliked. Journalists such as Ernie Pyle, who wrote accounts of the ordinary GI, described war as cruel and dirty and attempted to humanize the soldiers.

✣ CIVIL LIBERTIES AND THE WAR

Most conscientious objectors were permitted to serve in noncombatant roles in the military or to do essential civilian work. Of the more than 5,500 sent to jail for refusing to serve, more than three-fourths were Jehovah's Witnesses, who requested exemptions on grounds that they all were ministers. Because they did not oppose combat under all conditions and because most had nonreligious jobs, they were denied status as conscientious objectors.

Prosecutions for sedition were rare, yet some publications, including Father Charles E. Coughlin's *Social Justice,* were banned from the mails. And in July 1942, a federal grand jury indicted 28 native fascists for undermining military morale. Among them were Elizabeth Dilling, an anticommunist and anti-Semite who hated FDR; Joe McWilliams, former organizer of the Coughlinite Christian Front; James True, inventor of a billy club he called the "kike-killer"; and Harvard-educated Lawrence Dennis, author of *The Coming American Fascism.* The defendants, charging that the indictments were part of a Jewish conspiracy, sometimes wore Halloween masks or signs reading, "I Am a Spy." A mistrial was declared when the judge died, and after the war ended the indictments were dropped.

The most blatant violation of civil liberties was the internment of some 117,000 Japanese Americans, two-thirds of them United States citizens (Nisei), in ten camps in seven western states. Logistical difficulties and racism account for why the Japanese, not the Germans and Italians, were rounded up: there were far more German and Italian Americans, and they were not geographically concentrated. In the early months of the war, furthermore, it was the Japanese who inflicted an unrelieved succession of defeats upon America's armed forces. The Germans, who lacked a large navy, seemed a more distant threat. Finally, European aliens and descendants could blend more easily into the American population as a whole than could the Japanese.

The camps, although uncomfortable, were not comparable to Nazi concentration camps, and there was no starvation or deliberate brutalization. Still,

Japanese Americans, many of them United States citizens, were interned in several western states during World War II, the greatest violation of civil liberties in wartime. This family, from Hayward, California, awaited relocation.

many of the Nisei had to dispose of property at a fraction of its value, and they resented the stigma of disloyalty. Hostility toward Japanese in the United States declined once America went on the offensive, and early in 1943 the army began accepting recruits for an all-Nisei combat unit. Some 1,200 served in the 442d Combat Team, which earned fame for its bravery in the Italian campaign.

In 1944 the government began to release the internees gradually, and by 1945 most had returned to their homes. In 1944 the Supreme Court ruled in the *Korematsu* case that the government had the right to exclude the Nisei from the West Coast but in a companion case, *Ex parte Endo,* ruled that the War Relocation Authority could not detain a person whose loyalty had been established. In 1988 Congress acknowledged the wrongness of internment by passing legislation that included a formal apology and about $20,000 in restitution to each internee.

Blacks made significant economic gains, thanks to the greater need for labor in wartime. More than 1 million blacks migrated from the South to the North to take jobs in war industries, and many blacks who remained in the South moved from rural areas to cities for employment. In manufacturing the number employed rose from 500,000 to 1.2 million, and labor unions were increasingly hospitable to blacks. In government jobs, the number of blacks increased from 50,000 in 1939 to 200,000 in 1944, and some 250,000 black veterans attended college with government benefits after the war.

The gains did not come without tension, however. Many whites resented competition from blacks, and war industries did not hire blacks until the labor shortage became acute. Incensed because some war industries refused to employ blacks, A. Philip Randolph threatened a march on Washington in 1941. FDR, fearing racial violence, agreed to issue an order prohibiting job discrimination in defense industries and in the government, but he refused to desegregate the armed forces. On June 25, 1942, the president issued an executive order creating the Fair Employment Practices Committee to prevent job discrimination. In return, Randolph reluctantly canceled the march.

Many whites, recognizing the inconsistency of fighting for democracy abroad while denying it to black Americans, came to feel that racism was morally wrong, a belief underscored by Swedish sociologist Gunnar Myrdal's massive study of race, *An American Dilemma* (1944), which concluded that America's greatest failure was racism. The struggle against segregation made little progress during the war, although it gained momentum for the postwar period. The NAACP grew from 50,000 members and 355 branches in 1940 to nearly 500,000 members and more than 1,000 branches in 1945; the Congress of Racial Equality was founded in 1942 in Chicago. In addition, in 1944 FDR finally began admitting black journalists to his news conferences, and the Supreme Court, in *Smith v. Allwright,* ruled that the Democratic party in Texas could not exclude blacks from voting in primary elections. Unfortunately, there were several race riots in major cities. The worst occurred in 1943 in Detroit, beginning when fights erupted between blacks and whites at Belle Isle, a park on an island in the Detroit River. Looting and burning raged for several days in June before federal troops quelled the riots, which left 25 blacks and 9 whites dead. Two months later, a riot occurred in Harlem after a confrontation between a white policeman and a black soldier. Blacks attacked policemen and burned businesses. Six blacks died, and 300 blacks and whites were injured.

Racial tensions were also high between Mexican Americans and Anglos in California, where Mexican American teenagers, in defiance of conventional codes, sported ducktail haircuts and flashy, broad-shouldered zoot suits with thigh-length jackets. Gangs of zoot-suiters allegedly attacked sailors who dated Hispanic women, and soldiers and sailors roamed through Mexican American neighborhoods in Oakland and Los Angeles, beating zoot-suiters in May and June 1943.

Also in California, American Indians sued the federal government for $100 million to pay for the state taken from them in the 1850s. A bill to compensate the Indians passed both houses of Congress, yet Roosevelt vetoed it on the grounds that the government's responsibility "is a duty to the future, not the past." Litigation continued for 35 years until a compromise was reached, paying the tribes 47 cents per acre. Other wartime changes in Indians' lives were more immediate. Many left reservations to work in war plants and did not return to tribal life when the war ended. Some came back to the reservations, bringing modern technology.

Chinese Americans enjoyed the sympathy of most Americans because China was an ally of the United States. Worker shortages and their status as allies opened many hitherto closed areas of employment to the Chinese, and war workers moved from ghetto Chinatowns into the mainstream of American life. In 1943 Congress repealed the Chinese Exclusion Act of 1882, thus permitting Chinese immigration four years before the War Brides Act would permit Chinese women who had married American citizens to enter the United States. Moreover, Congress granted all Chinese immigrants the long-denied right to become naturalized citizens.

For American Jews, the chief concern was the rescue of European Jews threatened with annihilation in Hitler's Holocaust. Roosevelt, having refused to request relaxation of immigration quotas to admit refugees, sought a haven elsewhere for Jews, but other nations refused to accept them. FDR insisted that the question of a homeland in Palestine be deferred until after the war.

Even when reliable information reached the administration about Hitler's gassing of Jews, the president would not authorize attempts to rescue them. He rejected pleas to bomb gas chambers, crematoriums, and rail lines leading to death camps on the grounds that doing so would divert air power from military targets and prolong the war. With creation of the War Refugee Board in January 1944, the United States sought to rescue Jews in occupied Europe through ransoms, false passports, and other subterfuges. Thousands were saved, yet millions might have been saved if the United States had acted earlier. The Nazis, for their part, continued to exterminate the Jews even after realizing that Germany would lose the war. Ultimately, world leaders recognized that Jews needed a refuge from persecution, which would lead to the founding of the state of Israel after the war.

As with minorities, the employment of women grew as labor in general became scarce, and the female labor force increased by more than 50 percent between 1940 and 1945. Employment grew in every field except domestic service, with the most spectacular increases occurring in factory work, particularly in defense industries. Black women moved out of farm and domestic labor into service and manufacturing. The female proportion of the labor movement increased from 9.4 percent of union members in 1940 to 21.8 percent in 1944, and nearly 1 million women were hired by the federal government. More married women, mothers, and older women took jobs, and for the first time there were more married than single women in the labor force. Women met domestic responsibilities in addition to outside work by sacrificing sleep and recreation. The government and employers provided some child care, but most

Women were essential to the war effort and took over some jobs previously performed by men, including the building of a bomber.

working mothers relied on relatives. Women's wages increased in absolute terms and in relation to men's. In 1942 the National War Labor Board ordered equal pay for women who did the same jobs as men, and four states enacted equal pay laws during the war, yet there was still no equal pay for comparable work.

The proportion of women enrolled in college increased, although more than 50 percent of students remained male. The number of married students also increased. Women still concentrated in the arts and humanities, and most expected to work only until marriage or motherhood.

A higher percentage of women married in the 1940s than ever before; hasty marriages led to higher divorce rates and, beginning in 1946, a baby boom. Many women practiced contraception, and illegal abortions were common. The rate for children born outside marriage, however, doubled between 1940 and 1950. And with heterosexual marriage the ideal, homosexuality continued to be stigmatized.

In politics, women increased their participation, even though they continued to vote in smaller percentages than men. More women served in state legislatures, increasing from 144 in 1941 to 228 in 1945, and as delegates to national conventions.

❖ GROWING DIVERSITY IN THE ARMED FORCES

As Americans realized that discrimination at home was incompatible with the cause for which they were fighting overseas, so, too, did they realize the shame of segregation in their armed forces. Integration nevertheless came slowly to the military, although such change came to that sphere more rapidly that it did in civilian society.

At the time of Pearl Harbor there were just 5,000 black troops in the army of 230,000; many draft boards, considering them unfit for combat, were reluctant to draft blacks; the Marine Corps had no black personnel; and the navy accepted blacks only as cooks. Attitudes changed when the government realized that discrimination represented a waste of vital personnel. In September 1944, when the size of the armed forces peaked, 702,000 blacks were serving in the army, 165,000 in the navy, 17,000 in the marines, and 5,000 in the Coast Guard.

In all these services, however, blacks were assigned to separate units, and most training and base facilities were segregated. Most black units had at least some white officers, but no black officers were assigned to white units. The majority of blacks served in units that performed hard, physical labor such as building roads and unloading boats. In the navy, blacks were usually assigned to shore duty, and the Naval Academy would not have a black graduate until 1949. The persistence of discrimination did not prevent blacks from fighting capably in every theater of the war.

Nearly 12 percent of the Jewish population, about 550,000 persons, served in the armed forces. Some 29 percent of Jewish servicemen were in the Army

Air Force, and more than one-third of Jewish dentists and physicians volunteered for military duty. A significant number of Jews achieved high rank: 6 major generals, 13 brigadier generals, 1 admiral, and 2 rear admirals.

Nearly 300,000 Spanish-speaking troops served in the military, and Mexican Americans were overrepresented in comparison to their numbers in the country. They showed a propensity to volunteer for dangerous missions, such as paratrooper raids, and 11 Spanish-speaking soldiers received the Congressional Medal of Honor. Hispanics in the armed forces suffered little overt discrimination.

American Indians volunteered in large numbers, and some 25,000 served in the armed forces, most as enlisted men in the army. Unlike blacks, they were assigned to integrated units. Some were effective in communication teams; by using their own languages, they confused enemy interpreters. Many Indians were decorated for bravery.

That warfare had become increasingly technical, and that some 10 percent of all armed forces jobs were administrative and clerical, facilitated the employment of women, who were hired for office work, communications, and health care. Some 140,000 served in the Women's Army Corps (WAC), 44,000 in the Women Accepted for Voluntary Emergency Service (WAVES) of the navy, 23,000 in the Marine Corps Women's Reserve, and 13,000 in the Coast Guard. About 4,000 black women served in the armed forces. In addition, 31.3 percent of all women nurses enlisted, some 60,000 in the Army Nurse Corps and about 14,000 in the Navy Nurse Corps.

Still, there was substantial resistance to women in the armed services. Some feared that war would harden women and cause them to lose their femininity. The most common charge was that female soldiers would encourage promiscuity. An Arkansas radio evangelist told listeners that WAC recruits were paraded naked before male officers, and citizens near a WAC training center at Daytona Beach, Florida, reported that army women "were touring in groups, seizing and raping sailors and Coast Guardsmen."

But traditionalists' fears were never realized; incidences of venereal disease, for instance, were lower among servicewomen than among civilian women. More women served in the armed forces than in any previous war, yet their roles were limited. Although some WACs served abroad, federal law prohibited WAVES from serving outside the continental United States or aboard combat ships or aircraft. On most foreign bases, WACs lived in guarded, barbed wire compounds and could leave only in groups escorted by armed guards, thought necessary to protect them from sex-starved male soldiers.

✛ THE ARTS AND ENTERTAINMENT

During the war there was the greatest mass market for books in American history. The number of volumes published almost doubled, and book sales increased more than 20 percent each year. Bibles and dictionaries were in such demand they had to be rationed. Writers were less alienated than during the

1920s and 1930s, and sentimentality, nostalgia, and religion were popular themes. Many writers found the war the central experience of their lives. Among those who made their debuts in this era were Saul Bellow, Irwin Shaw, and John Hersey.

Richard Wright, a Mississippian who emigrated to Chicago, where he joined the Communist party, established himself as the major black writer of the period with the publication of *Native Son* in 1940. A riveting best-seller, it was the story of a Chicago black man who accidently killed his white employer's daughter. In 1941, Wright collaborated on a dramatic version of *Native Son* produced on Broadway by Orson Welles, and in 1943 he published the autobiographical *Black Boy,* expressing his rage at racism. Coming to believe that Communists exploited blacks for political purposes, he broke with the party in 1944, when he published "I Tried To Be a Communist" in the *Atlantic Monthly.*

Nonfiction turned increasingly conservative. In 1943, Ayn Rand published *The Fountainhead,* which praised individualism over collectivism, sold steadily during the war, then registered millions of paperback sales. But the favorite book of conservatives was *The Road to Serfdom,* written by an expatriate Austrian economist, Friedrich Hayek, who believed modern liberalism was the path to tyranny. Predicting that national planning would fail in Russia and America, he described fascism and communism as twin tyrannies.

The war produced few plays that represent remarkable literature, although toward the end of the period Arthur Miller and Tennessee Williams established themselves as top dramatists; Williams's *The Glass Menagerie* was produced on Broadway in 1945. Several successful musicals debuted during the war: Irving Berlin wrote the score for the popular *This Is the Army* (1942), and Richard Rodgers and Oscar Hammerstein II collaborated on *Oklahoma!* (1943), which played for 2,212 performances, the longest run for a musical comedy in the history of American theater.

On a less lofty note, the popularity of comic books was such that their readers were not limited to children. About one-third of those aged 18–30 read popular comics like *Superman,* and a special edition was printed for soldiers. Some adults read only comic books and newspapers.

More people attended movies during World War II than during the 1920s. The major studios turned out only 377 films in 1945 compared to 761 in 1939, yet over the period before-tax profits increased from $42 million to $239 million. War films, spy films, movies about resistance to nazism in the occupied countries, and musicals were popular. Two great films appeared in 1940: *The Grapes of Wrath* and *The Great Dictator,* Charlie Chaplin's antifascist comedy, in which he played a character who was a parody of Hitler. In *Citizen Kane* (1941), Welles directed and played the lead, loosely based on the life of William Randolph Hearst. That year, Alfred Hitchcock arrived in Hollywood from England, and the wizard of suspense and unnerving humor became the best-known director in America. The memorable films of 1943 were war pictures: *Guadalcanal Diary, Watch on the Rhine,* and *So Proudly We Hail.* In 1944, *Going My Way,* in which Bing Crosby played a Catholic priest, became the most successful hit since *Gone with the Wind.* Hollywood stars such as Bob Hope supported the war effort by entertaining troops abroad.

Many popular songs illustrated the national mood. Some were bellicose, such as "You're a Sap, Mr. Jap," "We're Gonna Find a Feller Who Is Yeller and Beat Him Red, White, and Blue," "In the Fuehrer's Face," and "Praise the Lord and Pass the Ammunition." Glenn Miller's swing band popularized the sentimental "Don't Sit Under the Apple Tree with Anyone Else but Me," and Irving Berlin wrote "White Christmas," the best-selling song of all time. Country music boomed, inspiring the hit "Pistol Packin' Mama." A skinny young singer named Frank Sinatra became the most glamorous male entertainer since Rudolph Valentino.

Sales of visual art soared, never to reach 1945 levels again until 1960. Most art was abstract and pessimistic. American art was enriched by Europeans driven from their homelands by the war, including Marc Chagall, Salvador Dali, and Max Ernst.

Architects found work plentiful, with entire cities springing up around war plants, many of them utilizing prefabricated housing. Great figures such as Walter Gropius and Ludwig Mies van der Rohe brought formal, structured, coherent theories of architecture when they fled Europe for America. Frank Lloyd Wright enjoyed a revival in popularity. Claiming the box was the shape of fascism and disliking the coldness of much modern architecture, he sought to endow simple structures with warmth.

Sports, despite being attenuated by the war, provided an escape. Baseball sent more than 4,000 players into the armed services, and such stars as Ted Williams went into combat. The minor leagues folded for the duration, spring training was canceled, and night games were discontinued until 1944. The World Series went on as scheduled, however, and Series games were broadcast to troops overseas to help maintain morale. The New York Yankees dominated the American League, and the Brooklyn Dodgers were the most formidable team in the National League.

Many high schools dropped football, and freshmen were allowed to compete on college varsity teams. Because of fear of Japanese attack, the Rose Bowl was moved from Pasadena, California, to Durham, North Carolina, for 1942 only. Army and Navy were the top college teams, and Army's halfback Glenn ("Mr. Outside") Davis and fullback Doc ("Mr. Inside") Blanchard were the two most famous players. Professional football continued on a reduced scale; players who were not drafted worked in defense plants and played on weekends.

Basketball lost fewer players because many were too tall for the infantry, the air force, or the navy. In the early 1940s there was an influx of huge centers, and rules to limit the dominance of big men were adopted, including the ban on goaltending and the implementation of the three-second lane. Western teams such as Wyoming, Utah, and Oklahoma A & M dominated college basketball.

The titles of boxers who were drafted, such as Joe Louis, were frozen for the duration of the war. Blacks increasingly entered boxing, and by the end of the war some 75 percent of all fighters were blacks.

⫥ POLITICS

The federal bureaucracy, which grew by 60 percent under the New Deal, grew even more during the war—by 300 percent. The president became increasingly active, and Congress delegated broad authority to him and to administrative agencies.

As prosperity returned, the electorate, which had more to conserve, became increasingly conservative. In the 1942 congressional elections the Democrats were hurt by a low turnout, and the Republicans gained 44 seats in the House and 7 in the Senate, leaving the House with 208 Republicans and 218 Democrats, the Senate with 38 Republicans and 57 Democrats. A coalition of Republicans and conservative southern Democrats, which increasingly dominated Congress, joined to terminate the Work Projects Administration, the Civilian Conservation Corps, and the National Youth Administration.

Roosevelt had no qualms about seeking a fourth term during wartime, and no one challenged him for the Democratic nomination. The chief suspense at the convention in Chicago was over the vice-presidential nomination, particularly because Roosevelt's health was failing. After telling Henry Wallace and James F. Byrnes that he would let the convention select the nominee, Roosevelt privately endorsed Missouri Senator Harry S Truman, a compromise choice. Wallace was unpopular with conservatives, and Byrnes was disliked by labor, blacks, and Catholics (because he had left the church), so FDR agreed that Truman had fewer liabilities. Truman's reputation had been enhanced by chairing a committee that revealed incompetence and corruption in defense production, saving the government billions of dollars.

The major candidates for the Republican nomination were Wendell Willkie, Thomas E. Dewey, Harold Stassen, Robert Taft, and Ohio Governor John W. Bricker. There was also a movement to draft General Douglas MacArthur. But after Willkie failed badly in the Wisconsin primary, he withdrew, and Dewey was easily nominated on the first ballot in Chicago. Bricker was nominated for vice president after California Governor Earl Warren declined.

Many considered Dewey, 42, inexperienced and arrogant. Cold, stiff, and condescending, he was unpopular with the press. "You can't really dislike Tom Dewey until you get to know him," one of his assistants said. And Alice Roosevelt Longworth, who thought he did not look presidential, said of Dewey, "How can we be expected to vote for a man who looks like the bridegroom on a wedding cake?"

Dewey's only real hope was for the war to end before election day. He tried to make FDR's health an issue, denounced Roosevelt for accepting support from the CIO, and accused the administration of being influenced by communists and extreme liberals. Roosevelt, who profited from his role as commander in chief and from American victories on the battlefield, condemned the Republicans for isolationism and blamed them again for the depression. He boasted of his accomplishments for veterans yet made few new promises.

Both party platforms endorsed membership in a postwar United Nations. Internationalism had another stimulus in Willkie's *One World,* in which he claimed the world was a single geographic and political unit. *One World,* written after Willkie's trip around the world in 1942 and published in 1943, the year before his death, sold 200,000 copies within 72 hours and 1 million copies within a few weeks. The Senate would endorse the United Nations charter on July 28, 1945, with only two dissenting votes.

Roosevelt won 36 states with 432 electoral votes to Dewey's 12 states and 99 electoral votes. With 25.6 million popular votes to 22 million for Dewey, FDR gained 53.4 percent of the popular vote, the lowest percentage in his campaigns. Democrats gained 22 seats in the House and lost 1 in the Senate, and several congressional isolationists were defeated.

Ominously, Roosevelt, 62, had aged dramatically by 1944, and his friends were shocked by his appearance. He had grown frail and thin, his hands trembled, and he had dark circles under his eyes. In March, his doctors found him to be suffering from heart disease and hypertension. Without informing him of the gravity of his condition, they told him to cut down on cigarettes and prescribed heart medication and at least ten hours of sleep nightly. The commander in chief was destined to become as much a casualty of the war as the soldiers who died at Normandy.

BIBLIOGRAPHICAL ESSAY

The best overall history of the home front during World War II is Geoffrey Perrett, *Days of Sadness, Years of Triumph: The American People, 1939–1945* (1973). Other excellent studies include John Morton Blum, *V Was for Victory: Politics and American Culture During World War II* (1976); Richard Polenberg, *War and Society: The United States, 1941–1945* (1972); Kenneth S. Davis, *Experience of War: The U.S. in World War II* (1965); and A. A. Hoehling, *Home Front, U.S.A.* (1964). Popular accounts include Cabell Phillips, *Decade of Triumph and Trouble: The 1940s* (1975); and Richard R. Lingeman, *Don't You Know There's a War On? The American Home Front, 1941–1945* (1970).

Politics is covered in Roland Young, *Congressional Politics in the Second World War* (1956); Robert A. Divine, *Second Chance: The Triumph of Internationalism in America During World War II* (1967); and Bruce Catton, *The War Lords of Washington* (1948). See also Bernard Asbell, *When F.D.R. Died* (1961); Harvard Sitkoff, ed., *Fifty Years Later: The New Deal Evaluated* (1985); Donald H. Riddle, *The Truman Committee* (1964); and Herbert S. Parmet and Marie B. Hecht, *Never Again: A President Runs for a Third Term* (1968). Economic mobilization is discussed in Alan S. Milward, *War Economy and Society: 1939–1945* (1977); and Elliot Janeway, *Struggle for Survival: A Chronicle of*

Economic Mobilization in World War II (1951). Specific aspects of the economy are described in Henry C. Murphy, *The National Debt in War and Transition* (1950); Howard World, *The Story of Scrap Rubber* (1943); J. M. Ball, *Reclaimed Rubber* (1947); Joseph R. Rose, *American Wartime Transportation* (1953); Walter W. Wilcox, *The Farmer in the Second World War* (1947); and Bela Gold, *Wartime Economic Planning in Agriculture* (1949).

The race to construct an atomic bomb is discussed in James Phinney Baxter, *Scientists Against Time* (1946); and Robert Jungk, *Brighter Than a Thousand Suns: A Personal History of the Atomic Scientists* (1958). Propaganda is covered in Allan M. Winkler, *The Politics of Propaganda: The Office of War Information, 1941–1945* (1978); and Robert K. Merton, *Mass Persuasion: The Social Psychology of a War Bond Drive* (1946). The best local study is Alan Clive, *State of War: Michigan in World War II* (1979). Books on labor during the war include Nelson Lichtenstein, *Labor's War at Home: The CIO in World War II* (1982); and Joel Seidman, *American Labor from Defense to Reconversion* (1982). Women's role is reevaluated in Sherna B. Gluck, *Rosie the Riveter Revisited: Women, the War, and Social Change* (1987). Race relations are examined in Richard M. Dalfiume, *Desegregation of the U.S. Armed Forces, 1939–1953* (1969); Robert C. Jones, *Mexican War Workers in the U.S.* (1945); and Robert Shogan and Tom Craig, *The Detroit Race Riot: A Study in Violence* (1964). The initially desultory efforts to rescue European Jews are discussed in Henry L. Feingold, *The Politics of Rescue: The Roosevelt Administration and the Holocaust, 1938–1945* (1970).

Treatment of conscientious objectors is the subject of Mulford Q. Sibley and Philip E. Jacob, *Conscription of Conscience: The American State and the Conscientious Objector, 1940–1947* (1952); and antiwar activities are discussed in Lawrence S. Wittner, *Rebels Against War: The American Peace Movement, 1941–1960* (1969). The incarceration of the Nisei is described in Roger Daniels, *Concentration Camps U.S.A.: Japanese Americans and World War II* (1971); Morton Grodzins, *American Betrayed: Politics and the Japanese Evacuation* (1949); Audrie Girdner and Anne Loftis, *The Great Betrayal* (1969); and Daisaku Kitagawa, *Issei and Nisei: The Internment Years* (1967).

CHAPTER FIFTEEN

WORLD WAR II

✢ THE COMMAND STRUCTURE

Roosevelt proved to be an inspirational leader who convinced Americans that they must sacrifice to win the war; he helped make the people confident, and no plans were made for surrender. Roosevelt's chief contributions were as a diplomat and an organizer of the home front. He did not participate in making tactical decisions, as Churchill did, nor did he hire and fire generals, as Lincoln had.

The Joint Chiefs of Staff, the highest-ranking military commanders, included two army and two navy representatives. Admiral William D. Leahy served as chair and as Roosevelt's representative. He was joined by Admiral Ernest J. King, General of the Army George C. Marshall, and General Henry H. Arnold, head of the Army Air Force. Although Leahy directed the discussions, the dominant personalities were Marshall and King. Marshall, demanding but even-tempered, was a statesman who selected able subordinates and built support for the army in Congress. King, a highly efficient administrator and a disciplinarian, inspired more respect than affection.

The eventual supreme allied commander in Europe was General Dwight D. Eisenhower, who had been an assistant to Marshall and had served on the staff of General Douglas MacArthur. Eisenhower's amiable personality helped smooth difficulties between the Americans and their Allies. The Atlantic Fleet had one commander, Admiral Harold Stark, and the Pacific was divided into two commands dictated by interservice rivalries. Admiral Chester W. Nimitz, who reported to King, commanded the Central Pacific and Pacific Fleet and MacArthur, who reported to Marshall, led the forces in the Southwest Pacific. The Pacific commanders differed radically in their styles: MacArthur, brilliant yet temperamental, was colorful, forceful, and dramatic; Nimitz was soft-spoken and relaxed.

The Allies decided that defeating Hitler would take priority over defeating Japan because Germany appeared the more dangerous foe and because Hitler's scientists might develop new weapons of mass destruction. A majority of army forces and equipment were devoted to the campaign in Europe; most of the navy, and almost all of the marines, were concentrated in the Pacific.

❖ THE WAR IN EUROPE

Control of the Atlantic was necessary for victory in Europe, and the first conflicts between American and German forces came at sea. The navy had three principal tasks: protecting shipping, supporting amphibious landings, and shelling invasion targets. The German surface fleet was never a major factor, despite some attacks on convoys to the Soviet Union, because it was no match for Britain's and had to retire to port or face destruction.

The chief German threat was the submarine. At the beginning of the war the Germans had only 30 submarines operating in the Atlantic; by the peak of the Battle of the Atlantic in 1941 they had 150. The United States was initially ill equipped to combat submarines, and the U-boats took a terrible toll, sinking 360 merchant ships in the first six months of 1942. After mid-1942 submarines operated in wolf packs in the mid-Atlantic, following convoys until nightfall, then converging to attack.

Allied technology and techniques improved, however, and by May 1943 the battle had been virtually won. The first innovation was to cluster ships in convoys so destroyers and planes could protect them. Destroyer escorts, smaller and faster versions of traditional destroyers, were constructed, as were escort carriers, which were miniature aircraft carriers built to provide air cover to convoys. Sonar improved, and by 1943 small units were being built for placement in planes and on small boats. Finally, the U.S. ability to construct ships faster than the Germans could sink them was critical.

The battle was costly to both sides. The Allies lost 2,828 merchant ships, 187 warships, and about 40,000 men; the Germans lost two-thirds of their U-boats, and by late 1943, losses had become so heavy that they suspended submarine warfare. Had the Allies lost the Battle of the Atlantic, there could have been no invasion of Europe.

Two weeks after Pearl Harbor, Churchill met Roosevelt in Washington for the Arcadia Conference, the first of the wartime summits. The leaders decided that the first use of American ground troops would be in North

Africa. They realized that the strategic importance of North Africa was limited, but it was the only place where the British were fighting the Germans on
land, and Roosevelt was determined to give Americans a sense of participation
in the war. Eisenhower led the invasion of North Africa, code-named
Operation Torch.

The principal adversaries of the British in North Africa were initially the
Italians. The British had moved into the upper Mediterranean coast of Africa
to defend Egypt and the Suez Canal, and Italy was there to protect its
colonies. Vichy France was in nominal control of Morocco and Algeria. The
major questions facing the Allied commanders were whether the French
would resist, whether the secrecy of the operation could be preserved, and
whether the Germans might intercept and sink the invasion fleet.

The fleet approached undetected and, with air support from escort carriers and bombers based in England, landed at Casablanca, Oran, and Algiers
on November 8, 1942. French resistance was light and ceased after the
Germans occupied Vichy France on November 11 and ended any possible
allegiance of the French in North Africa with the Vichy government.
Eisenhower was criticized for cooperating with Admiral Jean Darlan, commander of the French fleet, the second-highest Vichy official, and a notorious collaborator with the Germans. Yet after a member of the French resistance assassinated Darlan on December 24, the Allies used French General
Henri Giraud as a figurehead to command the loyalty of North African
troops.

Almost simultaneously, the British launched an offensive from the east.
General Bernard Montgomery defeated the German Erwin Rommel at El
Alamein in late October and early November, then began advancing westward
to link up with Eisenhower's troops, catching the Axis troops in a pincer
movement. The Germans rushed reinforcements to Tunisia, but they merely
slowed the Allied advance, and by May 11, Axis resistance in North Africa
had been broken. Germany and Italy lost almost 1 million soldiers killed or
taken prisoner. American generals George S. Patton and Omar N. Bradley
gained combat experience, and the United States perfected its amphibious
invasion techniques.

At the Casablanca Conference in January 1943, Roosevelt and Churchill
decided to follow the North African offensive with an invasion of Sicily. This
plan made the easiest logistical use of the troops in North Africa and was in
part an effort to divert some Axis troops from the Soviet front. Like the campaign in North Africa, however, the strategic significance of the campaign in
Sicily was limited, and it had the negative effect of delaying the planned invasion of France by Allied troops stationed in England. Eisenhower also commanded this invasion, code-named Operation Husky.

In the early morning hours of July 10, the U.S. Seventh Army under
Patton and the British Eighth Army under Montgomery landed in Sicily.
Stormy weather and the lack of a preinvasion bombardment helped preserve
the element of surprise. By the end of the second day the Allies had put ashore
80,000 men, 7,000 vehicles, and 300 tanks. Many of the tanks and mechanized
vehicles bogged down in the soft sand of the beaches, and some landing craft

were grounded on sandbars. Nonetheless, the Allied forces, which command-ed air and sea, withstood furious counterattacks.

Montgomery's forces were meant to advance up the southeast coast to capture Messina, the city at the tip of Sicily separated from Italy by the Strait of Messina. Patton's army was to advance from the southwest, offering sup-port to Montgomery and preventing Axis troops from thwarting the capture of Messina. After capturing Palermo easily, Patton decided to take Messina and beat Montgomery there by one day. The Axis lost 164,000 troops killed or captured in the month-long campaign, but most Axis soldiers escaped to Italy across the strait.

The campaign earned Patton a reputation as one of America's most aggressive generals, but he provoked controversy by slapping two soldiers hospitalized for nervous conditions and threatening to shoot one of them. Eisenhower forced Patton to apologize to the two and to his troops. Patton was not removed from command, although Eisenhower promoted the less controversial Bradley over him.

The conquest of Sicily precipitated the fall of Mussolini and the collapse of the Italian war effort. Italians had grown disillusioned with the conflict, and their army had little incentive to fight; Hitler thoroughly dominated the Axis alliance, and many Italians realized they had as much to fear from a German victory as from a German defeat. Two weeks after the Allied landing in Sicily, the fascist grand council voted no confidence in Mussolini and King Victor Emmanuel III ordered his arrest. Marshal Pietro Badoglio was appointed prime minister and began negotiating terms of surrender with the Allies. Secretly, Italy surrendered on September 3, and Eisenhower announced the terms five days later. German troops, whom Hitler immediately rushed to Italy, disarmed the Italian army, and paratroopers, in a daring commando raid, rescued Mussolini from a mountain prison. Hitler installed him as ruler of a small German puppet state in northern Italy.

The Allies decided to invade Italy next, and on September 9 the American Fifth Army under General Mark Clark landed at Salerno. After meeting little resistance at the beachhead, the troops, with air and naval support, repelled a strong German counterattack on September 12. On October 1, 1943, the Allies captured Naples and hoped to reach Rome by Christmas. Their esti-mate was too optimistic by nearly a year.

Few regions were less conducive to ground operations than the mountain-ous peninsula of Italy, traversed by streams and dominated by rugged terrain that made tanks useless. The mountain fighting favored the defenders, and the campaign included some of the closest, most intense combat of the war. Moreover, with opposing lines only yards apart, supplies had to be brought in at night, on the backs of mules and men.

Germans blocked the Allied advance at Monte Cassino, site of a 1,400-year-old Benedictine monastery. Monte Cassino proved so formidable that the Allies decided to outflank it with an amphibious assault at Anzio, com-manded by Major General John P. Lucas. The landing surprised the Germans, and conditions were favorable for pushing out boldly from the beachhead into the lightly defended surrounding countryside before the Germans could reinforce their troops. Instead, Lucas, afraid to incur casualties, concentrated on building up troops and supplies at the beachhead while awaiting a counterattack. The Germans were able to send reinforcements, and when the counterattack came it nearly drove the Americans into the sea. Anzio was the only amphibious invasion of the war in which the Americans failed to break out of their beachhead.

Simultaneous with the invasion at Anzio was another offensive against Monte Cassino, which also failed. Reluctantly the Allies bombed the historic monastery, yet the Germans constructed defenses in the rubble. The war in Italy settled down to a bloody stalemate with the longest-lasting static front in the European theater. Finally, French forces broke through the German lines and opened the road to Rome. The city was occupied on June 4, 1944, two days before the Allies invaded France.

The invasion of Italy had little impact on the overall war effort. Although it diverted 26 divisions of German troops from the eastern front and secured air bases for bombing central Europe and southern France, it also diverted Allied troops from the major invasion in France. The worth of the campaign is still debated.

Some American planners hoped that Germany could be defeated by air power without an invasion of France. The leaders of the army and of the Army Air Force differed in their estimate of the efficacy of air power and in how planes should be used. Everyone acknowledged that air power could win battles, and some proponents thought it could win the war. Army leaders wanted to use air power tactically, to support ground operations, but air force leaders believed the first priority should be strategic bombing to destroy the German infrastructure of industry and transportation.

The Royal Air Force, which carried the main burden early in the war, concluded that daylight raids were too costly in terms of bombers lost and resorted to night operations. The chief American bombers, the B-17 Flying Fortress and the B-24 Liberator, were more heavily armed with defensive machine guns than the British bombers; they were also equipped with accurate bombsights that made precision bombing of specific targets during daylight more feasible. By mid-1943 around-the-clock bombing was taking place, by the Americans during the day, by the British at night.

The British preferred to saturate an entire area with bombs so as to destroy everything within it, a tactic called area bombing. The Americans believed their operations were sufficiently accurate to knock out specific targets, such as airplane factories. Allied reports, though, would conclude that 65 percent of all bombers failed to come within 5 miles of their targets, and Americans grew skeptical of their ability to bomb accurately anything smaller than a city. By the end of the war, joint fire-bombing raids had largely replaced precision bombing, with particularly grim results. The raid on Dresden in February 1945, for example, killed 135,000 people, the most destructive bombing in aviation history.

Whether they used precision bombing or area bombing, the raids did not eliminate German transportation and industry, but they did damage the Nazi war effort. The Germans were compelled to devote significant resources to combating the air offensive: By 1943 some 1 million troops were assigned to antiaircraft duty, and it took a labor force of 1.5 million men to repair damage. Further, the air war decimated the Luftwaffe and made it unavailable for tactical support of ground troops. Initially, the Allies discovered that the Luftwaffe was more lethal to their bombers than antiaircraft fire; bombing raids without fighter escorts were costly. Then by early 1944, the range of the P-51 Mustang and the P-47 Thunderbolt had been extended with detachable fuel tanks so they could accompany bombers. From that point, the Luftwaffe was ineffective in defending German cities, and the Germans began to respond selectively to raids because they were losing too many planes and pilots.

Although air power alone did not bring Germany to its knees, it was a significant factor in winning the war. Air superiority deterred an invasion of England and ensured the success of the Normandy invasion. Air power was also important in the Battle of the Atlantic, in which planes proved more effective than ships in antisubmarine warfare. Planes sank 62 submarines and accounted for 4 of the 6 sunken German battleships.

After the war turned in favor of the Allies, Hitler put his hopes for German victory in new secret weapons. The first pilotless flying bombs, or V-1s, appeared over London in June 1944, and by the time the threat ended in March 1945, some 6,000 British civilians had died and about 17,000 had been wounded. Germany escalated the air war in September 1944 with the launching of the first V-2 supersonic rockets at London. Before the last of the V-2 bases was captured, nearly 3,000 Britons had been killed and about 6,500 had been injured. Such weapons heralded a new age in warfare and had a profound psychological effect upon their victims, yet fewer people died from them than from a single conventional air raid. Jet fighters, another German innovation, were first used in July 1944. Vastly superior to any Allied plane, they were few in number, and few pilots were capable of flying them. Furthermore, the war ended before the weight of German science could be brought to bear, justifying the Allies' decision to make defeat of Germany their chief priority.

In November 1943, Roosevelt met Churchill and Chiang Kai-shek at two conferences in Cairo, sandwiched around a conference with Stalin and Churchill at Teheran. Few strategic decisions were made at the Cairo conferences, but Teheran marked the first conference at which the Big Three met personally. The main decision made at Teheran, the last of the summits devoted chiefly to wartime strategy, was to set the invasion of France for the spring or summer of 1944.

At Teheran, Stalin agreed to time an offensive to complement the Normandy invasion. Since 1941 his armies had carried the brunt of the fighting on land and prevented Hitler from taking over the Soviet Union. The Germans had driven to within 25 miles of Moscow in 1941, but then winter arrived, and the Soviets had launched a counteroffensive. The next spring, the Germans resumed the offensive, which again stalled before winter. In 1943 the tide turned on the eastern front, and the Germans were defeated at Stalingrad and Leningrad. By 1944 Hitler's designs had been thwarted, and his armies were on the defensive on both fronts. If all went as the Allies had planned, his troops would be crushed in the massive vise of two great armies advancing simultaneously from the east and west.

Elaborate efforts to confuse the Germans about the point of attack set the stage for the Normandy invasion, the largest undertaking in the history of warfare. Allied air superiority prevented German aerial reconnaisance, and the Allies dropped strips of foil and used barrage balloons to make it appear to German radar than an invasion force lay off the Pas de Calais, north of the real objective. They also broadcast simulated radio traffic and bombed more heavily near Calais than near Normandy. The Germans were predisposed to believe that the invasion would come at Calais, because the English Channel was narrower and calmer there. In fact, for days after the landings the Germans refused to commit their forces at Normandy because they still believed the operations there were a diversion.

Success in outmaneuvering the Germans was due partly to the Allies' ability to read some German codes. Hitler thought he had the most secure enciphering system for wireless communication ever developed, based on a machine known as the Enigma, and the Germans believed that only someone with another Enigma could read their code. Nevertheless, British cryptanalysts built one and eventually were able to decipher most messages within hours, material that came to be known as Ultra. Without Ultra, the deception surrounding the Normandy invasion probably would not have worked. The Allies had to be careful in using Ultra so they would not reveal that they were reading the German code. Indeed, next to the atomic bomb, the Allies' ability to read enemy code in both theaters was the most closely guarded secret of the war.

Other preparations were effective. The air command bombed transportation facilities, and the French resistance sabotaged the rail system. Practically every bridge west of the Seine was destroyed, making it impossible for the Germans to deploy reinforcements rapidly. Naval commandos landed at night to inspect the obstructions on the beaches, and on the evening before the invasion minesweepers began clearing the ocean. Tanks were designed to operate on soft, wet beaches and to detonate land mines ahead of themselves. Because it was impossible to unload heavy equipment directly onto the beach, the Allies constructed two artificial harbors, which they towed across the channel, then sunk old ships to create breakwaters. Although a storm wrecked one of the harbors two weeks later, most equipment was ashore.

The weather was a key factor. The best tidal conditions occurred only three days, surface winds could not exceed 18 miles per hour, and paratroopers required moonlight for night landings. On the day the invasion was scheduled, June 5, Eisenhower's meteorologist predicted thunderstorms at Normandy. Eisenhower postponed the invasion until the next day even though conditions were not ideal. The inclement weather helped preserve the element of surprise.

As daybreak broke on June 6, German sentries were shocked to find the horizon filled with nearly 3,000 ships, which launched an intense naval bombardment before the invasion. Troops then landed at beaches code-named Utah, Omaha, Gold, Juno, and Sword; Utah and Omaha were American operations, and Gold, Juno, and Sword were the responsibility of the British and the Canadians. The troops suffered about 9,000 casualties at the five beaches, about 2,500 of them at Omaha, where the invaders faced their stiffest resistance. By the end of the first day 155,000 troops had landed.

Once the troops had established a beachhead, their task was to break out into the surrounding countryside, which was not conducive to tank operations because of the thick hedges and mounds of earth farmers used to fence their livestock. On July 3 the U.S. First Army broke out toward St. Lo, and captured it on July 18. By the end of July the German forces in Normandy were near collapse and the Allies began to advance more rapidly than they or the Germans had anticipated. On August 25, French and American forces liberated Paris.

Some of the German generals, believing the war lost and desiring to end it before they were humiliated, attempted to assassinate Hitler. In the spring of 1943 they had placed a time bomb in the Führer's plane, but it had failed to explode. Then, prompted by Normandy, on July 20, 1944, a young colonel, Count Klaus von Stauffenberg, planted a time bomb in his briefcase and carried it to a conference called by Hitler. The explosion killed four men, but Hitler escaped with minor injuries. Hitler purged the army and government of everyone suspected of participating; some 5,000 were executed, and 10,000 were sent to concentration camps. Rommel, who knew of the plot, was given the choice of suicide or trial and execution. He swallowed a cyanide capsule.

The reeling German army was exposed to a new threat when American and French forces under Lieutenant General Alexander M. Patch invaded the French Riviera on August 14. They landed 86,000 men and 12,000 vehicles the first day and moved quickly inland. Meeting little resistance, they captured 57,000 German troops within two weeks.

Eisenhower directed Montgomery's army group to sweep northward toward the Ruhr, while Bradley's army group, including Patton's Third Army, was set to move southward toward the Saar. They advanced so rapidly that by the end of August they had outrun their supplies. The groups competed for scarce gasoline; each claimed that if given everything available it could envelop the retreating Germans and bring the war to a quick conclusion. Eisenhower, instead of attacking either flank, decided upon a slower general offensive along a broad front because he feared that too rapid of an advance by tanks would leave them without gasoline.

In early September, Montgomery proposed a daring plan that Eisenhower accepted: airborne troops dropped behind German lines would take bridges in Holland intact, then Allied armor would close the gap. Operation Market Garden began on September 10 and employed 1,545 planes and 478 gliders carrying paratroopers, who made the first daylight drop of the war. A limited success, the operation failed to meet Montgomery's ambitions and incurred heavy casualties.

None of the Allied generals considered the retreating Germans capable of an offensive, so when Hitler's troops struck at the lightly defended line in the Ardennes Forest, creating a bulge in Allied lines, it came as a surprise. Hitler had ordered the audacious Panzer offensive, with the port of Antwerp his objective. The German army was incapable of sustaining an offensive, however, and Hitler's overly ambitious attack would accelerate his defeat.

With fog grounding the Allied air force, the Germans, striking in bitterly cold weather and 6 inches of snow, penetrated 60 miles in the Battle of the Bulge, their last offensive. On December 22 they surrounded the crucial road-junction city of Bastogne and sent an ultimatum to the Allied commander to surrender. Brigadier General Anthony McAuliffe replied with one word: "Nuts!"

The skies cleared the next day, and Allied fighter-bombers pounded German tank columns as the Panzers sputtered for lack of gasoline. Three days later the Allies relieved Bastogne, then gradually pinched in the top and bottom of the bulge and extinguished the offensive. The Battle of the Bulge, which involved 600,000 American troops, was the largest ground battle ever fought by American arms. The United States incurred 81,000 casualties, including 19,000 killed, yet the Germans, who could not replace their losses, suffered more than 100,000 casualties. The Battle of the Bulge delayed the Allied offensive in the west for a few weeks, although it contributed to the attrition of the German army. And while the Allied advance temporarily stalled in the west, the Soviet army in the east surged toward Berlin.

With the battle for the European continent raging in 1944 and 1945, the Allies held a series of diplomatic meetings to plan the postwar world. In July 1944 a conference chaired by Treasury Secretary Henry Morgenthau met at Bretton Woods, New Hampshire, to plan economic recovery. It recommended establishment of an International Monetary Fund and an International Bank for reconstruction and development. Two months later FDR and Churchill met at Quebec amid an atmosphere of imminent victory and preliminarily approved a plan to dismember Germany, destroy its industrial base, and make it an agrarian nation. Still, this scheme, the Morgenthau Plan, was later scrapped. Meanwhile, representatives of the United States, Britain, China, and the Soviet Union were meeting at Dumbarton Oaks, an estate in Washington, D.C., to discuss the charter for a new international organization, the United Nations.

The last meeting of the original Big Three Allied leaders occurred at Yalta, in the Russian Crimea, in February 1945. Roosevelt, who had lost weight, was ill and frail, but he dominated the discussions. The chief issues discussed were Poland, the war with Japan, and the United Nations; the most acrimonious discussions concerned Poland. Churchill feared that the Soviets planned to install puppet communist governments in Poland and the other eastern European nations that the Red Army was liberating. Stalin agreed to broaden the communist Lublin government to include all factions and to hold democratic elections in Poland, although he argued that the country was within the Soviet sphere of influence and insisted on a friendly government there. With his army occupying Poland, there was little the British or the Americans could do to prevent Stalin from imposing a government. Such territorial conflicts, arising during the last months of the fighting in Europe, sowed the seeds for a cold war between the United States and the Soviet Union.

Roosevelt was more successful in his other objectives. The Soviet Union agreed to participate in the United Nations and to join the war against Japan within three months of the conclusion of the war in Europe. In return, the Soviet Union received three votes in the UN General Assembly and territorial concessions in the Far East. It was also agreed that the Soviet army would liberate Berlin, a controversial decision. Churchill wanted to beat the Soviets to Berlin, but Roosevelt deferred to Eisenhower, who did not consider the city an important military objective. Instead, Eisenhower turned his troops toward the Danube, to isolate and destroy the remaining German armies, partly in response to intelligence reports that the Nazis had constructed a national redoubt in the Alps.

First the western armies had to cross the Rhine. Continuing to advance along a broad front, the Ninth Army reached the Rhine at Düsseldorf on March 2 to find the bridges destroyed. On March 7 the Ninth Armored Division of the U.S. First Army was fortunate in taking the major bridge at Remagen intact. Taking advantage, the army raced 8,000 troops across the bridge in the first 24 hours. The German counterattack, including a V-2 barrage, was unsuccessful. American troops continued to pour across the bridge until March 17, when it collapsed; by that time pontoon bridges had been erected across the Rhine. On March 22, Patton's troops crossed the river, and on March 23, Montgomery's men followed suit.

As April opened, the German army was on the verge of total defeat. Each Allied division was taking at least 2,000 prisoners per day, and further resistance could be justified only on the grounds of seeking a warrior's death. On April 4, Patton's troops liberated the Ohrdruf Nord concentration camp, confirming the malignant underside of nazism, the slaughter of gypsies, Soviets, and homosexuals in addition to the principal victims, the Jews. Patton vomited when he saw the prisoners, and the mayor of Ohrdruf and his wife, after being forced to tour the camp, went home and hanged themselves. On April 11, the Third Army liberated Buchenwald, where the commandant's wife had collected the skin of prisoners to make lamp shades. "It was like stepping into the Dark Ages," an American sergeant wrote.

The war was also coming to an end in Italy, where Allied forces opened their final offensive on April 9. On April 28, Mussolini and his mistress, Claretta Petacci, were murdered by Italian partisans, who brought the bodies to Milan and strung them up by the heels. German forces in the country surrendered on May 2, the day the Allies captured Berlin.

Hitler, who had trained for a sprint, had found himself competing in a marathon, and he was suited neither by temperament nor resources for a long war. His army could win campaigns, but not a protracted war against the two greatest powers on earth. Unable to face the consequences of his blind fanaticism and obsessive bigotry, Hitler took the easy way out, poisoning his dog, his wife, then himself; fearing the poison would not work, he shot himself in the head. Thus his Third Reich, which he had predicted would last "a thousand years," died in the ashes of Berlin after 12, fulfilling his promise to make Germany the greatest nation in the world or to destroy it.

On May 8, Victory in Europe Day, Germany surrendered. The lights that had gone out on the European continent in 1939 began to blaze again. Sadly, one man who had done so much to turn them on did not live to enjoy the victory.

Franklin and Eleanor had grown apart during the war, and the president started seeing the widowed Lucy Mercer Rutherfurd again. On April 12, Rutherfurd, visiting him at Warm Springs, asked him to pose for a portrait. Sitting for the painting and chatting with Rutherfurd and two other women, Roosevelt raised his left hand to his temple, complaining, "I have a terrific headache," and slumped in his chair. He never regained consciousness and was pronounced dead of a stroke at 3:55 p.m.

Millions were shocked by the death of the only president they had ever known, a president who had served longer than any other. Almost all Americans could remember what they were doing when they heard of Roosevelt's death. A Milwaukee laborer, who spent most of his income collecting photographs and mementos of FDR, stopped each of the dozens of clocks in his house at the time Roosevelt died and never reset them.

The consensus of historians is that Franklin Roosevelt was the greatest president of the twentieth century, and polls of historians and of the public consistently rank him as the third greatest chief executive behind Lincoln and Washington. By no means unflawed, Roosevelt was an inefficient administrator who sometimes used questionable means. Nevertheless, he transformed the presidency, liberating it from the inhibitions of the past. His New Deal, although it never ended the depression, saved the country from chaos and gave birth to the modern welfare state. Long after specific programs had faltered, the principle of government intervention in the economy and the extension of a helping hand to the needy would persist. Roosevelt's accomplishments as a wartime president were greater: he helped to mobilize America, to save the world from tyranny, and to transform the planet. Much of what the United States and the world became was due to his influence.

✤ THE WAR IN ASIA

In Asia the United States had to transport men and arms over thousands of miles of ocean to land on hostile shores. They also faced Japanese soldiers who proved to be tenacious fighters in the tropical jungles. Considering surrender a disgrace, the Japanese adopted suicidal tactics, and in each engagement they had far higher casualty rates than the Americans.

Naval air power was the decisive factor in the Pacific. Never before had ships and planes been so closely coordinated. The Pacific Fleet was organized into task forces centered around aircraft carriers, including accompanying cruisers and destroyers. Battleships, too slow to accompany task forces, were most useful in shelling islands before an invasion. Submarines were used for scouting and for preying on merchant and military vessels. The Japanese aviators, who had been fighting in Asia for years, were more experienced than the American flyers, and until introduction of the F6F Hellcat, the navy had no plane as maneuverable as the Japanese Zero. But the Japanese could not replace the pilots, ships, and planes they lost as rapidly as the Americans could replace their losses.

The Japanese strategy was to seize, fortify, and defend Pacific islands and archipelagoes within a radius of thousands of miles of the home islands, making the price to retake them too high for the Americans. Like the Germans, they did not consider the Americans a match for their troops, and they believed that if they made a war of attrition costly enough, the United States would concede them a sphere of influence. They misjudged the American intention, which was to fight the war to a conclusion, not to a stalemate.

The war in the Pacific revolved around islands, many of them small, sparsely populated, and relatively worthless except for their strategic value. Strategists concluded that they did not have to take every island Japan defended. Rather, they frustrated Japan with the tactic of leapfrogging. They would fight to capture key islands, construct airfields and naval bases, and, with control of the air and sea assured, hop over strong defensive positions, leaving them isolated and impotent.

In the immediate aftermath of Pearl Harbor, the Japanese conquests were comparable to the Nazi Blitzkrieg. Simultaneous with the bombing of Pearl Harbor, air raids were made on Midway Island, Wake Island, Guam, Hong Kong, southern Thailand, northern Malaya, and the Philippines. Wake Island fell on December 23, and Hong Kong on Christmas Day. Rangoon was captured on February 8, 1942, Singapore was conquered a week later, and the Philippines surrendered on May 6. The western powers had been humiliated.

The first significant fleet action occurred in January 1942, at the Battle of the Java Sea, after an Allied naval force intercepted an invasion fleet bound for Java. In the engagement the Allies lost two cruisers and four destroyers, delaying the invasion only briefly. Japanese ground forces landed, overwhelmed the Dutch outposts, and proclaimed the addition of Java to their empire.

The longest and most arduous Japanese conquest was that of the Philippines. After destroying the U.S Air Force on the ground on December 7, 1941, the main Japanese force landed on Luzon on December 22. The Americans, commanded by General Douglas MacArthur, retreated to the mountainous jungle of the Bataan Peninsula after two weeks of heavy fighting. Short of food and drugs, 80 percent of the American frontline troops contracted malaria and 75 percent had dysentery; more died from disease and starvation than from combat. MacArthur established his command on the island of Corregidor in Manila Harbor, but in February, ordered to leave in order to assume command in Australia, he fled through Japanese lines aboard a PT boat. His successors were Lieutenant General Jonathan M. Wainwright on Corregidor and Wainwright's subordinate, Major General Edward P. King, on Bataan. Despite orders, King, facing starvation and annihilation, surrendered on April 9, and Corregidor was captured on May 6. Captured troops were forced to march about 65 miles in blistering heat without food or water, the infamous Bataan Death March that killed some 10,000 American and Filipino soldiers. The Japanese commanders were subsequently tried for war crimes.

In April 1942, a Japanese fleet set out to invade Port Moresby, on the island of New Guinea, which would put the Japanese within range to bomb Australia. The American fleet engaged the Japanese at the Battle of the Coral Sea, sinking a carrier yet losing one. A tactical draw, the battle was a strategic defeat for the Japanese because they were compelled to cancel their plans for an invasion. The battle, fought entirely by carrier-based planes, was the first

Brilliant but controversial, General Douglas MacArthur commanded the American forces in the Southwest Pacific. He fulfilled his vow to return to the Philippines after losing the islands to the Japanese.

naval battle in which surface fleets never made visual contact and did not exchange a shot.

Starved for at least a psychological victory, American aviators staged a daring raid on Tokyo on April 18. Under the command of Colonel James H. Doolittle, 16 B-25s took off from the carrier *Hornet* some 650 miles offshore. Lacking sufficient gasoline to return and unable to land bombers on an aircraft carrier, they planned to fly on to friendly airfields in China. Most of the planes reached China, but eight flyers landed in enemy territory, and the Japanese executed three for bombing residential areas. The raid inflicted little damage, although it raised the morale of Americans.

With Japanese strategists seeking a decisive battle to destroy the American fleet, Admiral Isoruku Yamamoto took most of the Japanese navy to attack Midway, preceded by a diversionary attack on the Aleutians. American planners, aware of the coming attack because of their ability to read Japanese codes, set a trap, and Admiral Raymond A. Spruance awaited Yamamoto to the north of Midway. When Yamamoto's planes attacked, leaving the carriers unprotected, American pilots decimated his fleet, sinking four carriers to offset the loss of one carrier. A devastating defeat for the Japanese, the Battle of Midway marked the end of Japanese expansion and broke Tokyo's offensive power. In another coup for American intelligence, cryptanalysts learned of Yamamoto's itinerary and timetable for an inspection tour of the Solomons. On April 18, American fighters shot down Yamamoto's plane, and he perished, depriving the Japanese of their best admiral.

The first American offensive came at Guadalcanal, a jungle-covered island in the Solomons. After the marines invaded on August 7, a series of naval engagements ensued as both sides attempted to reinforce troops. The ground battle raged for six months until the Japanese evacuated their troops in February 1943. After Guadalcanal, the Japanese were on the defensive, and the Americans did not lose a battle for the rest of the war.

By the fall of 1943 the American offensive was proceeding rapidly. Six new carriers, stocked with Hellcats, were available for the Pacific. Admiral Chester W. Nimitz was set to fight toward Japan through a line of islands including the Gilberts, the Marshalls, and the Marianas, while MacArthur was set to wage an offensive in the Southwest Pacific. On November 20 the navy attacked Tarawa in the Gilberts, followed by a landing of marines, who subdued the island by November 23. Nimitz then assaulted the Marshalls, a cluster of small islands taken by February 23, 1944, after stiff resistance.

The next campaign in the Marianas, the most ambitious to date, had three major objectives: Saipan, Tinian, and Guam. Control of the Marianas was important because B-29s based there could reach the Japanese home islands. The bloodiest campaign was on Saipan, the largest island. When the American invasion began on June 15, the Japanese sought another decisive naval victory, only to suffer another decisive defeat. The Japanese lost 273 of the 373 planes that attacked the task force at the cost of only 29 U.S. planes, and American submarines sank three carriers. Some 30,000 Japanese soldiers were killed on Saipan, and the Americans suffered 14,000 casualties, killed and wounded.

About 50,000 Japanese soldiers died defending the Marianas, which furnished air bases and an important harbor on Guam for the Americans.

MacArthur, when forced to flee the Philippines, had vowed to return, and he insisted on redeeming his promise even though some military planners wanted to bypass the islands. On October 20, 1944, as marines landed on Leyte, MacArthur waded ashore and announced, "People of the Philippines, I have returned." A huge Japanese fleet attempting to reinforce Leyte met the American fleet at the Battle of Leyte Gulf, the largest naval engagement in the history of warfare. For the first time, the Japanese used kamikazes, planes loaded with explosives and flown into American ships by pilots on suicide missions. However, in the last naval engagement of the war the Japanese navy was decimated, losing all 4 of its remaining carriers, 3 battleships, 6 cruisers, and 12 destroyers. Leyte fell to the marines.

On January 9, 1945, the marines landed on Luzon, the major Philippine island, and began a bitter campaign that killed nearly all of the 260,000 Japanese soldiers there. In Manila, the fighting was house-by-house, and some 100,000 civilians perished, but the Americans captured the city. Corregidor surrendered on March 2, and by June 30 resistance had ended. Fighting continued in the outlying islands until the end of the war.

The Americans also targeted Iwo Jima, a small volcanic island about midway between the Marianas and Japan. Planes bombed Iwo Jima for 74 days before 60,000 troops invaded on February 19. The Japanese, who had created a maze of caves and tunnels beneath the island, largely survived the bombing and fought to the death. Mount Suribachi, which dominated Iwo Jima, was honeycombed with caves, pillboxes, and bunkers that the Japanese defended ferociously. From its peak Japanese spotters directed artillery fire at the beaches. Nonetheless, the marines, using flamethrowers and explosives, gradually fought their way up Suribachi. On the third day of fighting five marines were photographed raising the American flag on Suribachi, a photograph that won the Pulitzer Prize and became the most famous picture taken during the war. Of the 23,000 defenders of Iwo Jima, about 21,000 died, while the United States lost about 7,000 dead.

The last American objective before the planned invasion of Japan was Okinawa, a 60-mile-long island 350 miles southwest of Japan. Preliminary bombardment began on October 10, 1944, and the invasion took place on April 1, 1945. Some 77,000 defended Okinawa against the assault of 183,000 American troops, and the Japanese lost 10 dead for every American killed. The Japanese held out for more than 100 days against a force more than twice their size, making American planners fearful of the cost of invading the home islands.

While the war raged for the Pacific islands, the Allies fought a frustrating war in China. America had few ground troops in China, but a group of volunteer pilots under Colonel Claire Chennault, the Flying Tigers, had been fighting in the air since 1940. Chennault believed that an air offensive against Japan by planes based in China could end the war, yet his hopes proved unfounded.

The United States sent Lieutenant General Joseph Stilwell to represent the

Americans in China and to serve as chief of staff for Chiang Kai-Shek. Chiang's army was corrupt, demoralized, and inefficient, and Chiang was reluctant to fight because he wanted to save his army for the civil war against the communists that he knew would follow the defeat of Japan. Chiang's refusal to fight aggressively and his forces' inability to recapture Burma frustrated the irascible, impatient Stilwell, who quarreled constantly with the arrogant, imperious, and secretive Generalissimo. In 1944, FDR sent a personal emissary, Major General Patrick J. Hurley, to resolve the dispute. After Hurley sided with Chiang, Roosevelt recalled Stilwell and replaced him with Major General Albert C. Wedemeyer. Unfortunately, Wedemeyer was no more successful than Chiang in getting the Chinese to fight or the rival nationalist and communist armies to cooperate against the Japanese. Roosevelt's attempt to treat China as a great power proved to be unrealistic, and the China campaign turned out to be one of the most frustrating of the war. The main contribution of the Allied forces in China was to tie down Japanese troops.

Like aviators in Europe, aviators in the Far East believed that air power alone might defeat their foe. By early 1944, the Allies had available the B-29 bomber, which flew at higher altitudes and had a longer range than the lighter, slower B-17. Based first in China, later in the Marianas, the campaign of strategic bombing, directed by Major General Curtis E. LeMay, devastated Japan. LeMay initially sought to cripple aircraft production but soon turned to area bombing with incendiary bombs that created fire storms in the cities constructed largely of wood and paper. A raid of 344 bombers on Tokyo on March 9, 1945, killed 84,000 persons, injured 41,000, and left more than 1 million homeless. Excluding nuclear bombs, the air raids destroyed 43 percent of 63 major Japanese cities, eliminated 42 percent of Japan's industrial capacity, and killed, wounded, or rendered homeless 22 million people. In the last seven weeks of the war, bombers, aircraft carriers, and surface vessels participated in the bombardment, and the United States tightened a naval blockade.

In July 1945, the Allies held their last wartime summit at Potsdam, Germany. Stalin alone remained of the original Big Three; Truman replaced the deceased Roosevelt, and during the conference Churchill was replaced by Clement R. Attlee, who defeated him in the British elections. The conference settled few issues permanently, and the British and the Americans were shocked by Stalin's demand for huge reparations in kind from Germany. The Grand Alliance was beginning to break up.

At Potsdam, Truman was notified of the successful detonation of the first atomic bomb in the desert of New Mexico on July 16, 1945. The United States, Britain, and China issued the Potsdam Declaration urging Japan to surrender or face annihilation, although the bomb was not specifically mentioned. Tokyo would not yield, and on August 6, three B-29s took off from Tinian bound for Hiroshima, Japan's eighth largest city. Hiroshima had been selected because it had been spared from heavy bombing and contained no prisoner-of-war camps. The lead bomber, the *Enola Gay,* piloted by Colonel Paul Tibbets, carried an atomic bomb, and the two escorts carried cameras and scientific equipment. The bomb exploded above the city, killing between 70,000 and 80,000 people and destroying more than 80 percent of the buildings in Hiroshima. A few hours later the White House announced the existence of the bomb and warned the Japanese that unless they surrendered "they may expect a rain of ruin from the air, the like of which has never been seen on this earth."

Predictions of bad weather advanced the date for use of the second bomb, sparing Kokura, the primary target, and marking Nagasaki for destruction. A few hours before, the Soviet Union declared war on Japan, an act that helped convince the Japanese that their cause was doomed. Some 35,000 people then perished at Nagasaki.

Even after the second bombing, though, the Japanese were reluctant to surrender. The ensuing scenario made it appear unlikely that anything short of the combined effects of atomic bombs and the Soviet declaration of war could have persuaded the Japanese to surrender. To Allied demands for unconditional surrender, Japan responded by asking for the right to retain Emperor Hirohito. The Allies agreed but specified that he was to be a figurehead subject to their command. Japan disliked the condition, yet the emperor called an

The atom bomb dropped on Hiroshima left almost total destruction near ground zero. Of all the technological transformations from 1921 to 1945, atomic warfare posed the most terrible threat.

imperial conference at which he announced his decision to surrender. That evening, as the emperor prepared to broadcast his decision to the nation, a group of fanatical army officers attempted a coup to assassinate the leaders of the government, seize power, and continue the war. The coup failed, and on August 15, Hirohito announced the surrender. The official treaty of surrender was signed in Tokyo Bay aboard the battleship *Missouri* on September 2.

In later years, use of the bomb has incurred more recriminations in America than in Japan, with considerable debate over whether Japan could have been forced to surrender without the horrible weapon. One must remember, though, that the alternatives were worse. Continued nonatomic bombing would hardly have cost fewer lives than the atomic bombs, and an invasion would have cost devastating losses on both sides, including Japanese civilians. Destruction of their islands in hand-to-hand combat, rather than swift, limited death from the air, would likely have left more bitterness among the survivors. There is, moreover, no question that the atomic bomb would have been used against the Germans had it been ready, nor is there any doubt that Germany and Japan, both of which had nuclear programs, would have used the bomb against their enemies. And in the long run, the destruction and revulsion of the bomb made future military use of nuclear weapons less likely.

The war left 22 million dead in the Soviet Union, 13.5 million in China, 7.4 million in Germany, 5.4 million in Poland (most of them Holocaust victims), 2.1 million in Japan, 430,000 in Britain, and 220,000 in the United States. Only 1 American serviceman in 10 was ever exposed to combat, and with an overall death rate of 5 per 1,000, the military was safer than the industrial home front, where the death rate was more than twice as high.

The American contribution to winning the war was substantial. At peak strength the U.S. Army was nearly as large as the Soviet army (12,294,000 to 12,500,000). While fighting a multifront war over vast distances the United States contributed equipment and supplies to its allies. The Soviet Union, for example, received more than 400,000 jeeps and trucks, more than 7,000 tanks, more than 14,000 planes, and nearly 2 million tons of food. Although the Soviet contribution to victory on the ground was the most significant, the Soviets fought a single-front war and made only small contributions to the war in the air and at sea. Without the Americans' efforts, the victory would have been impossible.

✦ THE TRANSFORMING INFLUENCE OF WORLD WAR II

World War II was the greatest transforming experience in human history. Its destructiveness was unprecedented, and the environmental damage would affect generations. It ended colonialism, required spending on a massive level, accelerated scientific development, discredited racism, precipitated substantial changes in the roles of women, and wrought a near-revolution in the American economy and society. It ended the depression and was a greater factor in redistributing income than any social programs in American history.

The America that emerged from World War II was not the same America that entered it. Facing great postwar obligations and often falling short, the United States was accused, with some justification, of self-righteousness and moral hypocrisy. Yet in many ways, it was a better, more sober, more realistic nation.

Like the war, the entire era from 1921 to 1945, for all its troubles, was cathartic, shaping America to a degree matched by few periods of comparable length. In meeting problems with vision or naïveté, in embracing the future enthusiastically or reluctantly, Americans showed a bravery and fortitude that most generations could not equal. With the victory over Japan, their nation reached the apogee of its influence as a global power. The challenges, however, were not over for the United States, or for the planet. Never before or since has the future seemed so promising, or so dangerous, as it did in the summer of 1945. In the postwar era the world would feel the tension between transformation and reaction that had dominated American life.

BIBLIOGRAPHICAL ESSAY

Among the general histories of World War II, including all participants, are B. H. Liddell Hart, *History of the Second World War* (1970); H. P. Willmott, *The Great Crusade* (1989); John Keegan, *The Second World War* (1989); Gordon Wright, *The Ordeal of Total War, 1939–1945* (1968); James L. Stokesbury, *A Short History of World War II* (1980); and Martha Hoyle, *A World in Flames: The History of World War II* (1970).

Histories of the United States in World War II include A. Russell Buchanan, *The United States and World War II*, 2 vols. (1964); and Kent R. Greenfield, *American Strategy in World War II: A Reconsideration* (1963). Roosevelt's role is described aptly in James MacGregor Burns, *Roosevelt: The Soldier of Freedom, 1940–1945* (1970); and Eric Larrabee, *Commander in Chief: Franklin Delano Roosevelt, His Lieutenants and Their War* (1987), which includes portraits of the leading generals.

The European theater is covered by Charles B. MacDonald, *The Mighty Endeavor: The American War in Europe* (1986); Dan Van Der Vat, *The Atlantic Campaign* (1988); and Stephen E. Ambrose, *The Supreme Commander: The War Years of General Dwight D. Eisenhower* (1970).

The diplomatic history of the war is discussed in Gaddis Smith, *American Diplomacy During the Second World War* (1965); Herbert Feis, *Churchill, Roosevelt, Stalin* (1967); Robert Dallek, ed., *The Roosevelt Diplomacy and World War II* (1978); and Gabriel Kolko, *The Politics of War: The World and United States Foreign Policy, 1943–1945* (1968), a provocative work. The Yalta Conference is the subject of Richard F. Fenno, Jr., *The Yalta Conference* (1972); and Russell D. Buhite, *Decisions at Yalta: An Appraisal of Summit Diplomacy* (1986).

Black soldiers are discussed in Mary P. Motley, ed., *The Invisible Soldier: The Experience of the Black Soldier, World War II* (1975). Cynthia Enloe, *Does Khaki Become You? The Militarization of Women's Lives* (1988), is a thoughtful study of women in the military.

The best account of the war in Asia is Ronald H. Spector, *Eagle Against the Sun: The American War With Japan* (1985). Also see two riveting biographies: William Manchester, *American Caesar: Douglas MacArthur, 1880–1964* (1973); and Barbara Tuchman, *Stilwell and the American Experience in China* (1975).

The use of the atomic bomb is covered in Martin J. Sherwin, *A World Destroyed: The Atomic Bomb and the Grand Alliance* (1975); Herbert Feis, *The Atomic Bomb and the End of World War II* (1966); and Paul R. Baker, ed., *The Atomic Bomb* (1976).

Index